THE MYSTERY
OF LIGHT

The Life and Teaching of Omraam Mikhael Aivanhov

THE MYSTERY
OF LIGHT

The Life and Teaching of Omraam Mikhael Aivanhov

by Georg Feuerstein, Ph.D.

Passage Press
Salt Lake City, Utah

Passage Press is a division of Morson Publishing
Morson Publishing
P.O. Box 21713
Salt Lake City, Utah 84121-0713

Published 1994

Printed in the United States of America
Printed on acid-free paper

Cover design by Steven R. Jerman

Library of Congress Catalog Card Number: 94-067979
ISBN 1-878423-14-2

In memory of Dr. Giovanni Boni

For all who understand that our life
is best lived as a pilgrimage.
May these pages help illumine their way.

CONTENTS

ACKNOWLEDGMENTS

I wish to record my gratitude to the following people:

— my spiritual friend Therese Boni, for making this book possible and for her boundless Mediterranean enthusiasm, which was manna for my psyche;

— the late Dr. Giovanni Boni, to whom this book is dedicated, for his ready appreciation of my efforts and his unfailing kindness;

— Paul Henri Gaillard, for his faith in me and for co-sponsoring this work;

— Sister Blagost, a longstanding disciple of Omraam Mikhael Aivanhov, for adding to the book's color by providing some anecdotal material and other valuable information about the life of her teacher;

— Cherry Frizzell, for freely sharing with me several anecdotes about Master Aivanhov during her and her husband's sojourn with him;

— Violet Nevile, for kindly supplying a substantial portion of the chronology (Appendix);

— the officials of Prosveta, France, for granting permission to quote copyrighted material free of charge;

— David Lorimer, for kindly providing information about Peter Deunov, the Bulgarian teacher of Omraam Mikhael Aivanhov;

— my wife, Trisha, for applying as usual her editing skills and sound judgment to this work;

— Larry Dossey, M.D., for generously giving of his time to furnish this book with a much-appreciated foreword;

— Robben Hixson, proprietor of Passage Press, for enthusiastically adopting this book and ushering it into the English-speaking world.

FOREWORD
by Larry Dossey, M.D.
Author of *Recovering the Soul; Space, Time, and Medicine; Meaning and Medicine, and Beyond Illness*

There are rare moments in our life when the discovery of a particular book, teaching, or piece of wisdom simply stuns us and leaves us breathlessly filled with awe, gratitude, and joy. We recognize immediately that we have come upon a great treasure. As we stand in its presence and yield to its brilliance, we can sense immediately that it has begun to change us. That has been my response to encountering the work of the remarkable Bulgarian spiritual teacher Omraam Mikhael Aivanhov.

The pages of history are littered with wise spiritual teachers. Regardless of the truths they have spoken, many of them have not made a great difference in people's lives or the world in general. What accounts for the transforming power of some of them? Whether or not a great spiritual teaching actually engages us depends on our openness to it, of course, but on other factors as well. It is not enough for the teaching to be true. In addition, it must be coherent not only with former wisdom but with the best current knowledge as well. It must convey relevance, immediacy, urgency. Above all, the teaching must somehow be right for the times, and it must *feel* right. At some point, if these conditions are met, magic may happen: We, and the world around us, can be transformed.

Not only is Aivanhov's teaching consistent with the greatest wisdom traditions of humankind, it is at the leading edge of our evolving knowledge about the world. This means that those who prefer their spiritual teachings to be dusty and crusty, archaic and arcane, will need to look elsewhere. Aivanhov does not advocate taking refuge in a sentimental

Omraam Mikhael Aivanhov
toward the end of his life

past. Using reason to the fullest, and supplementing it with his remarkable visionary powers, he enunciates a breathtaking picture of human transformation that is modern and up-to-date.

One of the most striking qualities of Aivanhov's teaching is the simplicity and clarity that shine through at every moment. His unadorned, uncluttered words are a refreshing contrast to the hopelessly obscure obfuscations that pass today for "spiritual" teachings. What a joy to rediscover that authentic wisdom need not be opaque and impenetrable!

Although Aivanhov's teaching is consistent with the best of the ancient wisdom that has gone before it, it is in many respects fresh and new. Aivanhov was obviously aware of the penetrating insights of modern science. He honored this window onto the world and, by applying his considerable intellect and understanding, opened this window even further. Unlike many spiritual teachers, Aivanhov never went *around* the modern picture of the universe; he marched straight *through* it and expanded it. This is one reason his teaching seems so relevant for our age.

There are probably more so-called spiritual teachers today than ever before. The West is flooded with them, and it has been difficult in many instances to sort out the sage from the scoundrel. Amid the current supermarket of offerings, the spiritual seeker's task of finding a genuine teacher can be daunting. That is one reason why it is a great honor and privilege to recommend the teaching presented in this book. It is in a class with few others.

Georg Feuerstein is uniquely qualified to bring the writings of Omraam Mikhael Aivanhov to our attention. Dr. Feuerstein is a world-renowned scholar in the field of spirituality and comparative religious studies, from whose books I have benefited for years. His writings — and his life — embody the same depth, integrity, and dignity of his current subject.

This volume is an enchanting, lyrical song between Feuerstein and Aivanhov — Aivanhov singing the melody, and Feuerstein rounding out the score with his skillful, unobtrusive interpretation.

I am frequently asked in lectures and seminars, "Who today is a believable, genuine, spiritual teacher?" Now I can answer without hesitation: Encounter Omraam Mikhael Aivanhov and see what happens.

Larry Dossey, M.D.
New Mexico

Omraam Mikheal Aivanhov

PREFACE

The present work is the product of a series of most felicitous circumstances. In 1989, I came across the English translation of Omraam Mikhael Aivanhov's book *Toward a Solar Civilisation*. I had requested it for review, and to my delight found the book absolutely fascinating. I gave it an appropriately laudatory review.

This is where Therese Boni appeared in my life. As the then director of the American branch of Prosveta, the publishers dedicated to promoting Omraam Mikhael Aivanhov's life work, she thanked me for my review with her characteristic enthusiasm. Before I knew it she had gifted me with a complete set of some forty volumes of Aivanhov's talks translated into English.

Soon afterward I met Therese in person, and we instantly struck up a wonderful friendship. I also found myself delving into Aivanhov's teaching with growing admiration and gratitude. I was amazed that I had never heard of him before, not even during my many years in Europe, although he had taught in France for nearly half a century. I particularly regretted that I did not know of him when he visited California in 1984. I would gladly have journeyed to Los Angeles from my home in Northern California to see him.

However, in the course of working on this book I came to appreciate the degree to which great teachers live on in their ideas. There were also many moments in which I felt an invisible presence supporting me. Sometimes writing can be a laborious task, but in the present case the work was filled with so much joy and luminosity that I almost regretted completing it.

I hope that this book will inspire you, the reader, as much as I was inspired by the powerfully transformative ideas that form its backbone. I am not referring to my own ideas, which merely serve to provide a context for Aivanhov's teaching, but to those potent thoughts and images that express a universal truth, crystallized by one of the finest representatives of perennial philosophy.

Omraam Mikhael Aivanhov was a simple and direct man. Sometimes simplicity and directness are merely the product of lack of sophistication. In Aivanhov's case, they are the fruit of a wonderful mental lucidity and great personal integrity. He presented even the most complex ideas in a clear and lively manner, and with an unpretentiousness that is deceptive.

Our age loves complicated matters. We pride ourselves in being sophisticated, and we generally assume that profound thoughts call for complex expressions. We always wonder whether an opaque thinker might not be incredibly deep. Aivanhov cut through all this pretense and confusion. His countless talks — he has not written any books — are uniformly simple, lucid, and deep.

Many who have listened to Aivanhov during his nearly fifty years of teaching found him to be too simple and moved on to other, more complicated-sounding teachings and philosophies. We discover the depth of his ideas only when we approach his teaching without intellectual snobbery and preconceptions. As the American physician and writer Larry Dossey, M.D. remarked:

> A mark of a great spiritual teacher is to convey wisdom of such luminous clarity that it seems genuinely simple — as if we might have known it all along, as if it is innate in everyone. Such a teacher is Omraam Mikhael Aivanhov, whose words have the ring of familiarity and truth. In an age that confuses profundity with impenetrable esotericism, Aivanhov is a refreshing discovery.

There is a traditional story about a somewhat presumptuous aspirant who came to a renowned spiritual teacher for instruction. When the teacher asked him to sweep the floor, the young man hesitated. When the teacher reassured him that this was in fact his teaching, the newcomer sneered and left. He had missed the whole point of the instruction and hence never caught even a glimpse of the teaching that would most certainly have transformed him.

In some respects, reading Aivanhov's published talks is like sweeping. Many of his ideas sound so familiar that we easily come to the hasty conclusion that we have already moved beyond them. But there is a vast difference between knowing something and living it. Aivanhov's talks and his exemplary life constantly remind us of this crucial distinction.

As we delve into Aivanhov's recorded talks, we are humbled by his tremendous depth of understanding. When we follow his thoughts attentively and gradually discover their profundity and beauty, we are touched and transformed by them.

In the present publication I have tried to express myself as simply as possible. Of course, I could never hope to successfully emulate Aivanhov's rich metaphoric language, and to compensate for this shortcoming of mine have interspersed my commentary with ample quotes from his vivid talks. The purpose of this volume is to introduce Aivanhov and his teaching to the English-speaking world and to provide the necessary background for understanding both.

I have focused on what I believe to be the salient features of his teaching. I have said nothing about the cultural and ceremonial life as lived by his community of disciples around the world. There are two reasons for this. First, while I hold Omraam Mikhael Aivanhov in the highest esteem and treasure his teaching, I have never been a formal student or a member of his community. My own path stems from a different tradition. For years I meditated according to the traditions of Yoga and Vedanta but for some time now have followed the Medicine Buddha practice of Tibetan Buddhism. Second, I feel that the communal dimension of experience is best discovered individually by those who desire to explore his teaching further.

More than my other books, the present work reflects my deep practical commitment to spiritual life. I have written it as a pilgrim on the path for others who have attained a similar orientation. May this little book prompt you, the reader, to want to refresh your whole being directly at the pure fountain of wisdom that flows so abundantly in Aivanhov's numerous published talks.

Georg Feuerstein

Note to the Reader

Over forty volumes of Omraam Mikhael Aivanhov's talks have so far been published in English. They can be obtained through the various branches of Prosveta, the publishing arm of the fellowship founded by Aivanhov. A list of Prosveta organizations and contacts is provided at the back of the book. The American branch is also publishing a newsletter, entitled *Circle of Light*, which can be obtained from Prosveta U.S.A., P.O. Box 49614, Los Angeles, CA 90049. Subscription is $9.00 per year.

PART I

THE TEACHER

1
THE EARLY LIFE OF
OMRAAM MIKHAEL AIVANHOV

THE PROPHECY

To a humble family will fair child be born
From a Balkan country will this Eagle fly
To dwell in the Land of the Rooster
His name the same as mine the world will long recall
His voice the peoples of the earth will hear
And following upon upheaval and disaster
A New Age will begin.

Thus reads a quatrain by Nostradamus, the great astrologer and prophet of the sixteenth century. This verse was found on an old parchment discovered in the South of France in 1957.

Over three hundred years later Mikhael Aivanhov was born in the Balkan country of Bulgaria. The "Land of the Rooster" is none other than France, which has the rooster as its emblem. It was Aivanhov who, in 1937, was sent to France to spread the spiritual teaching he had received from his teacher, the saintly Peter Deunov. The rooster is a symbol for the rising sun and for perpetual vigilance, and both the sun and vigilance play a central role in Aivanhov's teaching.

The eagle mentioned in the prophecy also represents the lofty sun — a fitting symbol for Master Aivanhov, who boldly soared in the dimension of the Spirit, close to the source of all light.

Finally, Nostradamus's full name was Mikaelis de Nostradamus, as inscribed on his tomb in the Church of Saint-Remy at Salon-de-Provence.[1] A plaque on the wall of the house in which he died on July 2, 1566, gives his name as Michel Nostradamus. The French name Michel is none other than the

*Omraam Mikheal Aivanhov
contemplating the morning Sun*

English name Michael, which is rendered as Mikhael in Bulgarian.

Is all this coincidence? Perhaps. But assuming that Nostradamus was not merely a madman but was in fact able to see into the future, and also granting the possibility that Mikhael Aivanhov's name might one day be more widely known than it is today, it does not seem too farfetched to connect Nostradamus's quatrain with him.

Be that as it may, the historical significance of Mikhael Aivanhov and his teaching in the spiritual field do not depend on our speculations about the possible meaning of such prophecies. Aivanhov's life and, even more importantly, his work speak for themselves.

Aivanhov himself had no doubt that one day his teaching of light, which has most ancient roots, would be universally recognized. But to understand this prediction correctly, we must also understand that he regarded his teaching as giving out universal spiritual principles. He did not immodestly expect a worldwide movement based on the particular form he had given those principles. Rather, with this prediction he simply intended to express his personal faith in the wisdom of human evolution, which one day would guide humanity to a universal spirituality.

Like many great spiritual personages, Aivanhov was naturally reluctant to talk about himself. He wanted people to focus their attention on his teaching rather than become attached to him. His own life mattered only insofar as it demonstrated the validity of the teaching for which he stood. Teachers, he once observed, are their own works of art. As he elaborated:

> I have immense admiration for the great cathedrals, symphonies and sculptures of the world, but the true ideal is to create such splendours inside oneself, to be one's own painting, one's own statue, poem, music or dance . . . A human being who is his own creation, his own work of art, does far more for humanity than all libraries, museums and masterpieces of the world because these are all dead, whereas he is alive![2]

Fortunately, over the years Aivanhov communicated just enough about himself in his lectures and private conversations to instill confidence and faith in his disciples. What we can gather from these various disclosures is that he led a quite extraordinary life, dedicated early on to higher ideals, and rich in experience, insight, and spiritual accomplishment.

CHILDHOOD IN BULGARIA

Bulgaria, as one of the Balkan states, is a country slightly larger than Tennessee but with historical roots that reach as far back as the early Neolithic. This was the time when the Great Goddess religion captured the hearts and imagination of the people, as the American archaeologist Marija Gimbutas has shown in her epochal work *The Goddesses and Gods of Old Europe*.[3]

Archaeological evidence dating back to over 9,000 years ago indicates a complex and diversified religious culture in the area of Eastern Europe. This culture knew sanctuaries, rituals, cult paraphernalia, festive attire, sacred signs, music, art, and mythology. Dominant were the vegetation Goddess, often shown in her bird or snake form, and the vegetation God, a forerunner of the later Dionysus. God and Goddess were complementary, with the Mother Goddess carrying the main symbolic and ritual load.

This Old European culture was the parent to the Minoan civilization. Both these great cultures appear to have been radically transformed when the Indo-European tribes arrived in the Mediterranean. However, they were not completely destroyed but continued to form a rich substratum in the newly emerging culture. Many of the old symbols persisted, largely kept alive by the female population. As Gimbutas notes:

> The Goddess's religion went underground. Some of the old traditions, particularly those connected with birth, death, and earth fertility rituals, have continued to this day without much change in some regions; in

others, they were assimilated into Indo-European ideology.[4]

Gimbutas continues:

> There is no question that Old European sacred images and symbols remain a vital part of the cultural heritage of Europe. Most of us were surrounded in childhood by the fairy world, which contained many images transmitted from Old Europe. In some nooks of Europe, as in my own motherland, Lithuania, there still flow sacred and miraculous rivers and springs, there flourish holy forests and groves, reservoirs of blossoming life, there grow gnarled trees brimming with vitality and holding the power to heal; along waters there still stand menhirs, called "Goddesses," full of mysterious power. The Old European culture was the matrix of much later beliefs and practices. Memories of a long-lasting gynocentric past could not be erased . . .[5]

Thus Aivanhov, who was born in the little Macedonian village of Serbtzi near Mount Pelister at the foot of Babouna Planina (Grandmother's Mountain) on January 31, 1900, was immersed in a culture that had longstanding and profound spiritual traditions that were once transmitted by women and that are still largely salvaged by women. His mother was a great healer and undoubtedly preserved ancient teachings in her healing practice. In a lecture given in 1969, when his mother was still alive, Aivanhov disclosed this about her:

> . . . my mother has always healed simply by acting on the navel. Today, even at her age, she is still healing many people. She makes them lie down and uncovers their navel, she places a handkerchief around her finger, dips it in some ashes, and applies it with a circular motion to the navel of the sick person. She says that there is an essential point in the navel, and that when it is out of place, the whole organism begins to deteriorate. So this point must be put back in place,

which is what she does. Many times she cured me in this way when I was young.[6]

Mikhael Aivanhov also spoke of the sacred way in which his mother related to his conception:

> My mother told me that when she conceived me and later, when she was carrying me, she did so with the idea of consecrating me to God's service. And, in fact, the day he baptized me, the priest was so happy that he got drunk for the first time in his life — normally he never drank! Afterwards he said that he had drunk too much because I was certainly not like all the other children he baptized, and he prophesied something about me . . . but I am not obliged to tell you what it was![7]

Aivanhov hastened to add that his mother's consecration of him did not make him an extraordinary individual at birth. But she lit a spark that would eventually become a blaze. Of course, in keeping with Aivanhov's teaching, we may also assume that it was his mother's moral stature and spiritual sensitivity that attracted him into her womb in the first place.

Aivanhov readily admitted the central importance his mother held on his life. Above all, she taught him to love and respect women. She showed him the greatness of motherhood, which knows no limits on self-sacrifice, patience, and love. "Never have I experienced anything comparable to the sublime life of a mother," he said, adding, "with the exception, of course, of my Master, Peter Deunov."[8]

We know little about Aivanhov's mother, who died in 1973 at the age of ninety-seven, but we can nevertheless tell that she must have been a remarkable woman. It was she who was his first teacher. She never yelled at him, hit him, or forced him to do anything. Instead she patiently and gently explained to him the options open to him and what consequences they would bring, leaving it to him to decide his own fate.

Aivanhov's attitude toward his disciples was similarly patient and tolerant. Even when he thought it necessary on

occasion to shake up a disciple, he never pushed anyone to
follow a particular path. He fiercely believed in a person's
freedom of choice. "Where would be the glory of God,"
Aivanhov once asked, "if we were not free to choose?"[9]

Of late, there have been too many reports of charismatic
teachers who, instead of setting their disciples free, have
placed them in shackles. Each person has his or her own song
to sing, and wise and compassionate teachers will do everything in their power to help disciples find their personal song,
their own unique way to communion with the higher reality.

Aivanhov recollected how his mother was always ready
to help and comfort others, and how she bore her own burden
without complaint. He remembered how she would occasionally weep, though never in front of people, not even in front
of her own family. She was unaware of young Mikhael observing her distress. He also noticed how, when a neighbor needed
help, she quickly wiped away her tears and patiently listened
to the other person's problems. "She always found the right
words to give courage and confidence to others," Aivanhov
remarked.[10]

His grandmother also was an exceptional woman who
knew the language of Nature. She would travel dozens of
miles for food, and in the deep of winter would make her way
through the forest if her services as a midwife were needed.

Little wonder that Aivanhov saw women as playing a
much more prominent role in the emerging new spiritual
culture than men. In many of his talks, he specifically addressed women, charging them with the obligation to instill a
spirit of love and harmony in their children so that the world
could be changed for the better. "A mother," he once noted,
"can accomplish great miracles because she holds the key to
the forces of life."[11] Women are power holders for Aivanhov.
"They must realize that great as their power is physically, it is
even greater in the higher world of emanations."[12]

In his high regard for the female gender, Aivanhov unknowingly concurred with another great sage of his day — Sri
Aurobindo, mystic, philosopher, and accomplished writer. Aurobindo once made this comment:

The mediaeval ascetics hated women and thought
they were created by God for the temptation of monks.
One may be allowed to think more nobly both of God
and of woman.[13]

It is clear from Aurobindo's further remarks that he held
women in the highest esteem and thought them capable of
getting in touch with the psychic dimension of existence more
easily then men. His longtime spiritual partner, known rever-
ently as The Mother, was still more complimentary when she
said that "women are in principle the executive power."[14] By
this observation she meant to empower the female gender,
which over many centuries has been systematically dis-
empowered by men. Aivanhov shared this enlightened point
of view with her.

Unquestionably, Aivanhov's father also was an important
influence during his formative years, but he died in his late
twenties of pneumonia when Aivanhov was a mere boy of
seven years. His father's death left his family destitute. As he
recalled:

> My father died when I was very young and we were
> very poor, so poor that my mother could not afford
> to buy books. Very often I went off to school in the
> morning with no breakfast and I was always a bit
> drowsy in class — sometimes I fell asleep. During the
> recreation periods I borrowed my class-mates' books
> and, in a great hurry, tried to learn a little of the day's
> lesson and then, when the teacher called on me I had
> to try to remember what I had read in those few
> minutes. In retrospect I see that all those difficulites I
> had to contend with awoke certain faculties in my
> character which stood me in good stead later on.
> When life is too comfortable it chloroforms us and
> puts us to sleep.[15]

Two years prior to his father's death, Aivanhov had an
experience that not only showed his spiritual sensitivity but
also left its imprint on his psyche. He had gone to the forest
with his father and other villagers to cut wood in order to make

charcoal. He delighted in watching the fires burn brightly. To keep him out of mischief, a friend of his father handed him St. John's Gospel. After devouring the story of Jesus, young Mikhael burst into tears: He realized that in comparison with Jesus he was a great sinner, and he vowed to himself to henceforth live a good and just life that would be pleasing to God.

However, Mikhael was not yet quite ready for such a noble path. The moment of insight and remorse was soon eclipsed by his boyish vitality, with all the attendant follies and pranks. But such moments are always formative and never entirely lost. They are stepping stones on the path to self-understanding and self-transcendence.

In those days, Aivanhov was apparently passionate about four things. He loved to climb trees — tall poplars as far as the branches would carry his weight. He liked the sense of being perched high up above and gaining an overview of life below. This foreshadowed his later desire to always keep the larger picture in mind, to consider life from the summit of enlightenment rather than the valley of egoic existence.

As a child he also loved to watch running water. Near his village a fountain bubbled up from seemingly nowhere, and its water was perfectly pure. He once remarked:

> I still remember some of the events that occurred during the few years I spent in that village, and one of my most vivid memories is of a discovery I made when I was four or five years old. Not far from our house I found a spring of water. The clear, transparent water bubbling out of the ground made such an impression on me that I stayed there watching it for hours on end. The image of that spring is still so vivid in my mind's eye that even now, when I picture it again, I experience the same sense of wonder and delight that I experienced as a child. I have often asked myself what it was about that water that made such a deep impression on me at such an early age.[16]

For Aivanhov, water was a potent expression of the feminine cosmic principle, just as fire was a manifestation of the masculine principle. In later years, he often admonished his disciples to be like a limpid stream and also to seriously work with the water element.

Climbing poplars and gazing into water were rather harmless pastimes. However, Aivanhov also was so enamored of fire that one day he accidentally burned down his parent's barn. He failed to understand why everyone was so distressed and rushed to put out the fire, which he thought was so extraordinarily beautiful. Nor was the parental barn the only one in the village that succumbed to Aivanhov's fascination with fire. Later he greatly regretted this childhood folly, which caused great pain and hardship to his parents and the village.

Like water, fire exercised a lifelong fascination on him. However, in his mature years, both assumed an altogether new significance for him. Water came to stand for the water of life itself and the feminine universal principle, whereas fire represented the Spirit, the eternal masculine principle. He transformed his fascination with fire into spiritual work, first kindling his own spiritual flame and then setting people's hearts on fire, instead of their property.

Aivanhov remembered another childhood prank in which we can also detect a deeper symbolism, as was pointed out by him in one of his lectures. One day he regarded the family loom with its numerous threads of wool neatly arranged. In an instant, he cut all the threads. The act that seemed entirely natural to him once again caused much distress to others, which he could barely comprehend. He simply had to have those threads, even though he could not think of a purpose for them. Later he explained:

> I didn't want the needles, they were not what appealed to me. It was the threads. . . How to interpret that? The needles were a masculine principle that I had already. I needed the feminine principle, matter, substance, threads, to be able to do the weaving. Finally, after a lot of work, God has given me these threads. I have them now. But you, I see that you have

never cut up woven material as I have. It was crimi-
nal, I admit, but I went [back to my village a few years
ago] and made amends for my crime.[17]

Life is nothing but tangled threads, as he was to philoso-
phize in his later years. Everything is interconnected, following the iron law of karma. People are enmeshed in threads of
their own making, yet they have cut the one vital thread
without which they are lost in the web of life, and that is the
golden thread connecting them to the Divine.

Aivanhov's spiritual work consisted in cutting karmic
threads and assisting disciples in finding and strengthening
their link with "Heaven," the great invisible world of luminosity and bliss. This task he understood to be real magic, and he
regarded himself as a bridge builder.[18]

But we are moving ahead of our story. In his early childhood years, no one could have known of Aivanhov's future
greatness. He was a thoughtful, sensitive child, but, as we have
seen, with some rather peculiar fascinations. He obviously
moved in a somewhat different reality from everyone else. The
universe was an enchanted place for him, and he was busy
trying to find his way around in it.

Among his favorite times were those occasions when his
grandmother or visiting elders told stories. He particularly
recalled one old man, also named Mikhael, who was very
wise.

Aivanhov said:

> When he talked he would measure his words and
> gestures. Like my grandmother, he would tell me
> fantastic tales of battles between the forces of good
> and evil, the powers of light and darkness, white
> magicians and sorcerers . . . and good always tri-
> umphed over evil in the end. Ever since, I have felt
> that by means of these tales this old man and my
> grandmother gave me an impetus towards the good
> and the light, and gave my heart a yearning to see the
> triumph of light over darkness.[19]

Aivanhov recognized that the moral lessons he imbibed through these stories were more character forming than anything he later learned from books. "Childhood," he noted, "determines the whole of one's life."[20]

Listening to his elders' tales, Aivanhov also discovered his own flair for storytelling. He endeared himself to some of his school teachers by his ability to embellish his scant knowledge so as to make it more credible. In later life, he gave few lectures in which he failed to insert an instructive anecdote or story.

He admired writers of fairy tales, mentioning by name Grimm, Andersen, and Perrault. "I prefer to spend most of the time in the fairy tale world," he admitted, "that is where I am elated and happy."[21] He also advised his disciples to read fairy tales, because these stories can put one in touch with the subtle, invisible realms of existence. These realms, Aivanhov insisted, are no less real than the world of ordinary experience; if anything, they are more real, because they are senior to the physical reality.

Aivanhov always looked for the beauty, the poetry in everything. This was so already in his youth. Hence disharmony, strife, and aggression were painful to him. But he was not exempt from experiencing them in his childhood environment. His country has been a troubled one for many centuries.

After Greeks ransacked their village in 1907, Aivanhov's family relocated to the town of Varna. Varna, which is situated on the Black Sea to the extreme east of Bulgaria, is today a city of 300,000 inhabitants, but in those days it was considerably smaller. Nevertheless, it was the second-largest city after Sofia, the capital.

It was in Varna that Aivanhov received most of his formal schooling. It was also here that his father died. Acting on a premonition, his father had enjoined his mother to marry a dear friend if ever something should happen to him. Soon after the death, his mother did indeed remarry in order to better provide for her two sons, Mikhael and younger brother Alexander. In due course, two girls and a third boy were added to the new family.

Like most intelligent children, Aivanhov found school rather limited. He used those years to develop a rich inner life. At the age of eleven, he experienced a second wave of spiritual concern, a burning desire to realign himself to the Divine. At that time he daringly led a group of friends to the Turkish legation in Varna to plant the Bulgarian flag in place of the alien banner. Bulgaria had been a Turkish province for almost five hundred years when, in 1878, it finally gained autonomy, though still under Turkish sovereignty. The Bulgarians were understandably bitter about the continuing Turkish involvement in their political life.

The young revolutionaries were spotted by the police. While his friends fled, Aivanhov bravely stood by his flag. The police officers took him to the station but, being Bulgarian nationals themselves, neither charged nor even reprimanded him. They were proud of what they perceived to be his ardent patriotism.

However, Aivanhov had acted on a different motive. He wanted to protest the injustice of the Turkish presence in his homeland. He was prompted to this youthful act of defiance by contemplating powerful spirits he thought resided in the mountains, from where they supervise our human destiny. Perhaps he saw himself as a heroic agent for their mission of preserving the good on Earth.

Aivanhov was eager to learn. He devoured any books he could lay his hands on. When he was about thirteen or fourteen, he also began to use school holidays to explore different trades. He worked in a sweets factory, where he quickly learned that moderation is a useful approach in all things. Work in a pastels factory gave him the opportunity to develop his keen sense of color, honed by his inner visionary experiences. As he explained:

> When I was a boy of fifteen or sixteen, I worked a great deal with colours. Not only did I picture them in my mind and meditate on them, but I daubed different colours onto the windows of my room to see what effect they would have on me. I would meditate in the room filled with the coloured light filtering

through the painted glass and observe the effects of each colour. Then I would wash off the first colour and begin all over again with the next one. I hardly need to tell you that my parents and the neighbours feared for my sanity! But I was quite unperturbed and went on with my experiments. When my room was filled with purple light I would soar away into other worlds and, one day, I invited some friends in to see what effect it would have on them, and all they did was to go to sleep![22]

Aivanhov also worked in a tailor's shop, but kept falling asleep from boredom, and at the end of the day decided that this job was definitely not for him. However, much later he humorously commented that he learned a valuable lesson even from this job. In his own words:

> . . . a day spent as a tailor leaves its mark and ever since I have always continued to sew, in my own way, without anyone noticing. I have never opened a boutique to make money that way, but I still continue to make my own clothes. Ah, you are surprised, aren't you? Yes, I go to certain shops I know, choose the very best cloth and make myself beautiful clothes, the most gorgeous tunics and coats that have ever been made. I let someone else make my exterior garments for me, or I buy them ready-made, but for my interior garments: that is my job.[23]

Young Mikhael also tried his hand at the blacksmith's art, working in the village smithy for several weeks. He operated the bellows, all the while carefully watching the blacksmith at work. "I can still remember," he said, how the sparks flew. It was magnificent."[24] The sparks also cascaded onto his feet, and since he only wore sandals he often returned home with blisters. He even got paid a few pennies for his pains.

But it was the experience rather than the money that he sought and enjoyed. Those were years of intense inner experimentation. He even discovered that he had considerable psychic abilities, and like any enthusiastic neophyte delighted in exercising and probing them.

Young Mikhael's experiments sometimes involved other people. While they were harmless enough, they fell short of the highest spiritual ideals, which he had yet to discover. In one of his talks, Aivanhov recalled how, by a mere act of concentration, he once rendered an unsuspecting friend incapable of walking. In due course he restored the friend's legs to full functioning.

Mikhael also was not above displaying his psychic powers to his peers, "just for fun." Thus one day he and a group of friends climbed to the top of Mount Musala, a 9,596-foot peak in the Rhodope mountains. The valley and the other peaks were shrouded in impenetrable fog. He asked which lake or peak they would like to see, offering to clear the fog around the mountain range. The boys named one of the five lakes in the valley below. Mikhael extended his hand, and to everyone's astonishment and excitement, lifted the fog above the lake so that the water became perfectly visible. Then he lowered his hand, and the fog rolled back over the lake.

Aivanhov told this story in 1967, solemnly assuring his listeners of its veracity. "I know that the invisible world is listening to me and I have no desire to lie to you."[25]

Evidently, more than fifty years earlier, young Michael had not yet integrated his magical talent with his otherwise remarkable moral sensibilities.

THE TURNING POINT

Mikhael's manipulation of other people through the power of thought was bound to have repercussions in the psychic and spiritual dimension. One day, while in a semilucid state of awareness, he had a vision of two figures. Here is his own description of this important psychic experience:

> One of them was very impressively built and everything about him spoke of strength and power, but the expression on his face was extremely harsh and there was something dark and terrible in his eyes. The

figure beside him, by contrast, was radiantly beautiful and his eyes expressed the immensity of divine
love. It was as though I were being told to choose
between the two. I was very impressed by the power
of the first, but my heart and soul were seized with
horror at the terrible evil I could feel in him and I was
more drawn to the other. I chose the one whose face
was the face of Christ, who was the picture of gentleness, kindness and self-sacrifice.[26]

This archetypal vision was very timely and made its point
in Aivanhov. He began to seriously apply his innate moral
sense to his psychic explorations. He admitted that, had it not
been for providence, he might easily have chosen the path of
black magic.

Heeding the warning contained in his vision, Aivanhov
henceforth assumed responsibility for all his actions and always sought to cultivate the good within himself, in other
beings, and in all situations. He had a highly developed moral
sense, and it was only a matter of time before he shook off his
incipient infatuation with power.

Just how mature his moral sense was in other situations
can be gleaned from a story he told about his days at Varna
College during World War I. Most teachers, he recalled, had
been drafted into the army to fight at the Front, and the College
had to resort to substitute teachers. One of these men, a
mathematician, regularly drew the ridicule and disobedience
of the students.

Feeling great compassion for the teacher, Aivanhov confronted his classmates one day, defending the teacher and
asking everyone to treat him with respect. For a few days at
least, his classmates mended their ways.

By the age of sixteen or so, his constant preoccupation with
the invisible reality had fanned the spiritual spark of his early
childhood into a blazing fire. As he explained:

I felt as though a fire burned within me and I wept
for joy; I was in raptures, in an ecstasy of delight; but
as I knew nothing about these things I did not

understand what it was. Thanks to my spiritual work
and all the exercises I had been practising, the divine
fire came and was beginning to burn me.[27]

This experience was precipitated by Aivanhov's intensive
practice of meditation and, somewhat later, of Hindu breathing exercises he had learned from a translation of
Ramacharaka's well-known book on Yoga. Ramacharaka was
the pseudonym of William Walker Atkinson, an American
lawyer, editor, and writer. He was born in 1862 and from 1903
onward produced books on Hatha-Yoga. The contents of these
books was entirely derived from other sources, but even today
"Swami" Ramacharaka is quoted as a Hindu authority on
Yoga in India.

Ramacharaka's writings unquestionably opened up the
tradition of Yoga philosophy and practice for many Westerners. However, despite Ramacharaka's claims his books
were hardly reliable manuals, especially not for someone of
the caliber and stamina of Aivanhov, who adopted the exercises with an extraordinary single-mindedness. Aivanhov
commented on that phase in his life as follows:

> . . . I had thrown myself totally into certain yoga
> exercises of breathing and concentration. One could
> say that I had lost my head. I spent days and nights
> studying, fasting, meditating, concentrating, breath-
> ing, and I became thin, pale, and very weak. My
> mother despaired, seeing that her son thought only
> of meditating, that he never went out, that he was
> becoming weaker, and that everyone made fun of
> him. She even wanted to burn my books because she
> thought they were the cause of all the trouble. She
> would beg me to go out into the park a little, but I was
> too infatuated with my exercises![28]

Still ignorant of the traditional Sanskrit maxim that Yoga
equals balance, Mikhael succumbed to the enthusiasm characteristic of beginners, and his exaggerated exercises made
him seriously ill.

> I was delirious, I was almost on the other side. . . .
> What's extraordinary is that in my delirium, I only
> asked for one thing: books, more books, all the best
> books. I didn't even want to live or be well, no, I just
> wanted to read all the books of all the libraries on
> earth. I asked for any books which dealt with philos-
> ophy, religion and science, and my poor parents had
> to satisfy me, to bring me quantities of books which
> they placed close to my pillow so I could see them and
> touch them. And it was the books that saved me! Yes,
> but when I was well again, this madness for books
> had disappeared.[29]

Even though Aivanhov's "madness" for books was cured
with the restoration of his health, nonetheless books continued
to play an important role in his life until he succeeded in
reading the Book of Nature itself. By his own admission, he
was an eternal student in his early years. Studying, however,
held a special significance for him. The information he so
eagerly sought was not mere theoretical knowledge but practical knowledge, gnosis, that would help him understand
himself and life and reveal the great secret behind appear-
ances. "True understanding involves every cell of your body,"
Aivanhov once commented.[30] In his talks to students he often
emphasized that he had personally verified everything he was
communicating to them. Often he would say:

> Do not rely on explanations from others or on books;
> they can do nothing for you if your whole being does
> not vibrate and throb with the fire within, if you are
> not ablaze with fire, like the sun.[31]

Aivanhov's dedication to the spiritual quest was rewarded
early in his life. Particularly his prodigious breathing exercises
paved the way for a spiritual breakthrough at the age of
seventeen. Before his episode of illness, one morning while
reading an inspiring book in a quiet orchard outside town, he
felt a fire enter his lungs and from there flood his entire body
and being. In a talk given in 1968 he recollected this mystical
experience as follows:

I did not understand what was happening, but from that time on, all kinds of strange, unimaginable phenomena began to manifest themselves. It was at that period of my life that I heard the Music of the Spheres. Only later did I realize that the fire that I had received was a particle of the ether, of the Cosmic Spirit.[32]

He commented about it further in another lecture, given in 1970:

I was snatched from my body and permitted to hear the Harmony of the Spheres. Never have I known anything to equal the intensity and richness of the sensations I experienced. There is nothing I can compare it to; it was indescribable, almost unbearable, so strongly did I feel that I was being stretched and diluted in space. It was so beautiful, so divine that I was afraid; I was afraid of that splendour, for I felt my whole being expanding to such an extent that I was in danger of dissolving and disintegrating into space. So I cut short the ecstasy and came back to earth. Now, I regret it, of course! But at least, for a few seconds, I actually experienced it, I actually saw and heard the whole universe vibrating. . . . When I heard the Harmony of the Spheres it was the crowning point of all my research, all my work, all my out-of-body experiences. And, ever since, it has remained as a criterion, an example, a touchstone, a model which enables me to understand and recognize how everything else fits in.[33]

For a brief period, Mikhael was tasting the unexcelled beauty of the higher realm. He was immersed in an ocean of light. In a talk given in 1975, he said:

It was an indescribable experience, I thought I was going to be ground to bits, dissolved in space . . . it was marvellous, and it was terrible. I was frightened! I did everything to come back into my body. No words can express the sensation, a rare one for anyone to have, even for the Initiates; I consider it a great privilege.[34]

In another lecture, Aivanhov described his spiritual awakening as a *kundalini* experience. He said:

> It was a terrible sensation, as if my head was on fire; I was very afraid. I then made gigantic efforts to make it go to sleep again — yes, such efforts; and I succeeded. . . . What happened to me when I was young could have been the greatest disaster for me if I had not been capable of making this force go to sleep once again. Fortunately, Heaven was watching over me.[35]

The term *kundalini* stems from Sanskrit, the sacred language of the Hindus. It means literally "she who is coiled" and refers to the psychospiritual energy that in the ordinary person lies "coiled up" in the lowest psychoenergetic center at the base of the spine. When this occult force is awakened, either deliberately or by accident, it shoots upward along the spinal axis of the body, rushing toward the head.

Ideally, the aroused *kundalini* energy dynamizes the topmost psychoenergetic center (*cakra*) at the crown of the head, which induces a state of ecstasy. However, in those who are unprepared the *kundalini* energy wreaks havoc in the body and mind. The best known instance of a spontaneous *kundalini* experience that caused tremendous physiological and psychological problems is that of Gopi Krishna.[36] It took Krishna, a native of Kashmir, years before he had brought the adverse manifestations of the *kundalini* under control.

Aivanhov was indeed fortunate to have bypassed the physical pain and psychological trauma of a *kundalini* gone haywire. His account of this experience is, however, too perfunctory to determine whether or not he experienced a full-fledged awakening of the *kundalini*.

At any rate, his various descriptions indicate that, at an early age, he enjoyed a rare mystical experience. They also show Aivanhov's characteristic deep feeling and grateful attitude. As with any experience, mystical realizations need to be integrated with the rest of one's life and being. Otherwise they are little more than fascinating fragments in one's life experience. To integrate them, we must reflect upon them and allow them to inform all aspects of our lives.

In other words, we must ground even the most extraordinary and elevated state of consciousness, and we can do so through the medium of feeling. As Aivanhov explained, feeling "is the lever capable of touching matter."[37] It is a true vehicle of personal transformation, as modern psychotherapy has rediscovered for our time.

Aivanhov's experience of what he called the Harmony of the Spheres was, in Hindu terms, a very high form of *savikalpa-samadhi* or "ecstasy associated with ideation." During the brief span of this experience, Aivanhov in some sense was the cosmos he had been contemplating so intensively.

But the ego-sense, which is deeply rooted in the human psyche, did not allow this process of spiritual identification with the universe to take its full course. Young Mikhael recoiled in fear at the prospect of his imminent dissolution as a separate being. He was promptly snatched back into the limited form of his ordinary body-mind, but immensely enriched by what had been revealed to him.

The experience thoroughly transformed him. He was never to be the same again. He had firmly entered the spiritual path to full illumination, and was now ready for the next important step: the arrival of his outer teacher.

NOTES

1. See P. C. Renard, *The Solar Revolution and the Prophet: The Role of the Sun in the Spiritual Life* (Frejus, France: Prosveta, 1980), p. 182.
2. Aivanhov, *The Living Book of Nature*, p. 216.
3. See M. Gimbutas, *The Goddesses and Gods of Old Europe* (Berkeley and Los Angeles: University of California Press, 1982).
4. M. Gimbutas, *The Language of the Goddess* (San Francisco: Harper San Francisco, 1991), p. 318.
5. Ibid., p. 320.
6. Aivanhov, *Harmony*, pp. 194–195.

7. Aivanhov, *Education Begins Before Birth*, p. 29.
8. Aivanhov, *Spiritual Alchemy*, p. 215.
9. Aivanhov, *Cosmic Moral Laws*, p. 191.
10. Aivanhov, *Hope for the World*, p. 184.
11. Aivanhov, *Education Begins Before Birth*, p. 29.
12. Aivanhov, *Hope for the World*, p. 196.
13. *On Women: Compiled from the Writings of Sri Aurobindo and The Mother* (Pondicherry, India: Sri Aurobindo Society, 1978), p. 1.
14. Ibid., p. 46.
15. Aivanhov, *Education Begins Before Birth*, p. 142.
16. Aivanhov, *The Mysteries of Fire and Water*, pp. 16–17.
17. Aivanhov, *Cosmic Moral Laws*, p. 234.
18. See Aivanhov, *Cosmic Moral Laws*, pp. 236–237.
19. Aivanhov, *Education Begins Before Birth*, p. 116.
20. Ibid., p. 117.
21. Aivanhov, *On The Art of Teaching* (Part III), p. 204.
22. Aivanhov, *The Splendour of Tiphareth*, p. 112.
23. Aivanhov, *The Living Book of Nature*, p. 110.
24. Ibid., p. 111.
25. Aivanhov, *The Splendour of Tiphareth*, p. 102.
26. Aivanhov, *The Book of Divine Magic*, pp. 19–20.
27. Aivanhov, *The Splendour of Tiphareth*, p. 245.
28. Aivanhov, *Harmony*, pp. 231–232.
29. Ibid., p. 232.
30. Aivanhov, *Harmony and Health*, p. 45.
31. Aivanhov, *The Living Book of Nature*, p. 115.
32. Aivanhov, *The Splendour of Tiphareth*, p. 247.
33. Aivanhov, *Harmony and Health*, pp. 42–44; an earlier translation of this talk can be found in *Harmony*, p. 28.
34. Aivanhov, *On the Art of Teaching* (Part III), p. 51.
35. Aivanhov, *What Is a Spiritual Master?*, p. 47.
36. See G. Krishna, *Kundalini: The Evolutionary Energy in Man* (London: Robinson & Watkins, 1971).
37. Aivanhov, *The Powers of Thought*, p. 88.

2
SPIRITUAL
DISCIPLESHIP

ENTERING THE STREAM

As is evident from Omraam Mikhael Aivanhov's various remarks about his ecstatic experience at the age of sixteen and his spiritual experimentation surrounding it, he was an intrepid explorer of the invisible dimension. He regularly practiced astral projection, leaving his physical body behind to reconnoiter the psychic realms of existence.

Astral projection, or the deliberate induction of out-of-body experiences, is a phenomenon that is recognized in most spiritual traditions. In particular it is part of the paranormal repertoire of yogins and is, for instance, referred to in Patanjali's *Yoga-Sutra,* the standard Sanskrit work on Classical Yoga, which was probably composed some time in the second or third century A.D.[1]

Spontaneous out-of-body experiences are fairly well documented in the parapsychological literature. They have been reported to occur during medical surgeries, after accidents, in moments of danger to the physical body, or during lovemaking, exhaustion, or sleep. A comprehensive collection of such case histories can be found in psychologist Robert Crookall's widely read book *The Study and Practice of Astral Projection.*[2] The most extensive first-person accounts of controlled out-of-body experiences are those by Robert Monroe, an American businessman who started to have spontaneous experiences of this type at the age of forty-three.[3]

Like Monroe and others, Aivanhov used the mind's natural ability to separate from the physical body to pursue his occult research without being hampered by the slow, tedious process of acquiring knowledge in piecemeal linear fashion.

Peter Deunov (Beinsa Douno),
the teacher of Omraam Mikhael Aivanhov

Omraam Mikhael Aivanhov, Paris 1940

He had an unquenchable thirst for knowledge, wanting to understand the ultimate structure of the universe, to read Nature like an open book. All his early esoteric research culminated in the ecstatic experience during which he, however briefly, participated in the Music of the Spheres.

This lofty realization of the eternal symphony, played out in the ocean of universal energy, gave him the sought-after vantage point. He had known instinctively that to comprehend anything in depth, one must first find its highest form of manifestation — at the level of laws and first principles. But like an ill-equipped mountaineer he had climbed to the mountain top only to discover that the descent was more difficult and perilous than the ascent. His young body gave way under the strain of his incessant inner work.

Aivanhov's illness, which rendered him bedridden with a high fever for weeks, was a necessary crisis. It confronted him with his physical limits and prepared him for a more mature orientation to spiritual practice and life. The illness left him weakened but even more determined to study the hidden code of existence and apply it in life.

Soon after his recovery, young Aivanhov met his beloved teacher. This statement fails to convey the momentousness of this event. Perhaps no words can do justice to that decisive moment in a seeker's life. When we read in the gospels that Jesus summoned the fishermen Simon Peter and Andrew to follow him and that these good men obeyed at once, we can only guess at the amazing psychic process that must have occurred between them and the radiant stranger.

Possibly only another disciple can understand what it means to find one's predestined teacher. In any event, Aivanhov's life changed radically. He was no longer a lonely adventurer risking his life and causing his relatives and friends to fear for his sanity and bodily well-being. He now had the wisdom of an experienced adept to guide him. That adept was Beinsa Douno or, as he is also known in the West, Peter Deunov.

MASTER PETER DEUNOV

Peter Konstantinov Deunov was born July 12, 1864. He was the youngest of three children. His father Konstantine Dunovsky was a priest and something of a rebel. He was the first to use his native Bulgarian instead of the prescribed Greek in reading the Bible during the liturgy. This deliberate break with tradition was in keeping with the liturgical reforms that had been initiated in other parts of Europe. Yet these contemporaneous precedents elsewhere do not diminish the boldness of Konstantine Dunovsky's innovative step. He was a man of courage all round, for he was also a prominent political activist in the Bulgarian national liberation movement, which sought to shake off the yoke of the Turks.

Peter Deunov was educated in Varna and Suishtov, and for a short period of time taught in a small village named Hatantsa. At the age of twenty-four he obtained a stipend and went to the United States. For seven years he studied medicine and theology in Boston and New York. Little is known about his time in America. However, according to some accounts, he was very popular with students, and when on excursions with them, he would typically withdraw after a while and then be found meditating in a quiet spot.

After his return to Bulgaria in 1895, he published his doctoral dissertation, entitled "Science and Education." For the next few years he was an itinerant teacher and also spent prolonged periods of seclusion in the mountains. In 1898 he surprised his countrymen with the following announcement:

> The Truth of Life descends from the world of Eternal
> Light to illuminate the minds, regenerate the hearts,
> raise and renew the souls of all the sons of Truth
> destined to constitute the nucleus of the new human-
> ity of which the Slavs will be the cradle.[4]

Deunov adopted the spiritual name Beinsa Douno and, in 1900, founded the Universal White Brotherhood. The fraternity was inaugurated at a convention held in Varna on April 6 of that year. Only three people showed up! But Deunov was not in the least discouraged, prophesying that one day there would be thousands. He would be proved right. When he passed away in 1944, he had a following numbering around forty thousand.

This is a large number for a small country with a population of maybe six or seven million inhabitants at the time. The corresponding membership in the United States would be around seven million people, which is almost the size of the Anglican Church.

For many years Deunov traveled throughout his homeland, constantly teaching and healing. Every year, more people gathered at his congresses. The Church watched his activities with growing discomfiture and finally excommunicated him.

In 1914, he was under house arrest in Varna. That same year Deunov had a vision of Christ and dedicated his life to him. Later he said, "What Christ said and what I am saying come from one and the same source."[5]

According to Deunov, 1914 also ushered in the Age of Aquarius, the Era of the Waterbearer, the time in which the "Third Testament" will be revealed to humanity. Deunov saw it as his mission to help in the birthing of this new spiritual cycle.

Four years later, he was free to return to the capital. In 1922, he started an esoteric school for serious disciples, continuing to give public lectures as well. There also were summer camps every year, except in 1927 when the authorities banned all larger gatherings of the fraternity. His disciples are still gathering today in the mountains of Bulgaria, as they have done since the 1920s.

During the course of his life, Peter Deunov gave over 7,000 talks. He was an immensely charismatic and gifted man — a mystic, theologian, philosopher, healer, clairvoyant, and, by all accounts, a wonderful musician. He understood his teaching as a revival of esoteric Christianity, which he felt had been suppressed and lost to the people.

The bishops of the orthodox Church completely misunderstood his intentions, or else were only too well aware of the consequences of an esoteric gnostic community growing stronger. As so often has happened in the history of the Christian Church, the authorities felt threatened by this original and empowered representative of the esoteric tradition that had its roots in the Gospel of John.

The outbreak of World War II in 1939, when Germany attacked Poland, also had its repercussions in Bulgaria. Roughly four months before D-Day, at the beginning of 1944, Sofia was bombed. Deunov moved to safety near Mount Vitosha. Later that year he told a disciple that he had completed his task on earth and was going to depart. He died at 6 a.m. on December 27 of the same year, with a beautifully intonated *aoum* — the sacred Sanskrit syllable *aum* (*om*) — on his lips.

Two days later, the Communist authorities came to arrest and presumably execute him. His grave at Izgrev ("Sunrise"), the fraternity's center just outside the Bulgarian capital, is unnamed. It is simply marked by a pentagram inscribed with the words "Love, Wisdom, Truth, Equity, Virtue": the legacy of a great soul.

DISCIPLESHIP

It was while Deunov was under surveillance in Varna that Aivanhov met him for the first time in 1917. The young seeker felt he had come home, and a great joy welled up in his chest. As he put it:

> If I described the extraordinary joy and happiness I experienced when I first met my own Master, you would not believe me. And that state has lasted until today.... When I met my Master I had the impression that all the treasures of the universe had been poured into my heart and head. I felt rich, fabulously rich![6]

Aivanhov's love for Deunov continued to burn brightly even after he had attained mastership himself. In a talk given in 1938, he said this about him:

> He is a being of very high spirituality, and all of his
> life he has been an example of purity, wisdom and
> intelligence ... With his powerful radiance, with his
> words and example, the Master performs miracles
> around him.[7]

In Peter Deunov he had found the human embodiment of
the spiritual ideal he had been searching for so avidly. He
knew instinctively that this great man could show him the way
to the Divine, and he dedicated himself wholeheartedly to the
disciplines of a disciple. As in so many other things, he was
exemplary in his devotion to his teacher. But the gift of his
devotion was reciprocated in countless ways by Peter Deunov.
As Aivanhov recalled:

> I cannot describe here in great detail the outings made
> at sunrise on the hills of Varna. You cannot imagine
> the beauty of the morning colors and the splendor of
> the sun rising over the Black Sea. How many times
> the Master and I sat together under the caressing sun!
> We would both leave our physical bodies, and he
> would lead me to the invisible world so that I could
> learn its realities.[8]

Deunov also healed his young disciple's liver complaint
by making him sip hot water several times a day while thinking of the water.[9] Although the instruction made no sense to
the apprenticing Aivanhov, he followed it implicitly and
reaped its fruit. He still had to learn that a master's words are
empowered: Spoken from truth, they work their transformative magic in a disciple's heart and body.

When a few months later, in 1918, the authorities allowed
Master Deunov to return to Sofia, Aivanhov followed him
without question. Deunov noted his new disciple's eagerness,
dedication, and love, and quietly watched over his spiritual
growth. Few words passed between them, but whenever
Deunov addressed his pupil directly, Aivanhov would respond quickly and with great eagerness. Occasionally, when
Deunov responded to one of his questions, Aivanhov would

aspire to listen to his teacher with complete attention while at the same time remaining sensitive to the feeling he instilled in him.

Sometimes Aivanhov found it difficult to remember everything his teacher had said to him, and then he would spend as much time as was necessary to reconstruct every moment of the conversation. It was unthinkable for him that he should ask the same question a second time. Deunov's every word and gesture were precious to him, and he wanted to be sure to miss absolutely nothing. In this way, he developed a wonderful facility for memorization.[10]

For the most part, however, Aivanhov anticipated his teacher's expectations of him. One day Deunov said to him approvingly, "For you, a glance is enough."[11] Aivanhov was puzzled by the remark but studied himself and found Deunov's observation to be true. "The Master," he noted, "had seen into the depths, the roots, the structure of my being."[12] Aivanhov did indeed only need a single look from his teacher. Later he learned to cultivate that same special glance and use it to hallow the lives of others.

The eyes are very important conduits for the life force, more so in the case of an adept whose body-mind is supercharged with spiritual vitality. This is the reverse of the "evil eye." It is instead the eye that purifies and sanctifies. In one of his earliest talks, Aivanhov stated: "The eyes are linked with truth."[13] More will be said about this in Chapter 3.

Aivanhov always remembered those days at Izgrev with great fondness. In one of his early talks, when the memory of his teacher and fellow disciples back in Bulgaria was still extremely vivid, he told his French audience:

> We are overjoyed that we have a chance to live with such a luminous being, full of love and goodness, and to be able to listen to him and see him in the simplest details of daily life. It is the greatest fortune to have a Master capable of answering the most obscure questions. . .[14]

Still speaking as a disciple, Aivanhov added:

> When the Master arrives at our colony of Izgrev,
> where he lives among the brothers and sisters, every-
> one is immediately aware of his presence. Even the
> air seems to vibrate differently when he is there . . .
> The way the Master speaks is amazing. When he
> lectures, he never reads or quotes other authors, as
> most lecturers do. He lets inspiration guide him. He
> is aware of what is bothering his listeners, and speaks
> to answer their inner questions so as to help them to
> solve their problems . . . All the disciples know that
> the Master is aware of what people think.[15]

Many years later, Aivanhov's own disciples would say the same things about him. But at that time, in the late 1930s, he was still "Brother Mikhael" to everyone, an inspiring disciple of the great Peter Deunov.

During the early years of his discipleship, Aivanhov was rather poor. He owned a bed, some books, a violin, and a few shabby clothes. He cared little for possessions or the way he looked. He was working hard on purifying his inner being. However, he treasured the violin given to him by Deunov. This gift meant all the more to Aivanhov because he knew that Deunov was a marvelous musician and composer. The gift was a token of his love for Aivanhov, and undoubtedly also had deep symbolic significance. Perhaps it was Deunov's way of saying that he wanted Aivanhov to play the game of life as well as he himself did, to be as attuned to the Divine as the master himself.

Aivanhov spent most of his time on spiritual retreats in the mountains, where he studied and meditated. Occasionally he took a job to earn enough for his upkeep. Yet, he considered himself "fabulously rich."

We catch occasional glimpses of the intense, tender relationship between master and disciple. One day, Deunov tested Aivanhov's knowledge about palmistry. In front of the entire fraternity, he asked his disciple which line of the hand appeared first and which next.[16] Aivanhov correctly replied the life line, the heart line, and finally the head line. Deunov seemed pleased with the response, because the answer could not be found in any books, which told him that Aivanhov had acquired his knowledge through keen observation of life and understanding of life's fundamental patterns.

Deunov encouraged his disciple's penchant for contemplation and esoteric studies. However, he also obliged him to broaden his conventional knowledge by pursuing studies at the University of Varna. Aivanhov enrolled in courses on psychology, education, philosophy, physics, mathematics, chemistry, astronomy, and medicine. He admitted to learning just enough to obtain the requisite diplomas and was often absent, preferring to spend his time reading other books and meditating. As he put it, "I gave only fifty percent to the world."[17]

To others it seemed that he was an "eternal student." Aivanhov wanted to assimilate as much as possible, while at the same time being careful not to stultify his inner life by too much academic cerebration. When he left the university, he was spiritually not only intact but very much alive. His next step was to deliberately "forget" many of the things he had learned, "because I understood that they were a veil between myself and reality."[18] Instead he cultivated his reading of the Book of Nature through psychic means, by developing the "single eye" spoken of in the Bible.

Deunov tested his young disciple in many ways. Aivanhov shared his memory of one particularly difficult test with his own students. One day, Deunov announced to him that he was to climb to the top of Mount Musala in the middle of a moonless night. He simply said, "The experience will make you understand many things."[19]

Aivanhov waited for a moonless night and then, equipped with some provisions and a walking stick but no torch, made his way up the mountain. He had to pass through a forest and was soon enveloped by a thick silence. He could hardly see his own outstretched hand. Not only was the forest infested with bears, wolfs, boars, and other wild beasts, on one side the path dropped into sheer nothingness. Aivanhov knew that his teacher would never abandon him, but the palpable silence and total darkness made his heart pound nonetheless. He stopped to pray.

> I can assure you that in such moments one prays with great fervor; I felt that I had never before prayed like that. A few moments after this ardent prayer, I saw a light which lit the way before me for some two meters: from then on, I walked in the light and I was full of joy. I sang and I felt something moving inside of me, as if new currents of energy had passed through me.[20]

Aivanhov probably thought that his trials were over, but then he heard the barking of two large dogs. He assumed they were wild and dangerous. He also knew that retreating would not help him, as their barking came closer and they would not hesitate to follow and attack him. So he bravely continued on his upward course, trusting in his teacher's presence. What happened next is worth telling in Aivanhov's own words:

> The day was beginning to break, and the dogs were soon at a distance from which they could see me. They began running and howling terribly. At a distance of two or three meters they stopped, ready to spring on me. Each was the size of a small donkey, one white and the other grey. Everything happened very quickly and words are too slow to tell about it. With their jaws wide open and menacing, the dogs were ready to spring, but as I felt so full of light and confidence, I thrust my right hand in their direction with unimaginable force. It was an exceptional instant, where I sensed the presence of invisible entities and of the Master; what I saw then is enough to prove to me the existence of the divine world even if I would never have had any other proof. At the moment when I thrust my hand forward, I heard the dogs cry out with an atrocious and rending howl, and they were both lifted by an invisible force and literally thrown several meters away from me. Then they lay howling on the ground in a terrorized attitude, immobile, silent, not looking in my direction.[21]

Once he had recovered from the shock of the encounter and the surprise at the unexpected turn of events, Aivanhov apologized to the dogs but explained to them that they should have known he was a disciple and therefore was protected. Several hours later he reached the summit, just as the sun was rising. He was filled with joy and gratitude for the experience. Deunov once commented about this test:

> If you cannot climb up and down Moussala [Musala] ... you cannot be disciples. Climbing Moussala is a difficult examination, especially in the evening or on a snowy winter's night ... The person who performs this experiment will acquire something fine in his character ... People grow when they find themselves between opposing sets of conditions. In this way they get to know themselves and become acquainted with the great and sublime in the world ... The peaks a person climbs in the course of his life are a measure of his achievements.[22]

Deunov had a great love for the mountains, which he considered tremendous reservoirs of energy useful to spiritual life. Aivanhov shared that love, as he also shared many other traits of his teacher. "Mountains," he once observed, "serve as immense aerials by means of which the earth communicates with heaven."[23] He elaborated:

> During the twenty years I spent with the Master Peter Deunov in Bulgaria, mountains occupied a very prominent place in my life. Every summer the Master would bring together the whole Brotherhood in the Rila Mountains. We would stay up there for several weeks, sometimes two months, depending on the weather. During the rest of the year the Master and many of the brothers and sisters lived in Sofia, but even then we used to spend almost every weekend in the mountains, for Mount Vitocha is only a few miles from the town. Sometimes we would stay up there for several days, and thanks to the Master, we always came back from those days in the mountains loaded

with heavenly gifts, for it was he who taught us the attitude we should have towards nature, towards streams and rocks, lakes, waterfalls and mountain peaks. From the moment we set out until we got home again the Master would use each of these as an occasion to teach us something.[24]

Aivanhov was constantly working on his inner being and on ways to understand and communicate with the invisible realms. He tolerated no weakness in himself. Earlier he had cured himself of his acute shyness by means of autosuggestion. Now he applied his formidable will power to other aspects of his life, using even sleep to reprogram his body-mind with spiritually sound patterns. He pushed himself to conquer mountain peak after mountain peak — those internal heights that can only be scaled by means of self-knowledge and unfailing dedication.

Once, while meditating in the Rila mountains, he experienced the intrinsic aliveness of all things:

> . . . Suddenly I thought I must be hallucinating, for everything around me seemed to come alive; the stones, the grass and the trees suddenly became vibrant and luminous as though by magic. The phenomenon lasted a long time, and my delight and wonder were so great I could not tear myself away from the spectacle. It was then that I realized how dreadfully ignorant we are about what nature really is. Behind her visible façade nature conceals realities such as human beings have never dreamed of.[25]

At one point, Deunov remarked that he, Aivanhov, had changed his skin.[26] Only much later did Aivanhov discover what his teacher had meant. He commented:

> The whole destiny of man depends on his skin, because his relationships with other human beings and with the exterior world depend on the skin . . . Every detail of the skin has a meaning. Even its consistency — smooth, supple, hard, flaccid, soft — reflects the

qualities, the essential characteristics of a person: his resistance, his will power, his activity, or on the contrary, his laziness and his deficiencies.[27]

Aivanhov had gone through the stages of caterpillar and cocoon and now was a butterfly ready to fly into the sun. He had engraved his teacher's magnificent ideals into his own soul, and was thoroughly groomed for the difficult task ahead of him: that of lighting the torch of wisdom in others. His whole being was ablaze with the divine fire. The birth of Christ had occurred in his soul, and after many years of discipleship Aivanhov was ready for the responsibilities of a spiritual teacher in his own right.

In 1937, one year before Germany annexed Austria and two years before the outbreak of World War II, Deunov read the signs of the time and charged his disciple with carrying the torch of his teaching to France. Aivanhov alone, among Deunov's forty thousand students, was found worthy of this immense responsibility.

NOTES

1. For an English translation of this Yoga scripture, see G. Feuerstein, *The Yoga-Sutra of Patanjali: A New Translation and Commentary* (Rochester, VT: Inner Traditions International, 1989).
2. See R. Crookall, *The Study and Practice of Astral Projection* (London: Aquarian Press, 1961). See also D. Black, *Ekstasy: Out-of-the-Body Experiences* (Indianapolis/New York: Bobbs-Merrill Company, 1975).
3. See R. Monroe, *Journeys Out of the Body* (Garden City, NY: Doubleday, 1971); *Far Journeys* (Garden City, NY: Doubleday, 1985).
4. Cited after D. Lorrimer, *The Circle of Sacred Dance: Peter Deunov's Paneurythmie* (Shaftesbury, England: Element Books, 1991), p. 2.
5. See D. Lorimer, *op. cit.*, p. 8.
6. Aivanhov, *Love and Sexuality* (Part II), p. 69.
7. Aivanhov, *The Second Birth*, p. 157.
8. Ibid., p. 165.
9. See Aivanhov, *Harmony and Health*, p. 124.
10. Aivanhov, *On the Art of Teaching* (Part III), p. 231.
11. Aivanhov, *Love and Sexuality* (Part I), p. 148.
12. Ibid., p. 148.

13. Aivanhov, *The Second Birth*, p. 72.
14. Ibid., p. 166.
15. Ibid., pp. 166–167.
16. See Aivanhov, *Life Force*, p. 13.
17. Aivanhov, *Harmony*, p. 224.
18. Aivanhov, *The Second Birth*, p. 168.
19. Ibid., p. 187.
20. Ibid., p. 188.
21. Ibid., pp. 188–189.
22. D. Lorimer, *op. cit.*, p. 181.
23. Aivanhov, *The Mysteries of Fire and Water*, p. 65.
24. Ibid., pp. 65–66.
25. Ibid., pp. 70–71.
26. Aivanhov, *Harmony*, p. 231.
27. Ibid., p. 233.

3
AIVANHOV: VISIONARY, TEACHER, AND HEALER

THE EARLY DAYS IN FRANCE

When Aivanhov received his teacher's commission to spread the teaching in France, he was not altogether surprised. Apparently the seed for his work outside his homeland had been planted long ago. As he told his students one day:

> I first climbed Mount Musallah when I was only seventeen or eighteen, and already in those early days, I thought of France and imagined myself taking the Master's teaching there one day. And years later what I had imagined came true; my destiny brought me to France. But it was from the peaks of Rila that I first touched your souls, long before I ever arrived here.[1]

Aivanhov arrived in France toward the end of July 1937, penniless and without any knowledge of the French language. His visa only authorized him to stay in France for the duration of the Universal Exposition. He had a round-trip ticket to Bulgaria and only a single contact person in France — a woman by the name of Stella Bellemin, who was known in the fraternity as Svezda (meaning "star" in Bulgarian).

She was an astronomer at the Observatory and was part of a small group of Bulgarian expatriates living in Paris who were students of Peter Deunov. In July 1937 Svezda read the book *The Master Speaks* by Peter Deunov and right away left for Bulgaria to meet Deunov. He told her that upon her return to France, she would be asked to work with someone, though he named no names. He also told her that she would serve that person for the rest of her life.

It was, of course, Aivanhov whom she was to receive and serve. She had been well prepared, for in her youth she had received (channeled) a spiritual teaching that later turned out to be identical with that of Deunov. She immediately recognized in Aivanhov a worthy and shining disciple of Deunov, and welcomed him with an open heart. As Svezda recollects:

> Above all, at our first meeting, it was the intense light that emanated from him that struck me, a light full of gentleness and pure impersonal love, pouring out like divine water on people and things. His look was the inner gift of himself, a total giving that belongs only to saints and Masters.
>
> Watching Brother Mikhael in action, one got the impression that his only concern was to offer this divine gift of love to all and sundry, with no restriction. This was all the more noticeable because of his inability to express himself in French, it made people conscious of what emanated from him. The radiance of his spiritual love shining through his unusual beauty touched everyone who came in contact with him.[2]

Aivanhov had left behind in Bulgaria his family, friends, and college students (he was a college principal). They had seen him off to the train station, waving after him with tear-filled eyes. Now he was in a new, strange country where he was unknown, with many people regarding him as a curiosity, but with a gargantuan task before him. But his deep knowledge, obvious wisdom, gentleness, and charisma soon won him admirers and supporters. They affectionately addressed him as Brother Mikhael, just as he embraced them as brothers and sisters. One of his students proffered this memory:

> On his arrival in France, the Master did not show what he was in reality. He was always self-effacing, humble, taking the back seat in a simple and modest way. He called himself Brother Mikhael. He did not reveal all his knowledge. He mixed with astrologers, alchemists, writers and because of his bearing, they

all thought that he knew little and they gave him lots of advice which he always listened to . . . he always was friendly, always obliging and smiling.

But when he began his public lectures, his friends among the astrologers and occultists who came to support and encourage him were amazed by all that he revealed.

It was so new, original, deep and, above all, true.[3]

Aivanhov gave his first talks in Svezda's Parisian apartment, addressing small groups of around twenty people. He had learned enough French to address his listeners in their native tongue when, on January 29, 1938, he delivered the very first of what would be literally thousands of "conferences." Aivanhov liked to communicate with people "in their own" language and demonstrated his remarkable linguistic facility when, at an advanced age, he visited England and promptly learned enough English in the span of a few weeks to converse with students.

On that important day in 1938, there was an inexplicable problem with the water supply in Svezda's apartment. Aivanhov was quite concerned about this and tried all the faucets, but to no avail. Then he and Svezda went out and upon their return found the whole place flooded. While everyone was disturbed about this mishap, Aivanhov took it as a wonderful omen, a sign of abundance, saying that everything would go well with his first lecture. He was proved right.

When the circle of friends in France had grown beyond the apartment's capacity, a lecture hall was rented. No entrance fee was ever charged in those days. In fact, Aivanhov never asked for a penny from his students in all his nearly fifty years of teaching.

There was one exception, though. When touring America in 1984, Aivanhov suddenly insisted that everyone pay a hefty entrance fee. His disciples were surprised, perhaps even shocked. His lectures were a success, and a fair-sized sum of money was made. He had one of his students deposit it in a special bank account. Later he told her that she was entrusted with the sum and would know what to use it for when the time came. Many years passed, and the student had almost forgotten about the account when the present publishing project was initiated, and she knew instinctively that this is what the money had been intended for all those years ago.

Aivanhov often acted in unpredictable ways, following his own intuitions. As a magus, he was constantly in touch with the invisible realms of reality, and at times admitted to listening to advice and instructions given to him from "the other side." Then he would take apparently nonsensical actions, but predictably his eccentric behavior would turn out to have been guided by considerable wisdom.

Thus not a few visitors were shocked and perplexed by Aivanhov when he spent the entire time of their visit talking about money, their house, or their sexuality. Not everyone realized that he was simply responding to their particular mental preoccupations.

One day, a woman disciple brought a male friend to see her teacher. Aivanhov recognized instantly that the man was spiritually quite immature and kindly offered him a glass of rakia. The disciple was flabbergasted, and more so when her beloved teacher offered her a glass as well. At first she refused and felt miserable because she never touched heavy liquor, but Aivanhov encouraged her to drink up. When she yielded to his friendly insistence, she found to her surprise that the rakia might as well have been plain water, for it tasted just like it and also had no effect on her at all.

The mirror principle could be seen in reverse when spiritually inclined disciples came to see him, for he would seriously consider their spiritual life with them and freely bestow on them the gift of his wisdom. Although he had a great sense of humor, he did not play at being a trickster, as some teachers have been known to do. Rather, he was simply responding to what was in front of him, faithfully reflecting the state of mind of his visitors.

Being an exemplary student himself, Aivanhov assumed that his listeners were prepared to put the profound metaphysical ideas he was expounding into daily practice. However, he soon discovered that most of the people who came to his public lectures were titillated by what they heard but scarcely ready to apply the wisdom he so generously shared with them. He had come to initiate people into the most sublime secrets of his esoteric tradition, but he quickly realized that he would have to proceed more slowly, to prepare a foundation in them upon which they could build the kind of virtues that distinguish qualified aspirants from mere dilettantes.

Fortunately, a cadre of more serious students started to form around him. They gathered into groups in Sevres, a settlement just outside Paris. Both Deunov and Aivanhov were from the beginning interested in making their teaching available to the largest possible number of people and to found a fraternity that would truly welcome everyone interested in the life of the spirit. Neither teacher was content with founding the kind of school that is known as an *ashrama* in India. This is the Sanskrit term for a hermitage — a sacred place, empowered by an initiate, and enlivened by a small group of disciples willing to exert themselves individually to realize the highest ideals.

Both Deunov and Aivanhov had their hearts set on something far more comprehensive and international. The fraternity's two main centers, Izgrev and Bonfin, were sacred locations that served primarily as gathering places for disciples who came to be with Aivanhov and listen to him expound his teaching. They continue to be pilgrimage centers for students.

Izgrev in Sevres was acquired in 1947. In addition to being a meeting place for students, Izgrev is also the administrative headquarters of the worldwide spiritual fraternity founded by Aivanhov. As mentioned before, the name means "sunrise" in Bulgarian. Aivanhov adopted this name from the principal center in Bulgaria, founded by Deunov, in order to emphasize the strong link with his master.

The small town of Sevres is situated to the west of Paris. Aivanhov once remarked that it was not by chance that Sevres houses the National Institute of Weights and Measures. Explaining his remark, he further commented that materialists admit that we need a fixed point of reference; similarly, we need a magnetic north pole in spiritual matters. Izgrev was meant to be just that for disciples.

From that center, groups spread out throughout France and also formed fellowship pockets in other countries. In 1953, the 65 acres of the Bonfin ("Good Purpose") on the French Riviera near Frejus were acquired. The initial land purchase was made possible by the generous donation of Brother Jehan, the author of the book *Who is the Master Omraam Mikhael Aivanhov?* When the first group of students pitched their tents on this isolated property, there were virtually no conveniences. For many years it was used mainly as a summer camp, but in the late 1960s several students and their families moved permanently to the Bonfin, forming a small but very active community. As funds became available they erected buildings — workshops, warehouses, a store, guest houses, private dwellings, and notably the Great Hall, capable of seating 800 people.

The Bonfin is bordered by a military compound and a commercial zoo — perhaps no coincidence considering that both represent areas of life that stand in need of spiritual purification: In both cases, the principle of nonharming (*ahimsa*) is constantly in danger of being violated. Zoos, after all, are based on the incarceration of sentient creatures.

Although Aivanhov would have preferred a different location because of the absence of water on that piece of land, he recommended it for the center largely because of a nearby idyllic outcrop, known as the Rocher, overlooking the ocean.

It is here that for years he and his students gathered to contemplate the rising sun during the spring and summer seasons. He would take his place at the top of the outcrop, surrounded by hundreds of disciples. Everyone was facing east to silently greet the sun on its emergence from the horizon, hands on their knees with the palms up to receive the solar energies.

Often Aivanhov would give a talk on that occasion, usually about the selfless nature of the sun and how we must incorporate its giving and forgiving ways into our own lives. Then he would make his way back down to the *domaine*, saluting and blessing his students with his raised right hand. Typically he also would hand out candies to the children.

Aivanhov thought that during the first century A.D. the renowned Greek philosopher and magus Apollonius of Tyana had visited the rock. According to tradition, Apollonius was a miracle-worker who was able, like his famous contemporary Jesus, to raise the dead. He belonged to the school of Pythagoras, which perhaps explains Aivanhov's interest in him.

In these two centers, Izgrev and the Bonfin, annual congresses are held. There Aivanhov used to address hundreds of students at a time. They would live communally for a period of time, bask in the same Light, learn to serve, and forget about their worldly problems and the ego that was responsible for most of them. They would eat, sing, dance, make music, exercise, pray, and meditate together at sunrise, just as Aivanhov had done with his fellow disciples during his long discipleship under Peter Deunov in the distant mountains of Bulgaria. Aivanhov once said about the Bonfin meetings:

> The Bonfin is like a clinic where you come for a cure of detoxification. All year long you have been living in conditions that were not particularly conducive to good health: your physical body and, especially, your etheric, astral and mental bodies are saturated with impurities that you want to get rid of in order to go back to the work that God is asking of you with renewed energy. Here you eat pure food, prepared and cooked by beings who are full of loving care; you breathe pure air; every morning you steep yourselves in the purity of the sun's rays, and now it is up to you to make an effort to introduce purity into your thoughts and feelings, your desires and plans. Take full advantage of the conditions you enjoy here, the beautiful weather and the peace and silence of the forest, to meditate and review your whole life and make up your minds, at last, to become true servants of God.[4]

This sacred tradition of periodic gatherings continues to this day, both in the school started by Aivanhov and the parent tradition established at the beginning of this century by Deunov.

THE UNIVERSAL WHITE BROTHERHOOD

Year after year, Aivanhov gathered his disciples around him, taught and inspired them, as well as healed them in body and spirit. Today the community has c. 10,000 members worldwide — a comparatively small number, but it seems to be growing steadily. Since 1938, Aivanhov's talks have been recorded first by shorthand and later, after 1961, by tape recorder. From 1981 until September 1985 they were video-taped. At this point, over sixty volumes have been published in French, and every year several more are released. Increasingly, these works are also being made available in other languages, notably English.

When Aivanhov started to teach in France over half a century ago, he named his school L'École Divine, "Divine School," and he always thought of his fellowship in this way. He regarded the Divine School as belonging to the Universal White Brotherhood, that invisible college of higher beings who have the spiritual evolution of humankind at heart. When the fellowship grew in size and became a legal entity, the name Fraternité Blanche Universelle, or "Universal White Brotherhood," was chosen.

In Western Europe and especially in America, this name has occasionally provoked consternation and misunderstanding, since the appellation "white" has widely assumed racial connotations. However, for Aivanhov and his fellowship, which incidentally includes nonwhites, the name evokes altogether different associations. "White" stands for all those inner virtues by which a person lives with integrity in the world, illumined by the radiance of the transpersonal Reality. Aivanhov regretted that some people would deprive themselves of the advantages of his fraternity only because of its name.

He always made it very clear that the Universal White Brotherhood is not an exclusive club accessible only to the privileged few. Rather it is an open community of beings who share the same level of existence, or vibrate in unison with one another, because they are absolutely dedicated to the highest spiritual ideals. And that community far exceeds the number of those who call themselves his disciples on earth. As Aivanhov explained:

> The Universal White Brotherhood is a power which extends to the limits of the solar system and beyond. You must not make the mistake of judging it by the Brotherhood that exists here, on earth: a handful of men and women who are not always very wise or enlightened. The true Universal White Brotherhood on high is composed of all the most highly evolved beings that have ever existed, whereas we are simply workers who are trying to benefit from the light and support of those beings in order to carry out their plans on earth. But the Brotherhood on earth must become a faithful reflection of the one on high; and this means that its members must become more and more keenly aware of the tremendous privilege they have received in belonging to this sublime entity.[5]

In another talk, Aivanhov said:

> The ideal of the Universal White Brotherhood is to teach human beings to work no longer exclusively for themselves, but for the whole world.[6]

Aivanhov, like Deunov, was an inveterate spokesman for the ideal of brotherhood between all people, regardless of their race, nationality, creed, level of education, or station in life. He once remarked that he had attended many meetings of other religious and spiritual organizations and was always struck by the lack of love and warmth and the presence of haughtiness and exclusivism. He always exhorted his disciples to cultivate the disposition of brotherly (or sisterly) love not only among one another but in their relationship to the world at large. He knew that individual and global peace and harmony can only emerge when love melts down the walls people tend to erect around themselves. "In harmony everything blossoms."[7]

Aivanhov, who never married, regarded the fraternity as his fiancée and wife. Nothing was more disturbing to him than quarreling or tension among his disciples. And nothing was more precious to him than those moments when he could sit with his disciples in deep meditative silence and harmony, greeting the rising sun. He loved to see their shining faces — sure evidence that they were in contact with the inner light.

Aivanhov tirelessly devoted his energies to the welfare of his growing community. True to his ideal of balance and harmony, he spent half his time in seclusion, where he did his inner work, and the other half in the company of disciples and visitors. When he was on his own, he would work, pray, meditate, and tend to his lush garden. He explained this careful partition of his day as follows:

> If you are always alone, without ever giving of yourself, you feel miserable and deprived, something is missing; and if you are with others all the time, everything you have inside slips away until the reservoir is empty, there is nothing left to give.[8]

For three-fourths of his life, Aivanhov was quite poor. He only started to receive an income from royalties on his books in the mid-1970s. It was then that he purchased a plot of land in the Pyrenees, with a small house, where he would retire whenever he needed to be away from the center. He also owned his own modest plot in the Bonfin. Students had built him a cottage there, which, ten years before his death, he donated to the fraternity.

Aivanhov lived very frugally at all times and was always an example of elegant simplicity and disciplined industriousness to his disciples. His daily routine was very full. During the seminar periods — from the beginning of July to the end of September — he came to the gathering at sunrise. Upon returning to his cottage, he attended to his mail and also to his spiritual work, which he seldom talked about. He made it clear that he did not want to be interrupted during this period of time. Then at noon he led his disciples in their daily exercises and took a silent lunch with them.[9]

This was followed by a talk that could be short or hours long. The rest of the afternoon and evening was taken up by seeing individual students and visitors. At night he often handled more correspondence and also watched the news on television. He felt it was very important for him to be informed about world events.

Aivanhov was very independent and, unlike many Eastern teachers, did not expect his students to serve him hand and foot. He even did his own laundry on Sundays. "The way of wisdom," he said once, "is to count only on oneself; to rely neither on family nor friends nor possessions, but on that tiny divine spark which lives in each one of us and which we must nourish."[10]

COMBATTING THE FORCES OF DARKNESS

Aivanhov had worked in France with great success for ten years before the seemingly inevitable occurred. According to esoteric understanding, whenever great masters spread the light in the world, the forces of darkness gather to strike back, trying to undermine what has been accomplished.

Thus, in 1947, Aivanhov was accused of espionage, was dragged into court, pronounced guilty, and sentenced to four years in prison. This episode in Aivanhov's life reads like a Hollywood drama or the good-fights-evil story of his childhood. Yet it was historical reality, and one that caused him considerable hardship and his disciples great distress. But, as in the stories, the hero emerged triumphant. Aivanhov was released after two years in prison where his behavior had not only been exemplary but transformative for his fellow inmates.

The incident made front-page news in France. The *Continental Daily Mail*, February 17, 1950, ran an article entitled "Spiritualist Cover For Espionage." The article stated that French counterespionage services discovered a Soviet plot to seize control of Mikhael Aivanhov's spiritual organization as a base for espionage. The reason for this was that several of Aivanhov's students were high-ranking government employees.

The plot revolved around the person of Cherenzi Lind, a Cuban who claimed to be "King of the World" and a descendant of the notorious Genghis Khan. He gave his full name as Prince Cherenzi Lind Kut Humi Maha Chohan, purportedly hailing from the subterranean empire of Agartha located somewhere in Tibet, and purportedly having been responsible for the defeat of Hitler by occult means.

The Russian traveler, artist, and visionary Nicholas Roerich wrote in his book *Shambhala:*

> Great is the belief in the Kingdom of the subterranean people. Through all Asia, through the spaces of all deserts, from the Pacific to the Urals, you can hear the same wondrous tale of the vanished holy people. And even far beyond the Ural Montains, the echo of the same tale will reach you.[11]

According to Tibetan legend, the kingdom of Agartha is ruled by the King of the World, who will appear to humanity in a final struggle of good against evil. This legend was popularized by the Polish writer and traveler Ferdinand Ossendowski in his book *Beasts, Men and Gods*.[12] Ossendowski, a Polish writer (1876–1945), travelled widely in Central Asia in the 1920s.

The Agartha myth was further popularized by Robert Ernst Dickhoff in his book *Agartha*. He claimed that this subterranean empire was established by Martians some 80,000 years ago. The underground tunnels extend from the Antarctica to Tibet, Brazil, and the Pacific islands. There is supposedly also a secret underground port for UFOs known as Rainbow City.

Interestingly, the Indian sage Ramana Maharshi once told Paul Brunton that he had visions of cities beneath the sacred mountain of Arunachala where he resided all his adult life. He was quick to add, however, that these cities were no more real than the cities above ground, which all arise within the universal Self.[13]

The newspaper article further noted that the Soviet communists had suceeded in a similar takeover in Bulgaria where, after Peter Deunov's death in 1944, they seized his spiritual movement. Then, in 1948, they sent forty-seven "emissaries" to Paris to usurp Aivanhov's branch of the movement. This tactical move failed, however, because Aivanhov and his trusted disciples valiantly resisted the takeover.

Then Lind arrived from the United States to oust Aivanhov. When he too met with firm resistance, he started a whispering campaign suggesting that Aivanhov had made improper advances toward female students. Several young women even registered a formal complaint with the police. This led to Aivanhov's arrest and sentencing. The article continued to state that the "French police are now convinced that the evidence on which he was convicted was faked by Communist agents to get Ivanoff [Aivanhov] out of the way ... Police are now anxious to question the 'King of the World.'" Lind died in obscurity soon after these events, while Aivanhov's work not only survived the onslaught but thrived in subsequent years.

In 1962, Aivanhov's case was opened up again and his name was completely cleared. His former rights were restored to him but he was still not granted French citizenship, for which he had applied. In fact, his citizenship papers arrived on his doorstep two days after he passed away. He was not to belong to any country during his lifetime, and he always considered himself a cosmopolitan.

TRANSFORMATIVE JOURNEY TO INDIA

In March 1959 Aivanhov left for the East. He spent several months in Japan, Taiwan, Hongkong, Thailand, and Sri Lanka. Then he went on to India. This was not a sightseeing trip for his personal pleasure, but a pilgrimage, an essential part of his spiritual work.

In India he went to the *ashrama* of Sri Ramana Maharshi where he was recognized as a Western master and made welcome by Ramana's disciples. Without hesitation he was granted the rare privilege of meditating in Ramana's room, now considered a temple. Ramana Maharshi — Maharshi meaning "great seer" — was one of modern India's greatest sages. Although Ramana Maharshi passed away in 1950 at the age of seventy-one, the sage's spiritual presence can still be felt in his hermitage, particularly his room, which is regularly served by disciples. Aivanhov mentioned he felt Ramana's presence there.

Ramana was made famous by Paul Brunton, an early pioneer of the East-West dialogue. Incidentally, Aivanhov met with Brunton and was happy to have been able to spend some time with him in his garden at the Bonfin. Brunton expressed his intention to write about Aivanhov but died shortly after their encounter, in 1981.

A memorable meeting was with Neemkaroli Baba. At the time, Neemkaroli lived in seclusion but sent a disciple to let Aivanhov know he was going to visit him. They ended up spending several days together. It was Neemkaroli who acknowledged Aivanhov's mastership by bestowing on him the honorific name Omraam. This name is made up of two famous Sanskrit *mantras* or words of power, *om* and *ram*. The former is the most sacred *mantra* of the Hindus. It stands for the Absolute, or Divine, itself. The syllable *ram*, which was rendered as "Raam" in French to assist with the correct pronunciation, is the *mantra* denoting the fire element.

We have already seen Aivanhov's connection with fire. His link to the sun is recognized in the syllable *om*, which is the name of the all-pervading spiritual light of which the sun is a manifestation and symbol in the physical realm. Aivanhov explained his initiatic name as follows:

> The name I was given in India, OMRAAM, corresponds to the two processes of "Solve" and "Coagula": OM dissolves all things, rendering them subtle and fine, and RAAM materializes them. The name OMRAAM is the symbol of the process of concretization, the invisible, intangible idea that must incarnate

on earth so that it can be seen and touched by the whole world.[14]

Another noteworthy sage with whom Aivanhov met was Ananda Mayi Ma. She is regarded by tens of thousands of Hindus as an incarnation, or *avatara*, of the Divine. Aivanhov also met with the famous Swami Shivananda of Rishikesh, a former physician who renounced his profession to become a healer of human hearts. Unfortunately, we know nothing about the meeting.

Aivanhov also visited Swami Nityananda, the guru of the world-famous Swami Muktananda who died in 1983. The Swami sat surrounded by disciples, wearing only a loin cloth. When he saw Aivanhov, he entered into a long meditation with his eyes closed. When he opened them, he addressed Aivanhov in good English with these words: "A pure heart, peace in his soul and all powers have been given to him." Next Nityananda pronounced the name of an ancient Hindu sage, explaining that Aivanhov was a reincarnation of that great yogin. It was presumably the same sage who also had written several Sanskrit books. Peter Deunov once mentioned to his disciple that a very long time ago he, Aivanhov, had authored books in India which he would discover again. Aivanhov never mentioned the sage's name.

Much of his time in India, however, Aivanhov spent alone meditating in the tranquillity of secluded places or temples. In this way he was able to enter into communion with the invisible reality without being disturbed.

The lives of the great magi are lived not merely to work out karma of their own but to work for the spiritual welfare of all beings on this planet. For us who are always caught in our own personal dilemmas and hectic programs, such a state of being is difficult to imagine. We have little idea of the kind of labor done by the silent sages. We tend only to see their external actions and then form quick opinions about them.

The sages of India have typically been criticized by Westerners and Indians under the influence of a Western-style education. Their apparent inactivity and silence have been taken as a sign of indifference and perhaps even indolence, which is seen as inexcusable in view of India's great economic plight.

Such critics forget, however, that the sages have their distinct individual tasks to accomplish. Not every sage is a political activist like Mahatma Gandhi or a philosopher like Sri Aurobindo. Some, like Ramana Maharshi, have the function of simply being present — a potent symbol of the spiritual efficacy of silence and powerful channel for the divine Light. Not every illumined adept is destined to be a teacher. Few have the destiny of an adept who is entrusted with the lives of thousands, as was Omraam Mikhael Aivanhov.

Perhaps Aivanhov's most significant meeting was with the legendary Himalayan adept Babaji. He first met a disciple of this great master, whose name was Hanuman Baba, the priest at Babaji's temple in Nainital. In obedience to his guru, Hanuman had taken a vow of silence for several years and so communicated with Aivanhov on a slate, in English. They spent several days together, sometimes until two or three in the morning. Subsequently, Aivanhov twice met with Babaji himself, though what passed between them will never be known. He met Babaji on June 17, 1959, in the mountains of Almora where Aivanhov was staying in the home of an American expatriate. It was also in Almora that he met the German-born Tibetan Lama Anagarika Govinda, who died in 1985. A great friendship developed between Aivanhov and the Lama. Apparently Govinda even performed a magical ceremony for his newly won friend.

When Aivanhov returned from India in February of 1960, he was a changed man. The change was so profound that even his physiognomy was visibly different. Several students went to Orly to welcome him back and were shocked by his transformation. As one of his disciples described the moment, not without some pathos:

> He is here. Stupefaction! We are struck dumb, frozen
> in this moment of history. He is no longer the same!
> Even his nose is different! There was no doubt about

it, he was the image of his Master, Peter Deunov. He looked like what we imagine the world's great Initiates looked like, proving that they all had the same model. The child I held in my arms said: "It's Moses." It was Moses.[15]

Aivanhov returned looking like the archetypal prophet, a look-alike of his own teacher. Henceforth he was no longer Brother Mikhael but Omraam Mikhael Aivanhov. Sensing more than understanding the overwhelming transformation that had occurred within him, his students acknowledged him as a master, a conductor of the numinous, who was to be approached with the greatest respect.

All this time he had refused to be addressed as master by his disciples. He had always regarded himself as their fellow-disciple of his own teacher. Now everything was changed. His disciples insisted on paying him due respect, and he finally accepted being called master. He explained his reluctance thus:

> . . . a true Master will never once say that he is a Master but rather he will let you feel it and understand it. He is in no hurry to be recognized. However, once a false Master has decreed that he is a Master, he will only be concerned with imposing his will on others.[16]

A true master, he explained, is one who knows the truth, is thoroughly familiar with and upholds the laws and principles of existence. He also has the will and ability to control his inner environment and to use this ability only in order to "manifest all the qualities and virtues of unselfish love."[17] Finally, a true master can be recognized by his disinterestedness.

Disinterestedness is unselfish love, which, for Aivanhov, finds its highest expression in the known universe in the sun. Light, he once observed, is so fast because of its disinterestedness.[18] Hence he also said:

> The ideal of a disciple is to free himself from all restrictions, to throw off everything that hampers him, and become like light.[19]

The restrictions Aivanhov had in mind are the boundaries erected by the ego-personality, which make it virtually impossible for the ordinary person to see things as they really are and to think, feel, and act in consonance with Reality.

A master, who is in control of the ego, is in tune with the Divine. Therefore his actions are fundamentally motivated by unselfish love. His disinterestedness is as flawless as is possible in creation. The only element of selfishness contained in it is the master's interest in fulfilling the will of the Divine, of furthering the spiritual evolution of beings. But, as Aivanhov noted in a talk given in July of 1973, this interest can hardly be called selfish.

Aivanhov returned to India for three months in the spring of 1982 at the invitation of a Hindu lady. Through her he met "little Babaji," a saint who "recognized" Aivanhov and reportedly saw the Goddesses Durga and Lakshmi standing to the right and left of him, bestowing upon him a "gift for all women." He never mentioned what that gift was.

MASTER OF THE ORDINARY

What, again, is a spiritual master? Aivanhov addressed this inevitable question in a talk given in July of 1947. He remarked that it is the truly great masters who rebuild the world by their teaching of love and freedom. He spoke of their power to unleash natural forces to wreak havoc on earth, though their goal is to change individuals and human society through love and patience.

Aivanhov responded to the same question again in greater depth shortly after his return from India. He then emphasized that in all but one respect a master is like any other human being: He experiences hunger and thirst and bleeds when cut. What distinguishes a master, however, is the fact that "he has achieved perfect control over himself."[20] He is, first and foremost, a master of his personality.

One of Aivanhov's first disciples, Frida Theodosy, recollected how she used to give singing lessons to some of her fellow disciples. One day she arrived early and caught a glimpse of Aivanhov sitting at a table in the garden taking lunch with several disciples. The image of her teacher engaged in such a mundane activity as eating startled her, and she quietly reflected on the fact that even a master needs to eat.

A short while later, Aivanhov went to her room and kindly said to her: "A Master needs to eat, drink, and sleep just as everyone else does. The difference is that he is in control of his cells, he gives the orders, and his consciousness is much wider, that's all."[21]

Aivanhov's down-to-earth remarks were intended to dispel the popular stereotype of great adepts as nearly disembodied beings who sustain themselves on air alone and who feel none of the needs and experience none of the temptations of their fellow humans. While their inner life is bound to be more rarefied, they are nevertheless still human beings and subject to the promptings of the body-mind.

However, their mastery is evident in how they relate to those stirrings. They are masters of self-transcendence, which means they do not succumb to the coarser desires arising within and also seldom yield to subtler manifestations of the ego-personality, such as pride and self-will. They are truly centered, and the excitements of the body-mind are peripheral to their life.

A master knows and obeys the invisible laws and abides by the higher principles of existence. His thoughts, words, and actions are shaped by his spontaneous submission to the Divine. Whether Aivanhov talked, walked, smiled, ate, slept, meditated, or engaged in any of the other many functions of a human being, he did so with a fullness and completeness that rendered the ordinary into something extraordinary. As his disciples recollect, he was always fully present in his activities, which gave them an unusual strength and grace.

Some of this elegant simplicity is captured in the video recordings of Aivanhov. He enters the lecture hall with resolute steps, firmly grasping his staff. His expression is one of

earnest collectedness. He raises his right hand, blessing everyone with solemn intent. His speech flows, transmitting the
wisdom won through his own spiritual work and self-trans-
cending labor. His words, charged with charisma, hold his
disciples spellbound. He breaks into a smile, radiating a rare
gentleness that seems to fill the hall. Or he bursts into an
infectious belly laugh. He gathers his energies again. His eyes
seem to scan eternity, and a palpable stillness descends on
everyone — a stillness that is archetypally communicated
even through the video.

Zen students will have no difficulty in seeing a consum-
mate Zen master before them. Yoga students will undoubtedly
see in Aivanhov a great *siddha*, or adept of Yoga. Students of
magic will see in him a magus of the first order. But beneath
all the power and charisma, we can sense a wonderful child-
like simplicity, gentleness, honesty, and humility before God.
It is these qualities in Aivanhov that are the most attractive to
the sensitive heart. One is reminded of the saying by the Sufi
adept Abu Sa'id ibn Abi'l-Khayr:

> The true saint goes in and out amongst the people and
> eats and sleeps with them and buys and sells in the
> market and marries and takes part in social inter-
> course, and never forgets God for a single moment.[22]

"Real mystics," observed Aivanhov, "are reasonable, normal people, with orderly, harmonious manners, gestures, and
looks."[23] Unlike some teachers who ensconce themselves in
remote retreats or who surround themselves with an air of
impenetrability, Aivanhov was always accessible to his disciples.

He traded in heavenly goods, and was always hoping that
some of his disciples would seriously want to shop at his
divine store. He worked hard to get at least a few individuals
to utterly commit themselves to the spiritual process, as he had
done. One day he offered the following simile:

> Yes, my dear brothers and sisters, I am like Stradivar-
> ius, I want to make violins; but these violins cannot

be made with just any wood or any varnish, because
I want to make violins on which Heaven can play —
I want to make some capable brothers and sisters.
Otherwise, I am wasting my time. Everybody has a
goal in life, and my goal is not to attract just anybody
here, but to prepare some workers for the Kingdom
of God.[24]

Aivanhov spared no efforts in bringing about such a transformation in his disciples. His patience was seemingly inexhaustible. Although his teaching was motivated by love and
compassion, he was yet quite capable of sternly reprimanding
faltering disciples. As he explained:

A Master's task is not merely to manifest much love
and tenderness. He must also be severe on his disciples by telling them certain truths for their progress
and advancement. It is hard luck if what he says does
not please the disciples! If I worried about your reactions and your opinions of me, I would get nothing
done at all. Some of you have told me that when I
showed you your weaknesses, you detested me. It
does not affect me at all if I am detested, because I
have a good thick skin, but if I am to help you, I am
obliged to shake you up.[25]

He continued:

Personally, I would love to make you happy, but my
work and my responsibilities have also to be considered. Moreover, a Master who shuts his eyes is not
useful.[26]

The typical disciple will always want to hear pleasantries
from the teacher, be flattered and adored, and given preferen-
tial treatment. This is the way in which the unenlightened,
egoic personality habitually operates. The master's sacred
obligation is to undermine all such expectations and always
to remind his disciples that spiritual life is about transcending
the ego, not massaging and pampering it. For the teacher-

disciple relationship to bear fruit, both master and student must be equally committed to the truth.

Aivanhov compared his role to that of a dentist, who must sometimes hurt a patient to stop a nagging toothache. He saw it as his duty not to leave disciples alone but to stir them up and remind them of their higher destiny.[27] It was his mission to be "a pain in the neck," so that his disciples would have to work on their character and change their way of life.[28] He said:

> My principle is precisely not to satisfy your personality. This makes you annoyed and discontented with me, does it not? Too bad. What I want is to feed your spirit, your divine side which is lying in a corner half dead because no one takes care of it.[29]

In our Western society, which celebrates the ego-personality above all else, the task of a spiritual teacher is extremely risky. Aivanhov was quite aware of this. One day he noted:

> I know perfectly well that each time I shake somebody up, I am running enormous risks … If he works for the radio, he will broadcast a talk against me … If he is a journalist, he will write an article criticizing me … If he is a painter, he will caricature me. I know all this, but I accept it all in order to help him see things more clearly. I am not concerned with what happens to me: he may become my enemy, and that is unfortunate; but I am doing this for his own good. Many years later, events will show that I was right; he will remember and will understand that I wanted what was best for him …[30]

Aivanhov's skillful combination of constructive criticism and compassion is best illustrated by the following incident. During his stay in Los Angeles, he asked one longtime disciple to prepare a group of people for their first meeting with him. The group included a well-known actor. Wanting to look her best, the disciple dressed up in Hollywood style for the briefing.

When she got back and excitedly reported to Aivanhov that the new people had been very responsive and were eagerly awaiting their meeting with him, instead of praise she received a barrage of criticism from her teacher. In fact, Aivanhov was furious. He reprimanded her for wearing an outrageous outfit that was utterly unsuited for the occasion. He thought the asymmetric top and the fringes on her dress gave off the wrong kind of signal and definitely did not contribute to people's upliftment.

Aivanhov told the woman that he had noticed how she would often wear completely disharmonious outfits, ill-befitting a disciple. Then, suddenly, he switched to a different mood and remarked: "I must admit you do have a unique quality of bringing joy to people. If dressing differently blocks that joy in you, then forget about it." He turned and left the room.

The disciple was reeling from this unexpected onslaught and the seemingly mixed messages. She looked through her wardrobe and found that she had very few clothes that met her teacher's criteria. Although Aivanhov had, in so many words, given her permission to wear whatever she wanted, providing she would remain joyous, she now found she could not follow her whim. Yet she was not in the least upset because she felt free to make her own choice. Thus, in his wisdom, Aivanhov had succeeded in getting her to dress appropriately and continue to express her joie de vivre at the same time.

While Aivanhov was not one to mince his words with longtime disciples, he was perfectly considerate and gentle with newcomers. He realized that they needed to be embraced and made to feel safe until they had come to understand his role in their lives.

People come to spiritual teachers for all kinds of reasons. Only one reason, however, is legitimate; that is to want to lower the drawbridge of the ego's castle and grant entrance to the higher Reality, or the Divine. The teacher's task is to assist disciples in lowering their defenses against the Spirit, and to shower them with blessings. The blessings of a true master are of inestimable value.

Our postmodern civilization has long forgotten the power and importance of blessing. The "bless you" we say nowadays when someone sneezes is a meaningless ritual, a mere parody of authentic blessing, which is always an empowerment.

When Aivanhov greeted his disciples with his right hand raised in blessing, he engaged in a sacred act. Only another adept or a clairvoyant would have seen that this symbolic gesture was accompanied by an actual transmission of spiritual energy. It was what is called in Sanskrit a *mudra*, or "seal," by which he freely communicated his own state of being with others — a confirmation of his feeling of brotherhood.

Aivanhov's glance had a similar purpose and initiatory power. One student recollects how she was discouraged by her own inadequacy in comparison to the palpable harmony and peace she found on her first visit to the Bonfin. Then the master's glance communicated a different perspective to her:

> As we got up from prayer to salute Master Aivanhov, he stopped right in front of me, looking straight at or, better, into me. Then something happened — beyond space and time. I caught myself saying, "OK, OK, I'll get back to work." For a moment I wondered whether I had spoken out loud. Question and answer seemed superimposed on each other.[31]

That student understood the teacher's message and, instead of succumbing to lethargy, stepped up her inner work. Several days later, after a prayer gathering, Aivanhov stopped briefly in front of her, acknowledging her spiritual efforts with a gentle nod. However, he studiously avoided making eye contact with her, which would merely have pampered her egoic expectations of winning approval. Another useful lesson.

We speak of the eye as a mirror of the soul. "In the eyes," explained Aivanhov in one of his earliest talks, "we can see the quality of wisdom, truth, and everything which is hidden in man."[32] We are affected by the appearance of things. Whether we are aware of it or not, we instinctively react to images of violence, just as we respond to images of beauty. The eyes of initiates convey the Truth, and adepts have utilized the archetypal power of glance since time immemorial to initiate disciples or silently encourage or warn them.

A glance from a master is enough to open the floodgate of tears of remorse, to unlock deep joy within a disciple's heart, or to freeze someone's evil intentions before they are translated into action. A glance may also suffice to restore an ailing disciple to health.

HEALER OF HEARTS

Stories about healings are associated with many, if not most, spiritual teachers. Aivanhov is no exception. Like his teacher, Peter Deunov, he worked many miraculous healings, always motivated by love and compassion. He once described this work humorously thus:

> When a person becomes ill, it is because he has committed some fault, a sin of some kind that he must pay for. I go to the celestial entities, and I say, "Look, I love this person, he has worked hard for the Brotherhood. How much does he owe?" And I pay. Right away, the person is healed! Yes, it is true, you can pay for someone else when you have that kind of gold.[33]

He was trying to make a point not about his healing abilities but about the spiritual symbolism of gold. We all need to pay for our demeritorious intentions and actions, but if we have accumulated enough spiritual gold, we can do so with minimal damage to our physical and mental well-being. A master is someone who has a large enough spiritual bank account to pay for some of the transgressions of some of his disciples.

A female disciple once badly sprained her ankle and had to be carried home. She braced herself for several days of bedrest. At ten o'clock at night, the pain suddenly vanished. Her ankle was completely healed. She was certain that Aivanhov had effected the cure at a distance, for he had been told about her mishap. When she saw him the next day she thanked him for his intervention. Aivanhov replied: "I'm sorry I couldn't get to it before ten o'clock, something else kept me until then."[34]

Aivanhov's healing power extended even to the realm of mechanics. One day, he was traveling with some students by car in the Pyrenees, the mountain chain separating France from Spain. They came upon a stalled truck, which blocked a narrow road. Apparently the gear shift was broken. Aivanhov got out of the car and inspected the broken gear shift, even though it was clear to everyone that he knew nothing about motors or gear shifts.

Then suddenly he announced that the truck driver should give it another try. The man complained that he had already taken the gear shift apart and could not repair it. Aivanhov persuaded the driver gently. The man climbed behind the wheel, started the engine, and to his utter amazement the truck started to move. It went just far enough to the side of the road to allow Aivanhov's car to pass.[35]

Renard's book contains several more miracle stories of this kind. They demonstrate that Aivanhov was a magus of the first order. Even though some of the stories told about Aivanhov may contain exaggerations or distortions, we need not disbelieve them in principle. Miracles are an integral part of the lives of most saints.

In the Yoga tradition, for instance, a whole range of paranormal powers called *siddhis* are known. Many of them are catalogued in the *Yoga-Sutra* of Patanjali, the standard text of Raja-Yoga. Some of these magical feats are quite spectacular, while others are impossible on the physical level of existence and must be understood as applying to the subtle realms of existence. For instance, the power of expanding infinitely or contracting to the size of an atom cannot possibly relate to the physical body. But this does not make such abilities any less breathtaking. Modern parapsychology has only begun to scratch the surface of what the esoteric traditions claim to be possible and even to be common experience among initiates.

Since ancient times, yogins have been treated with great respect by the villagers of India, because they were known to be not only spiritual personages but powerful magi. At times, their spiritual purity was seen even to lag behind their magical expertise. In such cases, the villagers would give them a wide berth, out of fear that the adepts' penetrating gaze might bring misfortune on them.

There was no need for such fear in the case of Aivanhov. He was a white magus. Nothing could have been farther from his mind than deliberately harming another being. Rather, he was always looking for ways to bring out the good in himself and others.

Although many miracles are reported of Aivanhov, he himself never made much of them. He is said to have remarked once:

> You can heal people, you can raise the dead . . . but then they only begin all over again with the same faults and the same illnesses. The real miracle is to save a soul by filling it with light so that it will not sin any more; the real miracle is to teach human beings to transform hate into love.[36]

Aivanhov was a superb healer of hearts, a bringer of light to human souls. He always sought to spiritually restore those with whom he came in contact, to reconnect them to the Divine. But he was also a healer in the conventional sense. Many healing miracles are told about him. Renard reported the following incident.[37]

In 1958, a male student was advised to have a gangrenous finger amputated. It had refused to heal despite medication. When Aivanhov heard about it, he went into a brief meditation. Then he started questioning the man, getting him to confess that before his present marriage he had lived with another young woman who he promised to marry. The man broke down and cried. Aivanhov told him that he was not judging him.

When the student asked what he was to do, Aivanhov advised him to make amends. He also told him that the girl had been unable to marry because she had the man's child and that both were ill and in need of help. He instructed the man to waste no time to come to their aid and that his finger would be healed.

A doctor who was present intervened, arguing that the finger could not be saved. But Aivanhov insisted that healing would occur. Filled with relief and gratitude, the man fell at Aivanhov's feet, kissing his hands, and then went at once to his old sweetheart to correct the damage. His finger did heal, as Aivanhov had promised. But more importantly, Aivanhov had succeeded in healing the man's heart.

Now that Aivanhov is no longer present in the physical realm, though he vowed to remain with his disciples on the subtle planes of existence, his healing power lies in his words. During a summer gathering in 1971, Mikhael Aivanhov charged his disciples to "do all you can to propagate the Teaching for the happiness of the entire world."[38] He knew that a true teaching always survives the teacher, but that, like a young plant, it requires tender loving care.

Today Omraam Mikhael Aivanhov's teaching is being preserved by the community of disciples he has created. Every year more of his inspiring talks are made available in book form to realize his passionate vision of a benign future in which humanity celebrates life in harmony with all other life forms. His teaching, which was presented by him with such deceptive simplicity, is a powerful tool of transformation. Its potency derives from the fact that it was empowered by an exceptional spiritual adept who lived by and for the truth — a truth that is revealed in the conjunction of wisdom and compassion, of *gnosis* and *agape*.

TRAVELLING WISDOM

Aivanhov was widely travelled and once hyperbolically remarked: "I have visited nearly every country." His travels, however, were not for his personal amusement. By his own confession, he was always at work, constantly seeking to bring the divine light down into this realm. Imperturbed by adversities and the sluggish response of disciples and the world, he unflaggingly dedicated himself to the spiritual betterment of humanity. What he called his "work" even extended to the invisible realms, as he would occasionally let on.

As one disciple recollects: "The thing that impressed me the most profoundly was that he used every moment and every occasion to do his work: to do whatever he deemed necessary to assist someone's spiritual growth. Sometimes he would do so even at the cost of his own person and well-being. At times, I must confess, I considered his willingness to sacrifice himself quite insane. In my exasperation I even once expressed my dismay to him. He merely said: 'Eat, drink, sleep, and dance. Live! That's all you are asked to do.'"

Aivanhov's response might seem enigmatic to the outsider. However, it was a clear message to his disciple that she should not concern herself with his affairs. He did what he had to do, and she should do the same: to live life as it wanted to unfold itself in her case; and to "dance," that is, to be joyous rather than concerned.

Travelling with Aivanhov, as can be expected, was always a time filled with lessons. The reminiscences of one of his disciples in England give us a sense of both the joy and the difficulty of being in the company of a spiritual master, who is always teaching and looking to improve his disciples' destiny. As Cherry Frizzell remarked in a personal communication: "He always surprised us. He was always totally unexpected. He was always making us laugh. We were certainly never allowed to stagnate."

Aivanhov had come to visit his British disciples in November 1982 and was staying at the Frizzell's home. The lessons started on that same day. Before retiring, Aivanhov went round the house turning off all the lights, even the electronic clocks. He explained that this will save electricity, and also remarked on the heat in the house. His hosts had lit a fire in every room and turned up the central heating to ensure that he would be warm. They found out that everything they had been told about their teacher's likes and dislikes was swiftly contradicted by his actions. "We were never allowed to presume anything at all," said Cherry Frizzell. "We were expected to be totally flexible at all times, to use our intuition to its maximum. The first day he told us: 'You must accept everything I do.' It was his first real instruction to us."

She was extremely nervous when she served her teacher his first meal the next day. Quite aware of her tension, he took to stroking her hand gently for several days, without saying a word. He also cunningly requested another disciple, who was to do all the cooking, to translate some of his books instead, thus bequeathing the kitchen duties on his anxious hostess.

The following day she served him a splendid four-course meal, and he promptly piled all the food into one plate — salad, fish soup, spicy sauce, and croutons. From then on the meals became far less formal.

Apart from the brief time during lunch and occasionally for a short while in the late afternoon, Aivanhov remained by himself. Day and night, he seemed to be focusing on studying English, and did so by memorizing long lists of words and watching TV programs. After only three weeks, he announced that the moment had come for his first public lecture. A large hall was hired, and packed when he gave his inaugural talk. He spoke English in a slow, deliberate manner, but apparently it was nearly perfect.

After a few months, in January of 1983, Aivanhov during the customary midday meal suddenly popped the question: "How about going to Egypt?" When his suggestion was met with enthusiasm, he wasted no time explaining his proposed route. He wanted to travel along the Suez Canal, and then catch a boat to an obscure village called Quesir, on the banks of the Red Sea. Within a week Aivanhov and a small group of disciples were on their way to Cairo. He wanted to be in Quesir in time for his birthday.

Since no travel agent had ever heard of Quesir, and even the hotel in Cairo proved unhelpful in arranging transport to the village, the party had to trek overland by taxi. Before leaving, Aivanhov invited his disciples to inspect his hotel room. To their amazement, he had tidied up and even made his bed — a very simple but poignant lesson: There are many, even quite ordinary ways in which the noble task of transmuting matter can be undertaken.

Once they had arrived in the village, Aivanhov walked every morning to a rocky outcrop by the shore overlooking the Red Sea, and from there silently welcomed the rising sun. After breakfast he headed out into the desert, doing his imponderable work. The villagers treated him with great respect, sensing that he was a man of God.

One young Nubian, who had been hired for a boat ride down the Nile, was eagerly listening to Aivanhov's explanations about his teaching and his disciples. By the end of the trip, he was ready to leave everything behind and follow the master to France. There was a touching scene later that day when the Nubian maneuvered his boat alongside the larger ship, which was about to leave on a Nile cruise with Aivanhov and his disciples. The young man reached up to the railing, while Aivanhov knelt down and leaned over to get as close to the Nubian as possible. He was clearly instructing him, for the man, with his head close to his newfound teacher's feet, was listening raptly. When he finally left in his boat, he looked sad but radiant.

"I SHALL ALWAYS BE WITH THEM"

Motivated by the impulse of a *bodhisattva*, welling up deep within the integrated psyche, Aivanhov dedicated his entire adult life to helping others find the way back to the Divine. Yet he remained an intensely private person, valuing his hours of solitude when he could do his work in the nonphysical realm. This is also how he died: in solitude, undisturbed by others. As one longtime disciple remarked in conversation: "He worked to the end for the good of humanity. He was aware of everything important that concerned the brothers and sisters, the people of France, the whole planet, and probably the universe."

We know from other great teachers that they are wonderfully attuned to the lives around them, especially the lives of those who choose to be in spiritual and emotional communion with them. Thus one day Aivanhov called one of the dogs roaming in his garden by the name of a young disciple living in the Pyrenees. Later it was learned that this brother had died around that time.

On another day, Aivanhov asked one of his disciples to walk around the summer camp to ensure that everybody had what they needed. She "chanced" upon a young sister who was rather upset and depressed. The disciple talked to her from the heart, and after a while succeeded in lifting the dark cloud from her. To consolidate the turn-about, the disciple had her repeat after her with solemn intention: "La vie est belle" (Life is beautiful).

Shortly afterward, the disciple returned to her teacher's quarters to handle other tasks. She found Aivanhov seated in meditation, with an incredible expression of ecstasy on his face. She went about her business as quietly as possible, when he slightly opened his eyes and said with a voice that seemed to reverberate through her entire being: "La vie est belle."

Aivanhov died at his beloved Bonfin on Christmas day 1986 at 9:25 pm. Only one close disciple, Sister Blagost, witnessed the passing. Aivanhov's final words and testimony were true to his *bodhisattva* mission: "If you knew how many thoughts of love I receive from everyone! Tell the brothers and sisters that I shall always be with them, that they may preserve unity and harmony, and continue to spread the Teaching in the whole world."

Sister Blagost waited for three days before announcing her teacher's demise, so that his transition to the subtle dimension of existence could be smooth. A few hours after his passing, his face apparently looked exactly as it did when he first came to France all those years ago, and there was a wonderful scent of sandal wood in the room.

Two other disciples, who were staying with Aivanhov at the time, had significant prophetic dreams. In the night of December 25, one of them dreamt that her teacher rose from his bed, took a few determined steps as if he were walking toward someone, and then, making a perfect circle with his lips, forcefully exhaled his last breath. The following morning, she announced to her friend that the master was passing away.

That night, her friend dreamt that she was seated to the right of Aivanhov at an immense banquet. Everything was bathed in a dazzling light, and the huge table was laden with food. It was toward the end of the festive gathering, and it was time for one person to pay for all the celebrants who had been invited. Next to her, she saw a cradle filled with gold, jewels, and coins. She placed a handful of treasures into her lap to count the appropriate sum. At that point, she felt Aivanhov's hand on her arm. He said: "No, no — I am the one who must do this!" She protested: "But Master, it all belongs to you!" He gently but firmly held her arm with his right hand, and she felt a strong current, and then she disappeared. It was Aivanhov's final sacrifice. Death, noted Euripides long ago, is a debt that we all must pay ourselves.

After his transition, students were given the opportunity over the next three days to pay homage to Aivanhov one last time. During this entire period his body remained intact, his face wearing a beautiful expression. Only the sages, who have seen through to the heart of all things, can face death in humility, but without fear. For they know that death is merely the other side of life, and that all endings are new beginnings.

NOTES

1. Aivanhov, *The Mysteries of Fire and Water*, p. 74.
2. P. C. Renard, *The Solar Revolution and the Prophet: The Role of the Sun in the Spiritual Life* (Frejus, France: Prosveta, 1980), p. 55.
3. [Brother Jehan], *Who is the Master Omraam Mikhael Aivanhov?* (Frejus, France: Prosveta, 1982), p. 35.
4. Aivanhov, *Sexual Force or the Winged Dragon*, p. 154.
5. Aivanhov, *A Philosophy of Universality*, pp. 85–86.
6. Ibid., p. 129.
7. Aivanhov, *Harmony*, p. 34.
8. Aivanhov, *A New Dawn* (Part I), p. 121.
9. The exercises, which are performed slowly and rhythmically, are described at the end of Omraam Mikhael Aivanhov's *A New Earth: Methods, Exercises, Formulas and Prayers* (Frejus, France: Prosveta, 1988).
10. Aivanhov, *Man's Psychic Life*, p. 142.

11. N. Roerich, *Shambhala: In Seach of the New Era* (Rochester, VT: Inner Traditions International, 1990), p. 215. This book was first published in 1930. In the words of President Mikhail Gorbachev, Roerich "was one of the cultural pillars of Russia."

12. F. Ossendowski, *Beasts, Men and Gods* (New York: E.P. Dutton, 1922).

13. See *Talks with Sri Ramana Maharshi* (Tiruvannamalai, India: Sri Ramanasramam, 1957), vol. 1.

14. Aivanhov, *A New Dawn* (Part I), p. 120.

15. Renard, *op. cit.*, pp. 50–51.

16. Aivanhov, *What Is a Spiritual Master?*, p. 17.

17. Ibid., p. 15.

18. See Aivanhov, *Light Is a Living Spirit*, p. 109.

19. Aivanhov, *Light Is a Living Spirit*, p. 110.

20. Aivanhov, *What Is a Spiritual Master*, p. 12.

21. Told in Renard, *op. cit.*, p. 57.

22. R. A. Nicholson, *Studies in Islamic Mysticism* (London: Cambridge University Press, 1921), p. 55.

23. Aivanhov, *On the Art of Teaching* (Part III), p. 188.

24. Aivanhov, *Harmony*, p. 30.

25. Aivanhov, *What Is a Spiritual Master?*, p. 77.

26. Ibid., p. 78.

27. See Aivanhov, *The Key to the Problems of Existence*, p. 74.

28. Ibid., p. 131.

29. Ibid., p. 172.

30. Aivanhov, *What Is a Spiritual Master?*, pp. 84–85.

31. *Circle of Light*, no. 2 (1991), p. 2.

32. Aivanhov, *The Second Birth*, p. 67.

33. Aivanhov, *The Egregor of the Dove or the Reign of Peace*, p. 60.

34. Told in Renard, *op. cit.*, pp. 57–58.

35. Ibid., p. 42.

36. Ibid., pp. 56–57; Renard is here citing the singer Frida Theodosy.

37. Ibid., pp. 44–45.

38. Aivanhov, *A New Dawn* (Part I), p. 37.

Omraam Mikhael Aivanhov always had
a special relationship with children

PART II

THE TEACHING

4
PHILOSOPHY AND THE
MYSTERY OF BEING HUMAN

THE ESSENTIAL QUESTIONS

Who am I? Sooner or later we all ask ourselves this question, often at a time of crisis. But we don't have to wait until a moment of tragedy strikes to ponder the mystery of our own existence. Nor do we need to shelve this question until the onset of our inevitable midlife crisis or, if we should have managed to avoid it even then, until we must face death.

In fact, we cannot ask ourselves this question early enough in life, because our answer, or the lack of one, defines our destiny. "Man's destiny," said Aivanhov, "is written in the stereotypes he brings with him when he is born on this earth."[1] These stereotypes comprise our deep-seated intellectual presumptions about life, our attitudes, and our desires. These are our answers to life by which we constantly shape and live out our destiny.

If we want to change our destiny, we must change those stereotypes; we must change the mental pattern on which our present life is based. Destiny is a habit, and habits can be altered. This requires a tremendous expenditure of psychic energy. But this is precisely what spiritual practice is about: transforming the personality by transforming its stereotypes from destructive ideas to life-enhancing ones.

It is quite tragic that our civilization does not encourage us to be more reflective about our lives. Being philosophical today is equated with being morose. In times past, however, philosophy stood for what the word means: the love of wisdom (*sophia*). And wisdom was understood to be the ripe fruit of self-knowledge. Over the temple of Apollo at Delphi in ancient Greece were carved the immortal words *gnothi seauton*,

Omraam Mikhael Aivanhov, performing a fire ceremony

"Know Thyself!" Many centuries later, the Latin writer Cicero repeated them in his own language, *nosce te,* and long before him the sages of India exlaimed in Sanskrit *atmanam viddhi.*

Who am I? This was the question that Sri Ramana Maharshi, the sage of Tiruvannamalai in South India, recommended to spiritual seekers. What he meant was: Who am I *really?* Who am I beyond the roles that I play in life, beyond the moods with which I tend to identify, beyond the ideas that I am inclined to defend?

This question implies another one: Why am I here? And this gives rise to a third question: Whither do I go? Finally, we must ask ourselves: What am I to do? The simplicity of these questions is inversely proportionate to the difficulty experienced in answering them. Yet, there are always answers, and some are more convincing than others.

Our answers to the Big Questions are only as good as our understanding of the questions. Every question already implies an answer. But we have to know how to dismantle the question to get at the best possible answer. If you want to know why your car has stopped working, you examine the parts familiar to you. If you still don't understand the problem, you consult a repair manual or call in a mechanic. However, unless you are willing to learn from the mechanic, you still will not know how to fix the same problem the next time it occurs.

But car problems are a crude analogy. When you suddenly develop strange palpitations of the heart, you can't open up your chest to see what is going on. Instead you seek out a qualified doctor, and possibly more than one. Similarly, in philosophical matters, we would be foolish not to make use of the very best advice available. We don't have to become converts to any belief system, which would be foolish anyway. But we must educate ourselves about the kind of sophisticated philosophical answers to the Big Questions that have been developed over many millennia.

The shocking truth is that our civilization is designed around ignoring the Big Questions, and so our education system leaves us philosophically illiterate. What is taught as philosophy in our colleges and universities is only a shadow of the real knowledge that is passed on in the initiatic traditions.

Fortunately, when we muster the courage to confront the quaternary of Big Questions, we find that we are not entirely on our own. Since ancient times there has been help for the philosophically awake in the form of the great spiritual or initiatic traditions. Indeed, these traditions purport to be an elaborate response to just those questions. Their answers are the most comprehensive and complete.

This is so for the simple reason that these traditions are the repository of the wisdom and knowledge of countless generations of sages who have peered deeply into the mystery of existence, who have plumbed the depths of the human psyche, and who have traveled the road of knowledge far beyond the ken of the ordinary person and even well beyond the vista of the sciences.

The sages are the true philosophers, for they have applied and tested their knowledge in daily life. They are not merely intellectuals considering matters in the abstract. Their understanding is superbly practical. Their knowledge is initiatic, not merely theoretical. Hence they are profoundly affected and changed by it. As Aivanhov observed:

> You will never improve nor transform yourself by accumulating knowledge in your head. To be sure, this knowledge can broaden your mind and your point of view, but that is only on the surface; you will always be the same underneath: remarkable as far as general knowledge is concerned, a veritable one-man information bureau!
>
> But as far as character, virtues and qualities are concerned, nothing will be changed; you will be just as timorous, weak, sensual and wretched as ever. Whereas spiritual knowledge, the divine Science, obliges you to penetrate to the depths and climb to the heights, and it is not possible to be unchanged by it.[2]

Aivanhov was very critical of mere intellectual learning, and elsewhere he stated:

> If you prefer book-learning, go ahead. But you will wither away and neither love nor kindness will emanate from you. You will be nothing but a cold, dried-up intellectual who discusses, criticizes and dissects everything, but who is incapable of escaping from his own inner disorder.
>
> This is one of the greatest dangers for philosophy students. By the time they finish their studies, they are disoriented by the jumble of contradictory systems and ideas they have had to study. It is to be expected . . . for in philosophical studies you will find everything except true philosophy.[3]

Aivanhov was very outspoken about the demerits of conventional philosophy as taught in the academic curriculum and which is based on materialistic rather than spiritual principles. He spoke of it as "brutalizing" students and, we might add, the teachers themselves.[4] Harsh as this criticism is, it appears to be valid in most teaching situations, and it also applies to subjects other than philosophy, as taught in colleges and universities.

In recent years, some sensitive academics have themselves boldly stepped forward to criticize the educational establishment for its lack of vision. Thus, a few years ago, the American social philosopher Allan Bloom caused a considerable stir with his book *The Closing of the American Mind*, which even placed number one on the bestseller list.[5]

In this book, Bloom lamented the tragic fact that modern education has impoverished the souls of students. He also debunked the false openness enforced by the modern liberal school curriculum, which fosters not originality and goodness but, Bloom contended, mere conformism and the erroneous notion that values are relative and that we can simply pick and choose those which suit us best. Bloom stated:

Liberal education flourished when it prepared the way for the discussion of a unified view of nature and man's place in it, which the best minds debated on the highest level. It decayed when what lay beyond it were only specialties, the premises of which do not lead to any such vision.[6]

Bloom proposed to remedy the situation by reintroducing classical studies into the curriculum. He wants students to feast on Plato and Shakespeare, since their works allow them to participate in what he calls "essential being" rather than indulging in their accidental lives. Bloom's proposal has a certain appeal, yet it is too limited, for he does not even consider the great classics of cultures other than the Greeks and the Romans. He also does not appear to have any knowledge of the esoteric traditions, and so the question arises as to what degree a person's classical studies would guide him or her to the kind of deep understanding that would lead to participation in "essential being."

More recently, psychologist Ron Miller offered a far more radical critique of the Western education system in his book *What Are Schools For?* Miller favors a holistic approach to education and life:

A basic premise of holistic education is the belief that our lives have a meaning and purpose greater than the mechanistic laws described by science, and greater than the "consensus consciousness" of any one culture. This transcendent purpose is a creative, self-guiding energy which we ought not attempt to suppress.[7]

Miller's model of education is expressly founded in spiritual principles, and it is one of the promising and encouraging manifestations of the "new paradigm" that is trying to emerge not only within education and the sciences but within our Western civilization as a whole.

For Miller, holistic education emphasizes not merely the ingestion of a select number of "Great Books" or the learning of a few "basic skills" but life experience. This is another important point his model has in common with the esoteric traditions. Initiatic knowledge is always lived knowledge, or knowledge acquired through and translated into personal experience. As Aivanhov explained in vivid terms:

> By living your knowledge, by tasting it, by verifying it, by practicing it until you feel it becoming your own blood, your own quintessence, this knowledge becomes truly yours, and no one, nor anything, can ever take it away from you.[8]

It is through the fire test of lived knowledge that we grow and mature and, one day, become philosophers. Aivanhov was such a philosopher-sage. He once said about himself: "Ever since I was very young, I wanted to adapt, to conform, to shape myself along the line of a better philosophy than my own, the philosophy of the Initiates."[9]

He labored hard to gain access to that philosophy and to make it his own. The way he acquired it was not only by carefully listening to the teachings of the great adepts but also through acute self-inspection. As he put it: "All my life I have been studying myself, measuring, learning my limitations, for food, for sleep, for everything."[10]

Hence Aivanhov was able to say in a factual tone of voice: "Everything I believe, everything I hope for, everything I do is founded on knowledge."[11] And: "I swim in the great truths I have discovered."[12]

TRUE PHILOSOPHY

In order to gain knowledge of anything we must first combine with it. The more we combine with it, the greater our access to knowledge will be. This is one of the key insights of the spiritual traditions. As Aivanhov put it: "Knowing is achieved by penetration: something penetrates or enters into us and becomes a part of us."[13] The truth that knowledge is participatory is being rediscovered by modern philosophers.

This fact has become most obvious in understanding the processes involved at the level of subatomic physics. Thus, the German physicist and philosopher Werner Heisenberg formulated the famous principle of uncertainty, which states that we cannot accurately determine both the momentum and the position of a particle. If our reading of the particle's momentum is accurate, its position cannot be accurately known, and vice versa.

This finding has led some thoughtful philosophers and scientists to call into question the scientific ideal of objectivity on which the entire enterprise of conventional science is based. In doing so they have, fortunately, opened the doors to a more humane understanding of the world, the purpose of science, and the social responsibility of scientists.

The new science is also far more open to nonrational modes of cognition, such as intuition, and this bodes well for a more integral worldview, which also gives due weight to the spiritual traditions with their emphasis on wisdom and transcendental realization.

Wisdom is participatory knowledge of the first order. As Aivanhov put it in a nutshell:

> True Initiatic knowledge is to fuse, to become one in an act of love, as the Bible tells us that "Adam knew Eve," or "Abraham knew Sarah."[14]

Thus, in the final analysis, true knowledge depends on complete identification with the object. More than that, it depends on complete identification with the ultimate Object, or Reality. Hence the sacred injunction "Know thyself" has a much deeper significance. It refers to self-knowledge not merely in the sense of knowledge of one's habits, preferences, or moods, but as Self-realization.

This is in fact implied in the ancient Sanskrit phrase *atmanam viddhi* cited above. The *atman* refers both to the personal self, or the ego-personality, and to the transpersonal Self. For self-knowledge to be complete, it must reach beyond the patterns of the personality. Aivanhov made this very clear:

> To know oneself does not mean to know one's character with all its faults and failings, nor to know the limitations of human nature. If it went no further than that even children could understand and know themselves.
>
> In this phrase, "Know thyself!," what is the "self"? Our limbs? Our brains? Our thoughts and feelings? No, it is none of that. The Self we must know is a part of God, a spark, an immortal spirit, something indescribable but real which exists on a far higher level. To find and unite with this Self, human beings must reach up to greater heights. They will know themselves only when they know that indestructible, omniscient, all-powerful being, the higher Self which is a tiny part of God Himself.[15]

True philosophy, then, is about Reality in its full depth and breadth. It is about wisdom and Self-realization. This is why Aivanhov calls it initiatic, since it does not depend on book knowledge, which can be acquired from without. Initiation, as he understood it, is to vibrate in unison with the Spirit, or Self.[16] Once we are attuned to the spiritual dimension, all our experiences and knowledge are anchored in the core of Being. We think, feel, intend, and act differently.

True philosophy is what he called the "philosophy of the Spirit."[17] He also spoke of this as the "new philosophy," noting, however, that it was as ancient as humanity itself, even though it was known only to "those exceptional beings who understood the true nature of purity, love and sanctity."[18] In other words, initiatic philosophy has been until recent times the prerogative of a small number of highly evolved beings who guarded their esoteric knowledge well, initiating into the mysteries only those duly qualified, and then only after submitting them to careful trials and tests.

Today, initiatic philosophy is freely available to anyone who cares to consider its premises and adopt its attendant disciplines. No special initiatory ordeal is necessary, though spiritual life itself is as much a test as it has ever been. Those on the path are always taxed. Acquiring the "new" philosophy is not like donning a new coat. We must absorb it into our bones. We must live it, breathe it, think it, speak it, act it, and grow with it.

Continuing to grow as a human being is one of the signs of true philosophy. If our philosophy curtails our growth, we must jettison it and look for a more accommodating temple of ideas in which we can worship. The great value of initiatic philosophy lies in that it puts no limit on our human potential but constantly encourages us to move on, to shed outgrown skins, and to raise our gaze to higher possibilities.

EVOLUTION AND THE PURPOSE OF LIFE

Who am I? Another way of putting this question is: What is the nature of humanness? That is to say, what makes us uniquely human? In posing these questions we desire to know our purpose on earth, the meaning of life. Even those who never consciously pose this question have an answer for it. This is so because the way we live our lives is itself an answer to the Big Questions.

In our postmodern society, the answer expressed in the form of people's lives is often sadly banal. Judging from the lifestyle and general demeanor of so many men and women, they define their meaning in gross physical terms. Aivanhov put it quite bluntly thus:

> Most people behave as though their only reason for being on earth is to eat and drink and have a good time or, alternatively, depending upon their point of view, to suffer and be thoroughly unhappy. The truth is that they are here in order to work at one great common venture . . . but they do not know it.[19]

Such people live in a state of blatant denial. While they fill their days with tasks and, if they can, with much pleasurable activity, they are often suffering from depression. The syndrome is known as Quiet Desperation. When they finally consult their doctor or therapist, the cause of their depression invariably turns out to involve a felt sense of meaninglessness.

More than half a century ago, the great Swiss psychiatrist C. G. Jung observed:

> We are living undeniably in a period of the greatest restlessness, nervous tension, confusion and disorientation of outlook. Among my patients from many countries, all of them educated persons, there is a considerable number who came to see me, not because they were suffering from a neurosis, but because they could find no meaning in life or were torturing themselves with questions which neither present-day philosophy nor religion could answer.[20]

Jung's observation has meantime become a statistical certainty. More importantly, though, Jung also remarked with characteristic sagacity:

> Man is never helped in his suffering by what he thinks for himself, but only by revelations of a wisdom greater than his own. It is this which lifts him out of his distress.[21]

This is a very insightful comment, on which we can expand as follows. If we agree that there are degrees of wisdom, it obviously pays to go straight to the source of the greatest wisdom, because our existential suffering cannot be overcome through half-baked knowledge. Hence we find that, after years of therapy, some people's thirst for deeper meaning is still not quenched. They then become spiritual seekers, eagerly drinking from the cool, refreshing fountain of the perennial wisdom.

What indeed is the meaning of life? I remember, when I was in my early twenties, putting this question to an old man whom I considered wise. His simple answer, which had me puzzled for many years, was: The meaning of life is to put one foot in front of the other. At first I thought he was teasing me, but he smiled at me gently and I knew he was not being flippant. His answer was something of a riddle, a *koan*, for me.

It annoyed me because I knew that hidden within it was a nugget of wisdom that stubbornly eluded me.

In retrospect, I feel it was an excellent response, which skillfully thwarted my youthful impatient need to sort everything into neat intellectual categories. It was a deliberately obscure answer, because the old man had used a simple everyday activity as a metaphor for the sweeping process of life itself.

Life is, above all, movement. But it is not random movement, as we witness it for instance in the Brownian motion of particles in water. Rather, life is a highly organized form of movement, an essential aspect of which is growing differentation, or unfolding. We call this evolution. As Aivanhov expressed it succinctly: "The whole meaning of life is evolution, the transformation of matter."[22] He explained:

> Everything that exists has to evolve: even minerals. The evolution of the mineral world is, no doubt, imperceptible but it is none the less real. A hidden force in the mineral world is constantly striving to bring to light all its potential, inherent qualities and virtues. Precious stones and metals are the most advanced mineral forms and they emanate something which can be beneficial to men. Plants evolve also and the more advanced they are, the greater the curative, nutritional and beneficial properties of their flowers and fruit. And the same is true of animals and human beings, and even of the solar system.
>
> Evolution is the law of life. Evolution, that is, meaning growth and development to the point of perfection.[23]

Aivanhov's understanding of evolution clearly goes beyond the textbook conception of it. Scientific evolutionary theory does not admit of perfection. Instead it sees a never-ending process of trial and error in which life forms engage in a fierce struggle for survival, being ruthlessly replaced by those that are better adapted to environmental conditions.

Alas, the scientific vision is inadequate, as a growing number of scientists realize.

Darwin appears to have been wrong. Nature is not an inchoate process devoid of purpose in which every individual and species selfishly fights for supremacy. Rather, it is suffused with a remarkable intelligence, and everywhere cooperative behavior rather than blind conflict is predominant. Robert Augros and George Stanciu, the authors of *The New Biology*, summarized their investigations into the new orientation within the biological disciplines as follows:

> The new biology is born of a new sense of nature. Conventional opinion holds that "the wisdom of nature is a sentimental notion," or worse yet, that nature incorporates an antiwisdom. Darwin exclaims, "What a book a devil's chaplain might write on the clumsy, wasteful, blundering, low and horribly cruel works of nature!"
>
> But the nature we have discovered . . . is a model for both engineer and artist. Her attributes of simplicity, economy, beauty, purpose, and harmony make her a model for ethics and politics. This rediscovery of nature's wisdom calls for a new biology.[24]

Struck by the order and directedness of the known universe, cosmologists have articulated what is called the Anthropic Principle. This principle recognizes that our cosmos, which some fifteen billion years ago emerged from an unimaginably dense energy soup, seems from the outset to have been designed for intelligent life to arise. As philosopher Henryk Skolimowski noted, to call this directedness "anthropic" is misleading, and he proposed the name Biotic Principle instead.[25] This leaves it open whether Homo sapiens is in fact the highest life form to emerge in the universe. After all, there could very well be intelligent life among the trillions of stars that has far surpassed humanity in knowledge, wisdom, and compassion.

At the same time, it is also clear that our species has not yet actualized its full potential. In fact, when we truly understand the present-day global crisis, we realize that our species is confronted with the challenge of voluntarily stepping up its own evolution. We are called upon to become what social scientist Duane Elgin calls a mature species civilization.[26] Writer John White has given this new humanity the name Homo noeticus. He said, "I see Homo noeticus as the next stage of human evolution precisely as Cro-Magnon superseded Neanderthal."[27] White added:

> The full emergence of Homo noeticus is probably several thousand years away. . . . But the forerunners of Homo noeticus are here now, in increasing numbers, making their presence felt, crowding Homo sapiens, creating their own niche in the eco-psychosystem and pointing out to him his own potential to change consciousness and thereby evolve, directing his own evolution and accelerating the process.[28]

PERSONALITY AND INDIVIDUALITY

The new concept of biological evolution comes much closer to the traditional understanding of the significance and purpose of human life. Our existence is not a matter of blind chance but one of purposive growth. This includes growing into new levels of awareness, which extend our perception from the purely physical realm to nonphysical realms. This expansion of our awareness and sensibilities redefines the reality in which we live.

An expanded awareness has long been at the heart of the esoteric traditions of the world. It was the privileged domain of the religious specialist — the shaman, magus, saint, and sage. However, for the first time in human history, this expanded awareness can become the common property of all human beings. In fact, perceptive observers of the contemporary crisis argue that this is the only way in which we will be able to survive as a species. But for this to come true, we as individuals must make a sustained effort to change ourselves.

The change required of us is quite simply one of making our lives conform to the highest possible ideals. As Aivanhov explained:

> A man's ideal determines all the rest, for it is an active agent in his life and produces specific results, digging deep into his being and cleansing and organizing all the disparate elements into a harmonious whole. Every aspect of a person's life is arranged, fashioned, modelled and formed in accordance with his ideal. If, rather than being very elevated and noble, it is prosaic and materialistic, then all the rest of his life, all his thoughts, acts and emotions will conform to it. . .[29]

Aivanhov regarded ideals as living entities that supply us with life force, though we must consciously relate to and cultivate them. Obviously, only high ideals have the power to aid our growth as human beings and especially to promote our spiritual evolution. "A high ideal is the only thing that can fill every void in man," he said.[30] To discover the highest ideals known to our species, we must consider the sacred traditions. It is in them that we find the most profound guidance to our evolutionary destiny.

The sacred traditions of the world have long understood that our biological development is merely a phase in a much more complex process of evolution. As they have maintained throughout the ages, the human destiny is not exhausted by biological reality but is focused on the spiritual dimension. We can foster that evolutionary process by adopting the Spirit as our guiding ideal. In the esoteric traditions, this is known as the spiritual quest, or the impulse toward self-transcendence. It is a powerful intention, as focused as a laser beam, that shapes every aspect of a person's life. Aivanhov described the alchemy underlying this overwhelming intention thus:

> This is one of the great secrets of Initiation: to make everything converge in the same direction; to convince all one's contradictory tendencies to pull together; to impose one's will on them and, if need be,

to reduce them to slavery. And when one has welded
all those unknown, hidden energies into one, when
one has learned to launch them all together towards
one glorious, luminous, beneficial goal, then one becomes a focal point of such intense, powerful light,
that one is free to send rays of light in every direction,
like the sun.[31]

Focusing upon one's chosen ideal is the essence of spiritual
life. This discipline can be described in many other ways,
because it consists of many different parts and extends over a
person's whole life. One way of talking about it is in terms of
cultivating what Aivanhov called individuality, or higher nature, as opposed to personality, which is the lower nature.

According to Aivanhov, the individuality, or Spirit, is of
divine nature. As such it is all-powerful and perfectly free,
constantly exerting a subtle influence on the personality to
conform to the principles and laws of the spiritual dimension.
By and large, we choose to ignore that influence.

The American transpersonal psychologist Ken Wilber
spoke of the Atman Project, which is the impulse inherent in
the Divine to realize itself in the finite realms.[32] It is present as
much in people's quest for power, security, and pleasure as it
is in the sages' path of peace and happiness. But the ways of
the world are unconscious forms of the Atman Project. In
spiritual life, this divine impulse is recognized and respected
as the deepest source of all human motivation. Spiritual practitioners seek to respond to it in the purest manner of which
they are capable.

Though omnipresent and omnipotent on the level of
ultimate existence, the spirit can express itself in the physical
dimension only to the extent that it is permitted to do so by
the ego-personality. As Aivanhov noted:

The individuality keeps trying to bring its good influence to bear upon the personality but, since the personality is interested only in being free and
independent, it listens only to itself and seldom obeys
the higher impulses. Although it is vivified, fed and

> sustained by the individuality, it remains opposed to
> it, and will continue to be so until the individuality
> finally is able to control the personality completely.
>   Once the personality gives in and is submissive
> and obedient, at one with the individuality, it will be
> a marriage, the only real marriage, the true love. . . .
> That is the goal, the aim of all the instruction, methods
> and exercises offered by an Initiatic School.[33]

The individuality, or transcendental Self, is supercons-
cious. It is the eternal witness. Aivanhov often spoke of it as
being "above" nature, "above" the human personality. Yet, he
also made it clear that such terms as "above" and "below"
must not be taken literally, in a spatial sense.

> In nature there is neither up nor down, right nor left.
> These words simply signify rapid vibrations or slow
> ones, intense vibrations or feeble ones. Up and within
> correspond to rapid vibration; down and without
> correspond to slow vibrations.[34]

Thought, for instance, vibrates more rapidly than matter.
But the highest vibration is associated with the Spirit. From
one point of view that vibration is sheer aliveness; from another, it is pure, selfless love — a compassionate resonance
with all beings. To realize the Spirit, we must vibrate at its
unsurpassed rate. Spiritual life can be understood as the discipline of voluntarily stepping up our rate of vibration. As
Aivanhov put it:

> You are only alive if you emanate love. It's so easy to
> practice! For instance, when no one is looking, lift
> your right hand high and project all your love to the
> whole universe, to the stars, to the angels and arch-
> angels, saying: "I love you, I love you, I want to be in
> harmony with you!" And in this way you form the
> habit of always emanating something vibrant and
> intense, you become a living source, a source of love.
> Humans think they are safer behind a grim face with

no expression, reflecting nothing alive, no kindness. They don't realize how dangerous this is. . .

We must form the habit of vibrating, night and day, thereby giving to all creatures in Heaven and earth something of ourselves, penetrating them with our love, like the Lord.[35]

Spiritual discipline is thus energy work, which takes seriously Einstein's great discovery that matter is a form of energy. Through this energy work, we discover that our visible physical reality arises against the backdrop of an infinite invisible reality.

NOTES

1. Aivanhov, *True Alchemy or the Quest for Perfection*, p. 85.
2. Aivanhov, *Life Force*, p. 250.
3. Aivanhov, *Education Begins Before Birth*, p. 165.
4. See Aivanhov, *Harmony*, p. 72.
5. See A. Bloom, *The Closing of the American Mind* (New York: Simon and Schuster, 1987).
6. Ibid., pp. 346–347.
7. R. Miller, *What Are Schools For?* (Brandon, VT: Holistic Education Press, 1990), p. 154.
8. Aivanhov, *Harmony*, p. 155.
9. Aivanhov, *The Key to the Problems of Existence*, p. 175.
10. Aivanhov, *Cosmic Moral Laws*, p. 129.
11. Aivanhov, *The Powers of Thought*, p. 103.
12. Aivanhov, *The Key to the Problems of Existence*, p. 72.
13. Aivanhov, *Man's Two Natures: Human and Divine*, p. 86.
14. Aivanhov, *Man's Psychic Life*, p. 204.
15. Aivanhov, *The Living Book of Nature*, p. 82.
16. See Aivanhov, *Man's Psychic Life*, p. 205.
17. Aivanhov, *The Key to the Problems of Existence*, p. 190.
18. Aivanhov, *Love and Sexuality* (Part II), p. 74.
19. Aivanhov, *The True Meaning of Christ's Teaching*, p. 111.
20. C. G. Jung, *Modern Man in Search of a Soul* (New York: Harvest Books/Harcourt, Brace & Co., 1933), p. 231.
21. Ibid., pp. 240–241.
22. Aivanhov, *The True Meaning of Christ's Teaching*, p. 115.
23. Ibid., pp. 115–116.

24. R. Augros and G. Stanciu, *The New Biology: Discovering the Wisdom in Nature* (Boston and London: Shambhala/New Science Library, 1988), pp. 230–231.

25. Henryk Skolimowski proposed this in a meeting at the California Institute of Integral Studies held on September 19, 1991.

26. See D. Elgin, *Awakening Earth,* (New York: Morrow, 1993).

27. J. White, *The Meeting of Science and Spirit: Guidelines for a New Age* (New York: Paragon House, 1990), p. 243.

28. Ibid., pp. 247–248.

29. Aivanhov, *Life Force,* p. 213.

30. Ibid., p. 215.

31. Aivanhov, *The Splendour of Tiphareth,* p. 257.

32. See K. Wilber, *The Atman Project* (Wheaton, IL: Quest, 1980).

33. Aivanhov, *The Key to the Problems of Existence,* p. 24.

34. Aivanhov, *The Second Birth,* p. 83.

35. Aivanhov, *Love and Sexuality* (Part I), p. 196.

5
THE MAGICAL
UNIVERSE

THE SUBATOMIC WORLD
AND SPIRITUAL PRESENCE

The Music of the Spheres, which is the ultimate living simplicity of the cosmos, can only be experienced in states of mystical elevation, such as Omraam Mikhael Aivanhov experienced at a young age. As soon as we return to our ordinary state of awareness, we find that the fullness that has been witnessed through direct participation cannot be conceptually expressed in ways that would satisfy the rational mind.

Yet, not too long ago, scientists believed in a universe that was rationally perfectly comprehensible and predictable, consisting of a certain amount of matter extended through three-dimensional space and obeying Newton's famous three laws of motion. This belief was badly shaken by Einstein's theory of relativity and the scientific discoveries to which it led. The new post-Newtonian cosmology operates with the concept of four-dimensional space-time, and the new universe has become rather less substantial and more subject to statistical probability.

Even the respectable electron is no longer thought of as an indivisible particle. According to quantum theory, it is something far less tangible and should properly be looked upon as a wavicle. In fact, the entire subatomic universe has become a jigsaw puzzle that is growing more and more complex as scientists seek to piece it together. First it was atoms, then hadrons, then quarks, which were thought to be the ultimate building blocks of the universe. But they have all seemingly yielded new subforms — the so-called "particle zoo."

Trying to bring unity to this profusion, some scientists in the 1960s invented the concept of strings. These are thought of as one-dimensional vibrating loops no longer than a billionth of a trillionth of a trillionth of an inch. Rather like a violin string, they produce different "tones" — quarks, leptons, gluons, and their derivatives — depending on the rate of their vibration. This idea in turn has led theoreticians to assume that strings vibrate in as many as twenty-five dimensions. In the mid-1980s string theory was extended to include superstrings. It is truly a case of the more scientists know the less they understand of the great mystery confronting them. How many would admit this, though?

Meanwhile, theoreticians are struggling to find a universal theory to explain literally everything. According to the spiritual traditions, their faith is quite misplaced. Reason can never grasp the mystery of existence in its entirety. Even though modern high-energy research has once and for all demolished our naive conception of the universe as a simple three-dimensional cosmos, quantum physics is still in many ways committed to materialism. Few scientists accept that their multidimensional universe, arrived at largely through mathematical speculation, is enfolded in transdimensional Being. However, it is encouraging to know that the very methods of science continue to produce information that undermines its philosophical foundations, which are anchored in materialist soil.

From the point of view of the esoteric traditions, the world as a whole is mysterious at its core. It cannot be reduced to mathematical or physical theories. In this sense it is a truly magical place. Matter, energy, and consciousness can only be separated in one's mind. In reality, they are all aspects of the same totality. Some scientists are beginning to admit this much, though they are still reluctant to admit that the cosmos, as Aivanhov believed, is ensouled.

Where physicists see cause and effect, Aivanhov saw intelligences at work. Such a view is generally dismissed as primitive animism. Hence scientists tend to find exactly what they expect to find, namely a universe without soul. From

Aivanhov's point of view, the only intelligence materialistic scientists discover in the cosmos is their own human intelligence, and that is indeed not very much. As Aivanhov quipped:

> To my way of thinking, a materialist is not very intelligent: he has not seen all there is to see because he has relied exclusively on his intellect and, as the intellect is the assassin of reality, the essence of reality escapes him. The intellect prevents man from seeing this essence, the prime cause, the living core, the source of all that is.[1]

Aivanhov was an inveterate critic of scientific materialism, in fact of materialism in any form or shape. He thought it narrow-minded and sectarian.[2] He spoke of materialist scientists and philosophers as the "curse of curses" and as opening up the abyss, "releasing the forces of destruction."[3] He observed:

> By choosing materialism humans are choosing the way of annihilation. They think they will be free, but instead they are burying themselves. They don't want to listen to Initiates, they feel they know everything, but the day will come when they will be completely crushed under their own load, this matter which they won't let go of and which they love so much.[4]

Aivanhov admitted, however, that there are a few thinkers who valiantly fight off the spell of matter, opposing materialism. Always looking for balance, he even admitted that materialists have a certain usefulness in creation: they are like earthworms transforming the soil.[5] But materialism is clearly a limiting vision, especially for those aspiring to spiritual growth.

For Aivanhov, materialism has no future. Its days are numbered, just as the days of Russia's communism were numbered, as he predicted in one of his first lectures over half a century ago:

At the moment, human beings are still a prey to the materialistic philosophy which has estranged them from true strength, and they are growing continually weaker. But a few years hence you will see materialism banished and rejected and everywhere, in universities, schools and families, human beings will be taught the science of the spirit. Then they will realize that, for centuries, they have simply been marking time, and that all their technical and scientific discoveries do not really constitute progress. True progress is progress of the spirit; there is no progress except that of the spirit.[6]

Aivanhov added: "Write these words down, they constitute a formula for the future."

The multidimensional reality conjured up by physicists who rely on mathematics more than on laboratory tests is a fragmented reality. Fragmentation is one of the hallmarks of the intellect that receives no nourishment from higher intuition, revealing the unifying spiritual dimension. That is to say, the universe depicted by physicists — though far more complex than the Newtonian universe — is a universe bereft of spiritual presence, a Godless place.

Despite the fact that quantum physics and modern cosmology have tremendously enlarged our understanding of the world we inhabit, these sciences are nevertheless still afflicted with a lingering materialistic bias. In a way, the scientific theories are ahead of the human beings formulating them. Another way of putting it is that scientists have not yet fathomed the full depth of their own ideas. Once the materialistic prejudice is lifted, science will rediscover the spiritual presence in the universe.

Some scientists have already broken through the existing bias. Thus physicist Harold K. Schilling wrote:

Nature has again become for the human consciousness a window open to the transcendental and immanental reaches of reality, whence come intimations of creative-redemptive divinity transcendent to and immanent throughout nature or the cosmos. This is mystery that evokes more than wonder, namely worship. It is the ultimately mysterious reality commonly called God.[7]

Contemporary physics has lent new credibility to the esoteric traditions, which also understand the universe as a multidimensional organism. However, unlike the esoteric traditions, contemporary science has not yet applied this knowledge to the human being. As faithful mirrors of the cosmos at large, we too are multidimensional. Most of what we are belongs to the invisible realms of reality.

MULTIPLE BODIES, MULTIPLE REALITIES

Our secular Western civilization, which has a pronounced visual bias, operates on the rationalist doctrine that "seeing is believing." We invoke this doctrine whenever we doubt the existence of something, notably metaphysical realities like the Divine or higher spiritual beings. This is accompanied by an almost desperate belief in the visible.

However, since the visible is so obviously not our exclusive reality, such people are destined for great disappointment. As the well-known Jungian therapist June Singer stated:

> The belief that there is only the visible world can be disheartening to the point of despair. It feeds a sense of hopelessness — this is what the world is and no one can do much about it. One must live for today, and only for today. But in the end, living only for today ends in disaster.[8]

Clearly, many of the things that are fundamental to our material lives are completely intangible and invisible: freedom, justice, happiness, success, power, love, loyalty. We cannot really see them, yet they exist and are very important to us. Aivanhov put it still more radically thus:

> Have you never realized that your whole life is based on things you cannot see? Only the invisible world exists for sure: all the rest is open to doubt. If you deny

the reality of the invisible world, you are sawing off the branch you are sitting on, and one fine day you will find yourself on the ground! . . . Someone who denies the existence of the invisible world is signing his own death sentence.[9]

We frequently refer to the many invisible realities and values that make our lives worth living, and scientists are even trying to understand them by a variety of scientific methods. However, because these methods are based on quantifying what are essential, intangible qualities, they have predictably been rather unsuccessful. How can you measure love, freedom, happiness, or life itself?

Even the hard sciences, which make no room for invisible metaphysical realities, constantly operate with the invisible. For instance, no one has ever actually seen Planck's constant, Heisenberg's uncertainty principle, entropy, evolution, the law of probability, or any number of mathematical and physical principles that are crucial to the work of scientists. Yet the same scientists who do not hesitate to formulate hypotheses, models, and theories on the basis of those invisible principles are extremely nervous about, and often even quite intolerant toward, the kind of invisible reality that concerns philosophers and theologians; they would readily dismiss Aivanhov's metaphysical framework and the mystical experiences on which it is based.

Fortunately, we are witnessing a felicitous change of attitude nowadays. Singer's book signals this change within the discipline of psychology, which not too long ago even refused to work with the concept of psyche, or consciousness. In physics, the work of David Bohm for instance spells out this new direction. His concept of the implicate order can be straightforwardly translated into the concept of the invisible.[10] For Bohm, the totality of existence is an undivided whole, or holomovement, which is multidimensional, and everything is enfolded in everything else. Thus the universe is a magnificent hologram, and most of its aspects are implicate (invisible) rather than explicate (visible).

According to Bohm's view, the human individual is merely a relatively independent subtotality that is stable enough to give one the impression of uniqueness. However, this explicate structure is not all there is to the human being. We also participate in the vast implicate order of the universe. Hence human nature cannot be adequately explained by purely mechanistic principles. Bohm's model is a modern restatement of ancient intuitions.

Like the notion of invisibility, the concept of mystery has also become somewhat more respectable in scientific circles. Thus, the American physicist Harold K. Schilling described nature as "unfathomable by scientific exploration and analysis."[11] However much scientists prod and probe the universe, it does not appear to have a bottom or a top but is an ineluctable mystery.

It was no less an intellect than Albert Einstein who wrote these oft-quoted words:

> The fairest thing we can experience is the mysterious. It is the fundamental emotion which stands at the cradle of true art and true science. He who knows it not and can no longer wonder, no longer feel amazement, is as good as dead, a snuffed-out candle. It was the experience of mystery — even if mixed with fear — that engendered religion. A knowledge of the existence of something we cannot penetrate, of the manifestations of the profoundest reason and the most radiant beauty, which are only accessible to our reason in their most elementary forms — it is this knowledge and this emotion that constitute the truly religious attitude; in this sense, and in this alone, I am a deeply religious man.[12]

Within the gargantuan mystery of existence are many mansions, of which those questing for knowledge can catch a glimpse now and then. To some extent, the mysterious multidimensional reality may reveal and even make accessible hitherto invisible dimensions of itself to persisting spiritual pilgrims.

They may even come to see, though not with their physical eyes, the hidden structures spoken of in the esoteric traditions, such as subtle bodies and realms. The idea that the physical body is only the outermost shell of an interlocking system of "bodies," or energy fields, is central to most, if not all, initiatic schools.

As spiritual practitioners expand their vision to include ever more subtle dimensions, they also become varyingly capable of being effective on those higher levels of existence. The spiritual adepts are both great gnostics and great magi. In Sanskrit parlance, the *yogin* is both a *jnanin* (knower) and a *siddha*, or thaumaturgist, endowed with paranormal abilities. According to the *Siddha-Siddhanta-Paddhati* (II.31), an ancient Yoga scripture, only those who know firsthand the "anatomical structures" of the *subtle* body can claim to be yogins.

To obtain a truly comprehensive understanding of human nature, we must therefore not only consult biologists, psychologists, sociologists, and philosophers but also listen carefully to the testimony of the great spiritual teachers of humankind. They have experiential knowledge of the invisible aspects of human nature that are equally as important, if not more so, than the visible dimension of the body. As Aivanhov remarked:

> Man is totally ignorant of his own structure and composition, and of the constant interaction that goes on between human beings and the invisible beings in the other regions of the universe. It is this ignorance which is the cause of his great misfortunes. Whereas the disciple who knows how he has been put together in the Lord's workshops and how he is in constant relationship with the inhabitants of other planes of the universe, becomes aware of the need to pick and choose: he eliminates certain elements, closing his doors to hostile forces and opening them to forces which are beneficial, harmonious and constructive.[13]

He also observed:

> The bodies of men and women epitomize the uni-
> verse as a whole and the disciple must learn to look
> at them with awe and wonder and, above all, to use
> them as a stimulus for a renewed attachment to the
> sublime world on high.[14]

During his nearly fifty years of teaching in France,
Aivanhov spoke at length about the subtle configurations that
make up the invisible aspects of the human being. By and
large, his explanations mesh with those found in other esoteric
traditions. Often, however, he was able to add from his own
experience surprising elements that shed new light on the
ancient teachings. However involved his discourses on the
invisible dimensions became, though, he always emphasized
that, ultimately, what matters in spiritual life is the Spirit itself.
"I deal in essentials," he once noted.[15]

According to Aivanhov, the human being is a composite of
six bodies, which are known as *koshas* ("sheaths") in the Sanskrit scriptures of Hinduism. The sheath that is most familiar
to us is the physical body. Surrounding it is the etheric sheath,
which is not always listed as a separate body. It is also known
as the double, or what Aivanhov called the "vapor" of the
material body.[16] However, as Aivanhov explained, the various
subtle bodies also have their double.[17] He spoke of the etheric
body as follows:

> Like vegetation, the etheric body penetrates down
> into the physical body, at the same time retaining
> ramifications in the higher regions in order to capture
> forces to introduce into the system. It vivifies matter
> by drawing out its hidden qualities and acts as an
> intermediary between the physical body and the sub-
> tle bodies. No one knows very much yet about the
> etheric body, least of all the medical world. Doctors
> do not realize that many physical anomalies are
> caused by upsets in the etheric body. Even spiritual-
> ists think of it as less important than the astral and
> mental bodies. It may not have as much power as the
> other bodies, but for life it is essential.[18]

Wrapped around and interpenetrating the physical body and its bioplasmic field are, in ascending order of subtlety, the astral body, the mental body, the causal body, the buddhic body, and the atmic body.

The astral body is the seat of our personal emotions and intentions, whereas the mental body, as the name suggests, is the locus of our intellectual activity. In Sanskrit the former body is known as the *prana-maya-kosha* or "sheath composed of life force," whereas the latter body is called *mano-maya-kosha* or "sheath composed of mind." Aivanhov commented on the astral body as follows:

> Greed, cupidity, the desire to possess, to satisfy oneself, are all manifestations of the astral body and if this body is not controlled and taught how to behave, it puffs up more and more, becoming like a monstrous tumour in man ...
>
> The astral body, that seat of all feeling and passion, begins to manifest in people at the beginning of puberty. Before this period it is the etheric body which is most active. Of course both the astral and mental bodies are alive and, to a certain extent, active; the child experiences strong feelings and understands what is explained to him but his astral body is not really formed until he is about fourteen and the mental body is not formed until he is about twenty-one.[19]

The causal body, or higher mental body, is the field in which the most luminous thoughts occur, which are not so much the creations of the individual as archetypal realities. This is the level to which the geniuses of humanity are attuned and from which they derive their inspirations. It is also the plane of genuine wisdom. This body corresponds to the *vijnana-maya-kosha* or "sheath composed of awareness" in the Hindu tradition.

The buddhic body is what Aivanhov called the seat of the soul. The word buddhic is the Anglicized form of the Sanskrit adjective *bauddha*, which stems from the noun *buddhi*, meaning literally "intelligence, cognition, wisdom." Sometimes

Aivanhov also explained the soul as being composed of the lower mental body and the astral body together.[20] However, assigning the soul specifically to the buddhic body is logical enough, for this is the level of lucidity and tranquillity characterizing the saints. It is also the level of unselfish love that extends to all beings. In Hinduism it is known as the *ananda-maya-kosha* or "sheath composed of bliss," because on this level there is not the least intrusion of pain or suffering.

The atmic body is the seat of the Spirit, or higher Soul, which is the ultimate identity of the human being. It is also known as the universal or higher Self. It gets its name from the Sanskrit word *atman*, meaning "Self." It is the divine spark within us, which can never become extinguished because of its proximity to, or identity with, the Divine itself. The Spirit is what the sun is to the planets of our solar system. This is the level realized by the great spiritual adepts. It is also the "Omega point," as the French paleontologist and theologian Pierre Teilhard de Chardin would say — the terminal point of all evolution, in which the cosmos, or a part of it, awakens to its divine, precosmic origin.

THE COSMOS, GOOD, AND EVIL

To realize the Spirit presupposes mature self-understanding, and to understand ourselves means to understand the universe. The structural parallelism between macrocosm (world) and microcosm (human being) belongs to the oldest philosophical insights. As Aivanhov explained:

> From time immemorial philosophers have recognized in man a miniature universe. In the temples of antiquity he was portrayed as the key to the door of the Great King's palace, because all that exists in the universe, whether it be energy or matter, exists to a lesser degree in man.[21]

In the Middle Ages, this arcane teaching was epitomized in the Zodiacal Man, a graphic representation known as a *vesica piscis*, which shows a human figure surrounded by the twelve signs of the zodiac which are linked to various parts of the body.

This illustration expressed the belief that the human being is snugly inserted into the large design of the cosmos, and the cosmic structures are in turn analogically represented in the human being. Echoing all spiritual traditions, Aivanhov spoke of this parallelism as one of symbiosis. "Life," he stated, "is nothing more than a ceaseless flow of give-and-take between man and Nature."[22]

In explaining life, Aivanhov used the image of the river. Rivers begin in the mountains and flow down into the valley. They are purest at their source and become muddier as they flow toward the ocean. The River of Life is purest at its divine source, gradually gathering impurities, until it is thoroughly polluted in the material world.

The interconnection between macrocosm and microcosm is established by the fact that both the universe and the human being, as an evolutionary form of the world, derive their existence from the Divine. Aivanhov spoke of the "boundless flow of life streaming from the Godhead, penetrating the furthest reaches of Creation, from the greatest start to the most minute particle of matter."[23] He also remarked: "Nature is God's physical body."[24]

Life is the vital connecting link between all creatures and things. Human beings imagine themselves as being apart from and superior to all other creatures — a misconception that gives rise to tremendous suffering in the world. This false notion underlies not only all conflict between people but also the terrible exploitation of animals, plants, and minerals by human beings. The truth is that we are an integral part of the cosmos. In Aivanhov's words:

> Man is not separate from Nature, we are part of it, our breath and life depend on Nature. We are influenced by Nature, and Nature is influenced by us.[25]

Aivanhov also spoke of Nature as a single vast organism.[26] A biological organism is able to function because all its numerous parts are cooperative and perfectly synchronized. Disease occurs when this natural balance is upset. The equilibrium in Nature, as in the individual human body-mind, is highly dynamic. It consists of a succession of states that include dramatic moments of crisis. Without such moments, there could be no evolution, no growth.

That is to say, Nature, like human life, incorporates aspects that in the short run seem cruel, evil, and undesirable but that in the long run serve the causes of evolution and therefore must be considered appropriate, beneficial, and good. Aivanhov made much of this point. He said:

> In Nature, everything is good. I am not saying that devils are good, no, but one day, when they have become tame, appetizing and well-seasoned, they will be a feast for us! It says in the Talmud that at the end of the world the monster Leviathan will be cut up and salted and served as a feast for the just. What a privilege if indeed we are among the guests, to dine together on the Monster at the same table![27]

He explained further:

> Light and shadow are symbols of good and evil, like the right and the left: often the right side is associated with the good and the left side with evil, but actually it is only a manner of speaking. Man has two sides, but he is nevertheless one single indivisible entity. Look, if your left hand slaps your right hand, it doesn't mean they are two separate entities at war with each other. No, it is the same person who does both the hitting and the receiving. Once you understand the law of polarity you will have the answer to a lot of things you now consider mysteries.[28]

For Aivanhov, Nature is essentially good because it is a manifestation of the Divine, which is the embodiment of goodness. More precisely, though, the Divine is beyond good and evil, and good is simply the highest manifestation of the Divine.

In the physical realm, good and evil belong together like
the two parts of a conch shell. They are like brother and sister.[29]
However, only the principle of good is eternal. In the lower
planes of existence, evil fulfills a definite function. As
Aivanhov commented:

> Nature uses evil in the same way as a pharmaceutical
> laboratory uses certain poisons in the preparation of
> very potent medicines. Evil is a poison which can be
> lethal for the weak and ignorant, but for those who
> are strong and intelligent it is a panacea; it can cure
> them. This is the philosophy of the third school: evil
> must be used.[30]

Evil must be used by being transmuted. We cannot simply
get rid of evil, for to do so would mean we would also have to
get rid of good.[31] Rather, we must adopt a new attitude toward
evil by adopting a broader perspective on life. In order to
explain this, Aivanhov availed himself of the image of a water
wheel. In bygone days, and still in some village communities
in India and the Far East, people used a wheel pulled by oxen
to draw water from a well. A nearby observer would simply
see a team of oxen pulling a wheel moving toward or away
from him. However, an observer looking at the whole scene
while standing on a hilltop would get a more complete picture
of what is happening. He would see the same team of oxen
going round and round in a circle. Aivanhov frequently used
the image of an observer at a higher altitude to explain the
initiate's vantage point.

Instead of blaming the Divine for evil events, we must
learn to understand evil as a byproduct of creation at a lower
level of operation. "Evil," Aivanhov remarked, "is the residue
of good."[32] He compared evil to waste matter that may fill us
with disgust but that is nonetheless useful fertilizer. As he
explained:

> No matter how pure, how saintly and good some-
> thing may be, there is always a negative side to it . . .
> the other side of the medal, it is called. Everyone

knows this, but no one draws a conclusion. At the Creation, when the world was formed, a place was set aside, symbolically speaking, for refuse such as broken glass, rusty nails, cracked bricks and so on, left over from the construction. The world's store of refuse is the dark cone behind it, the world's shadow...[33]

The world's shadow is of course Hell, the dumping ground of all that is evil, the antipole to the Divine. But even in Hell, Aivanhov contended, exists a glimmer of good. For the Divine interpenetrates everything.

The divine good is above all expressed in the laws governing the universe. Aivanhov noted:

Everything is linked. The moral domain is governed by immutable, indestructible laws which you should know.[34]

Why is it desirable to know those cosmic laws? The answer is quite simply that such knowledge will prevent us from running afoul of those laws. While the universe is essentially good, it is also indifferent and impartially metes out punishment to all those who transgress its unwritten code. As in civilized jurisprudence, ignorance of the law is no excuse. On the contrary, it is a very good reason for reaping retribution.

Our destiny depends on the degree of our voluntary collaboration with life, our obedience to the divine will as it is expressed in the evolutionary thrust of the universe. By following the cosmic laws we link up with the luminous aspects of existence, drawing closer to the Divine itself. In other words, we must become good in order to transcend good and evil by merging with the Divine.

However, if we go against the cosmic principles, whether knowingly or unknowingly, we invite a fate that is less than benign. Our intentions and thoughts determine our state of being. This is guaranteed by the mechanisms of the cosmos itself, which forgets nothing. As Aivanhov taught:

Nature has a memory that never forgets, and so much the worse for the person who does not take this memory into consideration! It goes on anyhow, registering his jangling thoughts and inner turmoil until the day when he can stand no more, he is overcome and gives up.[35]

Aivanhov explained that our intentions, desires, and thoughts are all recorded in the etheric body. He said:

The records preserved by the etheric body are comparable to a photographic negative or stereotype from which thousands of identical copies can be made. Once something has been recorded — whether it be thought, a feeling or an act — it must necessarily repeat itself over and over again. And this is how habits are born. If you want to change a habit you have to change your negative or stereotype.[36]

In Yoga philosophy, these records or imprints are called *samskaras* — a Sanskrit word meaning "activators." These reside in the depth of memory where they combine into strings known as *vasanas*, which we call habit patterns. The *samskaras* are blueprints for our subsequent thoughts and actions. They cannot be eradicated, though adepts can transform and transcend them.

These imprints in the subconscious — or in the etheric body — are transformed by creating imprints that are positive, leading to the realization of the Spirit. In the highest states of mystical ecstasy, they are even temporarily transcended. But we can never entirely rid ourselves of the subconscious baggage we have created during our present lifetime and all our other lifetimes.

Aivanhov, like most initiates, taught that the present life is likely to be one link in a long chain of lives, or reincarnations. This teaching was also part of early Christianity but was revoked at the Council of Nicaea in 325 A.D. While we do not need to believe in reincarnation to live a spiritual life, this belief can often help explain things that remain otherwise obscure.

More will be said about this in the chapter on spiritual discipline.

To speak of Nature's memory is a graphic metaphor for saying that the laws of the universe are profound moral laws. Of course, they are not "moral" in the ordinary sense of the word. Common morality and conventional law are no more than varyingly imperfect reflections of the moral order of the cosmos. For a universal morality that fully adheres to and honors the cosmic laws we must turn to the great initiates. They can teach us how to read the Book of Nature properly and with spiritual profit.

NOTES

1. Aivanhov, *The Splendour of Tiphareth*, p. 198.
2. See Aivanhov, *A Philosophy of Universality*, p. 13.
3. Aivanhov, *Harmony*, p. 161.
4. Aivanhov, *Love and Sexuality* (Part I), p. 191.
5. See Aivanhov, *Love and Sexuality* (Part II), p. 90.
6. Aivanhov, *The Powers of Thought*, pp. 135–136.
7. H. K. Schilling, *The New Consciousness in Science & Religion* (London: SCM Press, 1973), p. 32.
8. J. Singer, *Seeing Through the Visible World: Jung, Gnosis, and Chaos* (San Francisco: Harper & Row, 1990), p. 22.
9. Aivanhov, *Man: Master of His Destiny*, pp. 130–131.
10. See D. Bohm, *Wholeness and the Implicate Order* (London: Routledge & Kegan Paul, 1980).
11. See H. K. Schilling, *op.cit.*, p. 116.
12. A. Einstein, *The World As I See It* (New York: Philosophical Library, 1949), p. 5.
13. Aivanhov, *Man: Master of His Destiny*, p. 42.
14. Aivanhov, *The Living Book of Nature*, p. 136.
15. Aivanhov, *Looking Into the Invisible*, p. 76.
16. See Aivanhov, *Man's Psychic Life*, p. 94.
17. See Aivanhov, *The Zodiac: Key to Man and to the Universe*, p. 62.
18. Aivanhov, *Christmas and Easter in the Initiatic Tradition*, p. 117.
19. Aivanhov, *New Light on the Gospels*, pp. 88–89.
20. See Aivanhov, *Man's Psychic Life*, p. 80.
21. Aivanhov, *The Living Book of Nature*, p. 11.
22. Ibid., pp. 11–12.
23. Ibid., p. 12.

24. Aivanhov, *Spiritual Alchemy,* p. 64.
25. Aivanhov, *A New Dawn* (Part I), p. 59.
26. See Aivanhov, *The Yoga of Nutrition,* p. 56.
27. Aivanhov, *The Key to the Problems of Existence,* p. 57.
28. Ibid., p. 57.
29. See Aivanhov, *The Tree of the Knowledge of Good and Evil,* p. 39.
30. Aivanhov, *Life Force,* p. 72.
31. See Aivanhov, *The Tree of the Knowledge of Good and Evil,* p. 32.
32. Ibid., p. 36.
33. Ibid., p. 34.
34. Aivanhov, *Man: Master of His Destiny,* p. 17.
35. Aivanhov, *Cosmic Moral Laws,* p. 19.
36. Aivanhov, *True Alchemy or the Quest for Perfection,* p. 76.

6
DECIPHERING THE
BOOK OF NATURE

A DIFFERENT KIND OF BOOK

Francis Bacon, the great English philosopher of science, lawyer, and politician of the late sixteenth century, wrote:

> After the sacred volumes of God and the Scriptures, study, in the second place, that great volume of the works and the creatures of God.[1]

It is evident from this comment that Bacon was a scientific thinker first and an admirer of God's handiwork, Nature, second. This is why he chose a political career rather than a spiritual avocation and perhaps also why, toward the end of his life, his meteoric rise in society came to an abrupt and ignoble end: He was found guilty of having taken bribes — a widespread custom in his day, as it is today.

Obviously, Bacon had failed to understand the Book of Nature. For Aivanhov, by contrast, the Book of Nature came before all other books. In his youth, he read every book he could lay his hands on, and while at the University of Varna, his appetite for intellectual learning was so voracious that it could not be contained by the narrow specialized knowledge offered in the halls of academe. Yet, in due course, he understood that the only learning that has any lasting value is that which comes through personal experience. As he put it succinctly: "Life is more important than learning."[2] He continued:

> Nine tenths of humanity spend their time on the surface of life; they don't live, they don't feel — by which I mean that they don't live or feel what is essential. They read about it, they discuss it, but they

don't really and truly experience it. You have to live things and experience them on a deep level, then they will stay with you eternally. Yes, the only things you can take with you and which will never be wiped out even when you die, are those that you have verified for yourself in your own life, your own soul, your own heart. All the rest, everything you have learned at the university or from books, will have to be left behind when you leave this world.[3]

Aivanhov came to appreciate, like St. Bernard of Clairvaux and other great mystics before him, that trees and stones can teach us more than books.[4] He understood, as did Ralph Waldo Emerson, that the Book of Nature is the book of fate.[5]

In trying to explain to his disciples how purity is essential on the spiritual path, Aivanhov made the following comments:

I have told you that I do not like to read too many books because the greatest truths in life are not to be found in books written by men, but in the great Book of Nature. Everything has been written in that book, and what I am telling you now is drawn from the lessons I have learned from insects: roaches, ants, fleas, etc.[6]

Writing and reading, Aivanhov argued correctly, tend to weaken memory. This, in turn, undermines the world's rich oral traditions. It also would seem to be responsible, as apparently the Druids thought, for the diminution of our psychic powers. Hence, as Aivanhov noted, they refused to resort to writing.[7] Literacy is obviously tied in with the cultivation of the intellectual functions associated with the left cerebral hemisphere. The right hemisphere of the brain was dominant in premodern times, which may explain why psychic abilities were more readily accessible to our ancestors, as indeed they still are to tribal peoples around the world.

On the one hand, the progressive reduction of our memory and orally transmitted knowledge is regrettable. We have lost many vital values because of this. On the other hand, however, the reduction of memory historically coincided with a reduction of humanity's reliance on the past. Tribal societies are typically tied to the past, with their time-honored rituals and myths. Modern societies, by contrast, tend to be more open toward the future, and hence also more subject to, and capable of, rapid change. This important point was made by the Swiss cultural philosopher Jean Gebser in his epochal work *The Ever-Present Origin*.[8]

Clearly, we must find a balance between respecting the past and being open to the future. Aivanhov, it would appear, had established this balance in his own life. He was not only an eminently rational person, but also knew how to tap the imaginative powers and hidden paranormal potential of the human psyche. He was ruled neither by the left nor the right cerebral hemisphere. Rather, he exemplified an admirable symmetry between intellect and heart. He lived the *whole* brain, the *whole* person.

The "Book of Nature" was a key image in Aivanhov's teaching, as it had been in the teaching of Peter Deunov. Aivanhov stated:

> Nature is God's book, His own masterpiece in which He expresses Himself, and His laws are all written down there for anyone who takes the trouble to learn to read.[9]

Aivanhov elucidated this as follows:

> Nature is the great book in which we must do all our studying. Gradually, as our attitude toward nature is modified, so is our destiny. If we believe that everything in nature is inanimate, we deprive ourselves of a certain degree of life, but if we believe that everything in nature is alive, then everything — the stones, plants, animals, even the stars — will contribute to increasing the flow of life within us. And as the flow of life in our physical body intensifies and our spirit becomes stronger, true, perfect Life enters into us and circulates through the solar plexus, setting up a flow of harmonious energy. It is only then that we reach

true comprehension. And true comprehension is in feeling.[10]

Aivanhov also noted:

> For an Initiate, to read means to be able to decipher the subtle, secret dimensions of objects and of all living creatures, to interpret the signs and symbols traced by Cosmic Intelligence on every page of the great Book of the Universe. And to write is to put one's mark on that book, to act upon minerals and plants, animals and men, by the magic power of one's spirit.[11]

To appreciate Aivanhov's notion of the "Book of Nature," we must adopt a symbolic reading, but it is precisely this kind of symbolic interpretation that has been closed to us by our entire education, which is founded on the materialistic and reductionistic ideas of scientism. The American philosopher Jacob Needleman characterized this tragedy well when he observed:

> The view of man that arises out of modern biology is an inevitable result of modern man's loss of the symbolic understanding of nature. The moment we forget that real symbols can only be fully apprehended in another state of consciousness, in that moment all the ancient teachings about man's place in nature begin to seem absurd.[12]

Needleman went on to say that "perhaps there were once peoples who learned directly from nature as from a sacred teaching, and perhaps somewhere even today there are still individuals who learn that way."[13] There undoubtedly were such peoples — entire cultures. And equally certainly there are alive today not a few individuals — among the tribal elders in America and other parts of the world — who are skilled at reading the Book of Nature.

One such individual is Wallace Black Elk, a Lakota elder and shaman who was born in 1921 on an Indian reservation in South Dakota. In his preface to the book *Black Elk*, editor William S. Lyon made these relevant comments:

> For the Lakota shamans who believe in and use the spirits, sacred power seemingly has no limits. What may seem unusual, even paranormal to us, is an everyday part of their world. They do not question the existence of power, only its application. That is a universal concern among shamans.[14]

Wallace Black Elk's symbolic way of thinking about, and relating to, Nature is evident from the following explanation in his own words:

> So man was given one drop of wisdom, one drop of knowledge, one drop of power, and one drop of gift or love (or talent). Tunkashila [the Creator] is the wisdom in itself. The knowledge is a woman, and we call it the Earth. We call it fire, rock, water, and green.[15]

Earth is knowledge. This is another way of speaking of the Book of Nature. Trying to explain his metaphoric language, the Lakota shaman continued:

> There is an everyday language, but the spiritual language I speak is different. When the spirits talk, they speak really deep. Really deep! When they gave me that power I could also speak and understand that spiritual language. So those people on the surface, they speak shallow. Their minds are really shallow, and their thinking is light.[16]

THE ANIMATED UNIVERSE

For Aivanhov, as for Wallace Black Elk and other spiritual teachers, the entire cosmos is a living organism. Far from being a dead material object the Book of Nature is an ensouled entity of incomprehensible complexity and immensity.

While the mind can never grasp it, our purified intuition can come to appreciate the fundamental principles and laws governing the universe. As Aivanhov affirmed:

> Everything in Nature possesses form, content and meaning. The form is for the common man, the content for the disciple and the hidden meaning for the wise, for Initiates.[17]

What the initiates have discovered is that the cosmos is alive, suffused with spirit. Both matter and energy are sustained by, and manifestations of, the Divine. The universe of the esoteric traditions is a living being that fills any sensitive soul with awe and wonder. Aivanhov said:

> Very young children have an innate sense of the marvellous. They believe that everything is alive and intelligent. They talk to insects, stones, animals and plants. . .
>
> Once a child has lost his power of wonderment he has lost his most precious faculty. For you cannot think that it is any great proof of superiority for adults to maintain that the universe has no soul and no intelligence and that man is the only living creature who has the power of thought. The whole of nature is alive and intelligent and peopled with living, intelligent creatures many of whom are far more intelligent than man![18]

When we deny the universe such intelligence, we opt for a philosophy of nihilism. In that case, we deprive ourselves of any higher purpose, of any morality that elevates us, of any reason for being alive. Aivanhov wholeheartedly condemned this infelicitous orientation, which is so widespread among the followers of scientism (rather than science). He observed:

> From the pedagogical point of view this is the most detestable philosophy, because in order to educate men, in order to elevate them morally and spiritually, in order to lead them toward something magnificent

from the social and collective point of view, you must present the opposite to them, you must present intelligence, reason, meaning, the Lord, and if none of this existed, you would have to invent it in order to give a purpose, a destination, to human existence. Otherwise, it is the end![19]

Aivanhov was right of course. We cannot hope to grow beyond our species' present confusion and moral dereliction without reinstating a philosophy that holds before our eyes the highest possible ideals. The bankruptcy of materialism should require no special demonstration at this point in human history. All our noblest accomplishments have been the fruit of a reverential or sacred approach to life and Nature.

As we are becoming more aware of the extent of the ecological crisis into which scientific materialism has thrown us, we are perhaps becoming more willing to reconsider our relationship to Nature and to learn to read its great Book, as the initiates have done for millennia. Indeed, unless we do so we will suffer terribly from the consequences of the faulty thoughts and actions committed by our race over the past two of centuries under the baneful influence of scientific materialism.

It may of course be too late to prevent the imminent backlash of Nature. However, it is never too late to set in motion more benign patterns of thought, so that future generations may benefit from our personal and collective spiritual struggles. At any rate, we will find no personal happiness unless we restore order and balance in our own lives. This means we must become conscious participants, benign players, in the magical universe.

The universe is magical because, as modern physics has demonstrated, every part is related to every other part. I am of course not considering here the so-called magic of a Houdini or a Copperfield. Their spectacular acts are clever tricks. Rather, when referring to the magical Nature of existence, I mean the far more spectacular "acts" that are performed on the cosmic stage, which suggest as it were a great invisible magician of astounding intelligence. This understanding of magic coincides with Aivanhov's who said:

> For me, magic is life . . . the whole of life, the whole universe. The true book of magic is there, lying open for all to read . . . but we have not yet learned how.[20]

UNDERSTANDING THE LANGUAGE OF NATURE

Occasionally we urbanites look at the sky, and what we see is different from what a farmer might see. While for us clouds may be pretty or uninteresting, a farmer gleans from them all kinds of useful information, and sometimes his knowledge is even more profound and accurate than that of a trained metereologist. But what a shaman sees when he looks at the sky exceeds even the knowledge of the farmer. From the shape of clouds and other metereological phenomena the shaman may obtain information that is quite unrelated to the weather.

For instance, he may conclude from the shape of clouds that visitors are on their way. According to Aivanhov, his teacher Peter Deunov was able to augur in this way. Deunov also explained, in Aivanhov's words, "that by observing the cloud formations above a town we can even know the quality of the souls of the people who live there."[21]

When city dwellers venture into the forest for a picnic, they are apt to notice the relative silence and the ants crawling over their food. A forester is aware of so much more. He will notice which trees are flourishing and which are diseased, where new growth is occurring and how well it will do, which trees have nests, where mushrooms have made their home under a shady tree, where the fox has dug its burrow, or where rodents have done damage. Even more profound will be the knowledge of a tribesman living in the forest. He can read all kinds of subtle cues about the forest as a being that is alive. If he is a medicine man, he will be able to augur from the tracks of deer whether a sick tribesman can be healed, or from the rustling of the leaves whether the hunt will be successful. Compared to the sensitivity of the shaman or medicine man, we are truly illiterate when it comes to reading the Book of Nature.

Their knowledge is possible because all things are interconnected, all things contain symbolic information. To understand it, however, one must master the language of analogy. As Aivanhov explained:

> I have a key, a method which has allowed me to discover the most extraordinary truths and to see that the whole universe is governed by the same body of laws. That key is analogy.[22]

Analogy is based on the resemblances between things that are not ordinarily considered to be related. In one of his talks, Aivanhov furnished a good practical example of how this analogical method works. One day, the story goes, he stopped a snail and began to question it about its curious habit of carrying its house on its back. The snail told him it was the most economical way, and that it was not tiring at all. When asked how it started this habit, the snail told him that it was out of fear:

> "What made you form the habit?" "Oh, I don't trust people, I'm afraid that if I leave my house, a stranger will get inside, and that will be the end of me for I have no arms to fight with, I am too soft, too delicate and helpless. And so I avoid danger by carrying my house around with me." "Oh," I said. "This is a whole philosophy!" But what is your house made of?" "Of saliva. The saliva hardens when exposed to air, and that is what I build my house with."[23]

Aivanhov added:

> You see how interesting it is to converse with snails, besides which it helps you to understand how God created the world. He emanated a very fine subtle matter, His own essence, which then solidified. Between yawns you are thinking: silly bedtime story!

One day everyone including the most learned and erudite will stay awake to hear such stories.[24]

Next, using the principle of analogy, Aivanhov compared the snail's shell to the physical body, which in a way is the house for our spiritual essence. The trouble is, as he pointed out, that we identify with the house rather than with the power that formed it. As he put it:

> The body is not the man, the man is not his body! It is available for his use as a car, a horse, an instrument, a house. Man is pure Spirit, not matter, but all-powerful, infinite, omniscient Spirit.[25]

Nature is filled with instructions about ourselves. This is so because macrocosm and microcosm intermesh. The interconnection of macrocosm and microcosm, the structural homology between the universe and the individual human being, is a central teaching in the esoteric traditions. It is also an important aspect of the teaching of Mikhael Aivanhov.

AS ABOVE, SO BELOW

For Aivanhov, it is the correspondence between the cosmos and the individual that makes spiritual work possible and necessary. If we are not cut off from everything else, as tends to be our conviction, then we are responsible for all our actions, since our actions affect not only us but everything else as well. This is in fact the idea underlying the Hindu teaching of karma, which is also accepted by many other traditions.

Aivanhov called this essential interconnection the law of resonance or the law of affinity. He compared it to the echo on the physical plane. Another illustration would be throwing a boomerang, which in due course curves back and, if we are not careful, hits us on the head. Aivanhov used the example of a ball. As he put it:

> Basically the ball is obeying the same law as your voice: the boomerang effect. Here too, everyone knows this law on the physical plane but nobody

believes that it applies equally on the psychological and spiritual planes. Whatever you do, good or evil, will necessarily come back to you one day. Every feeling you experience falls into a certain category and it goes out into space, awakening kindred forces which then come back to you, according to the law of affinity. And it is thanks to this law that man can draw on the immense reservoirs of the universe and obtain all the elements he wants, just as long as he projects into space thoughts and feelings of the same breed as those he wants to attract to himself.[26]

Aivanhov added:

To my mind this law of affinity is the most important key, the great Arcanum, the magic wand. My whole life has been based on it.[27]

Combined with what Aivanhov called the law of records, the law of affinity is a formidable force in the universe. As he explained:

The knowledge of this law is the basis of all moral and spiritual life for, if everything is recorded, we can no longer allow ourselves to do, think, feel or wish whatever we please without discrimination, for everything entails certain consequences.[28]

On a humorous note he added: "Cosmic Intelligence has pioneered in the field of recordings."[29] Everything, as we have already discussed, leaves its imprint behind for eternity. This ineradicable record is also known as the Akashic Record. The word "Akashic" stems from the Sanskrit language, where *akasha* refers to the infinite ether-space in which the four elements arise.

This ether-space must not be confused with the ether pre-modern physicists postulated in order to explain the propagation of light weaves. As the famous Michelson-Morley experiment of 1887 demonstrated, light propagates at the same speed regardless of the velocity of its source. Thus the medium of a physical ether has been shown to be an unnecessary assumption.

However, the *akasha* of esotericism is of a different order altogether. It has the same nature as *prana*, the life force (or "bioplasma"), whose existence some researchers are beginning to acknowledge. The Akashic Record is generally conceived as an envelope that stretches around the earth. However, it might be more correct to think of Akashic memory fields as existing everywhere in Nature, including our own body.

By virtue of the law of affinity, all our personal imprints on the universe provoke reactions of a similar type. Hence the enormous importance of leaving behind only positive traces of our presence in the world. As Aivanhov reminded his disciples:

> Try not to let yourselves be led into chaotic, destructive, negative activities ever again; try to learn how to behave towards creation and all creatures. And everywhere and always, whatever you touch and wherever you go, remember to leave imprints of light and love so that, more and more, all human beings may vibrate in unison with the divine world.[30]

Attunement to the Divine, or *imitatio Dei* as this practice is called in the Christian tradition, is the only way to avoid the undesirable karmic consequences, brought about by our intentions and actions. The esoteric teaching behind this practice is contained in the following enigmatic maxim of Hermes Trismegistus[31], the Thrice Great Hermes, whom Aivanhov quoted more frequently than any other spiritual authority:

> That which is below is like to that which is above, and that which is above is like to that which is below in order to achieve the wonders of one thing.

"Above," as Aivanhov explained, refers to the transcendental realm, while "below" is the level of our physical reality. He also made it clear that the similarity between above and below is confined to the dimension of the unchanging cosmic laws, foremost among which is the law of affinity. Aivanhov confessed to feeling "extremely privileged" that he had been able to decipher Hermes Trismegistus' cryptic statement.[32] Elsewhere he remarked that he was not permitted to reveal everything about this subject matter but that, when it was revealed to him, he was "dumbfounded."[33]

But what is the "one thing" of which Hermes Trismegistus spoke? Aivanhov provided a clue for the correct answer when proffering this observation: Speech is accomplished by the tongue and the lips; a child is created by the joining of man and woman. Obviously Hermes Trismegistus' maxim can be interpreted in many ways. But from a spiritual perspective, the "one thing" can be none other than the realization of the Self, or Spirit, which comes about when we diligently abide by the cosmic laws. That this realization is a true marvel, a miracle, is beyond question. Interestingly, in some Sanskrit works, the transcendental Self is indirectly referred to as that which is "marvelous" (*adbhuta*). And the marvelous makes us speechless and fills us with awe.

The cosmic laws work with perfect precision. In fact, like Pythagoras and Galileo before him, Aivanhov believed that underlying the processes of the universe is mathematics — numbers as energetic and generative principles.[34] This belief does not contradict his vision of the spiritual nature of the cosmos. Aivanhov stated:

> In their principle, in essence, numbers are very remote from human beings. And yet rivers, trees and mountains are simply numbers, numbers that have been materialized. In fact, if you look a little closer at the question, you will find that nothing exists but numbers. Everything is "number". Nature, the whole universe is built on numbers, but they are so well-disguised that they can be neither heard nor felt nor comprehended. If you get closer to them, however, and actually penetrate them, you will discover that they speak and sing and emanate perfumes. No doubt this is something that is still difficult for you to

accept, but for me it is so. And I know, because I have touched and tasted this reality.[35]

Aivanhov's vision of the mathematical structure of existence is both ancient and modern. The first metaphysicians were astronomers/astrologers who struggled to understand the arithmetics of the heavens. Today, thousands of years later, our most advanced physics has formulated such a highly abstract model of the universe that only mathematicians can hope to grasp it.

To understand the workings of the cosmic laws, we must learn to read the great Book of Nature. For Aivanhov, the single most important source of inspiration in Nature was the sun. As he admitted:

> I read the Book of Nature and I read, too, what is written on your faces and in your hearts. And, above all, I read the sun, the sun is my daily reading. Every day he reveals something new to me and then I pass it on to you.[36]

In the next chapter we will see just how important the sun was for Aivanhov, and also why he attributed such importance to our star.

NOTES

1. J. Spedding, ed. *The Letters and the Life of Francis Bacon.* (London, 1861). 7 vols. (1861–1874)
2. Aivanhov, *Man's Psychic Life*, p. 107.
3. Ibid., p. 108.
4. See Bernard of Clairvaux, *Epistles*, no. 106. To Master Henry Murdach, the later Archbishop of York. St. Bernard also wrote that the oaks and beeches were his "only teachers in the word of God" (Vit. I, lib. i, auctore Gullielmo, c. 4 (23) (Mab., ii, col. 2109).
5. See R. W. Emerson, *The Conduct of Life* (London: Dent & Sons/New York: Dutton, 1908), p. 157.
6. Aivanhov, *Man, Master of His Destiny*, p. 44.
7. See Aivanhov, *Life Force*, p. 188.

8. See J. Gebser, *The Ever-Present Origin* (Athens, OH: Ohio University Press, 1985), p. 324.

9. Aivanhov, *The Living Book of Nature*, p. 182.

10. Aivanhov, *Spiritual Alchemy*, p. 63.

11. Aivanhov, *The Living Book of Nature*, p. 211.

12. J. Needleman, *A Sense of the Cosmos: The Encounter of Modern Science and Ancient Truth* (New York and London: Arkana, 1975), p. 77.

13. Ibid. p. 78.

14. W. Black Elk and W. S. Lyon, *Black Elk: The Sacred Ways of a Lakota* (San Francisco: HarperSanFrancisco, 1991), p. xix.

15. Ibid., p. 37.

16. Ibid., p. 42.

17. Aivanhov, *The Living Book of Nature*, p. 18.

18. Aivanhov, *Education Begins Before Birth*, p. 114.

19. Aivanhov, *Harmony*, pp. 160–161.

20. Aivanhov, *Education Begins Before Birth*, p. 154.

21. Aivanhov, *Spiritual Alchemy*, p. 175.

22. Aivanhov, *The Splendour of Tiphareth*, p. 227.

23. Aivanhov, *The Key to the Problems of Existence*, p. 28.

24. Ibid., p. 28.

25. Ibid., p. 29.

26. Aivanhov, *Man, Master of His Destiny*, p. 91.

27. Ibid., p. 91.

28. Aivanhov, *The Book of Divine Magic*, p. 126.

29. Ibid., p. 124.

30. Ibid., pp. 126–127.

31. Hermes Trismegistus, a figure of mythological proportions, was identified by the Greeks with the Egyptian Thoth, the God of wisdom and learning. The "Thrice Greatest" Hermes is credited with the invention of arithmetic, algebra, geometry, astronomy, and the alphabet. According to Iamblichus (300 A.D.), he wrote 36,525 books. But, as Aivanhov emphasized, Hermes Trismegistus was first and foremost a spiritual adept who had fathomed the hidden laws of the cosmos.

32. See Aivanhov, *Cosmic Moral Laws*, p. 134.

33. Aivanhov, *The Splendour of Tiphareth*, p. 124.

34. See Brian Clement, "The Computer We Call Nature," in *The Scientific and Medical Network Newsletter*, no. 45 (April 1991), pp. 10–12.

35. Aivanhov, *The Book of Divine Magic*, pp. 82–83.

36. Aivanhov, *Education Begins Before Birth*, p. 167.

7
THE SECRET
OF THE SUN

SOLAR INTELLIGENCE

There are an estimated billion trillion stars in the known universe, which is thought to be 13 billion years old. A billion trillion is 1 followed by 21 zeros. Our own galaxy, the Milky Way, alone comprises about 150 billion stars. Even if only every hundredth star were to have one or more planets and if life emerged only on every ten thousandth planet, our galaxy alone would include 150,000 planets on which intelligent life forms could have emerged. This does not sound like much, but multiply this by billions for the entire universe. And let us also not forget that scientists are constantly updating our picture of the universe, which appears to grow ever more complex and vast.

Since the early 1960s, astronomers around the world have been systematically listening in to deep space with big radio telescopes for signs of extraterrestial intelligence. So far their efforts have not borne fruit.

Even if they were to find signs of intelligent life in our own galaxy, with our present technology we would not be able to see those intelligences face to face for many generations. According to current mainstream thinking, the speed of light is the big barrier in crossing the vast distances between stars by means of physical travel. The nearest star is about four light years away, and our fastest spaceships presently operate at a miniscule fraction of that speed.

There are of course those who believe that the Earth has already been visited by aliens from outer space. But the field of Ufology is so riddled with fantasy and self-delusion that it is virtually impossible to arrive at a definite conclusion.

*Omraam Mikhael Aivanhov
carrying the staff of the magus*

At any rate, both astronomers and UFO enthusiasts assume that alien intelligence is more or less made in the image of the human being, and that intelligent life must necessarily be DNA-based. Hence both may have overlooked an intelligent "alien" being within our reach — no more than about 93 million miles away, a negligible distance in cosmic terms, which takes a beam of light just over eight minutes to cross.

I am referring to the sun, the star of our particular planetary system.

This, at least, was Aivanhov's firm belief, and in this he is in the illustrious company of many sages and seers of past civilizations. He said, challengingly:

> People sometimes wonder who was the first person to teach men the arts of writing and agriculture, the use of fire and certain tools. Various names are put forward but, in reality, it was no man but the sun who was at the origin of these discoveries. You will perhaps say that that is all nonsense! That the sun is not an intelligent being and that he has neither a brain nor a mouth with which to speak! According to you, then, ignorant human beings have a monopoly on intelligence! The one being to whom all life on earth owes its existence doesn't possess intelligence![1]

In another talk Aivanhov observed: "No one on earth is as intelligent as a ray of sunlight: no one, not even the greatest genius!"[2] The idea that the sun is intelligent may strike us as outlandish, if not completely ludicrous. After all, astrophysicists have probed its structure and have identified it as a rather average star, just over 4.5 billion years old. It is a giant nuclear fusion reactor, with a temperature of roughly 20 million degrees Celsius in its center and only about 6,000 degrees on the surface. No spectral analyses or other scientific probes have ever suggested anything other than that the sun is a huge conglomeration of atoms, which emits light as the result of a continuous process of conversion of hydrogen into helium.

No one has ever seen the sun demonstrate any intelligent behavior. It has never made any effort to contact us. It has never spoken to anyone. Or has it?

The scientific view does not take into account that the human body is also a conglomeration of atoms vibrating at a particular rate and even radiating heat and other forms of energy of different wavelengths. And yet there is an inwardness to our life, which we characterize as conscious and intelligent. Does intelligence occur only in association with complex biological organisms, or is it not conceivable that it might also arise in complex high-energy bodies like a star?

Certainly science-fiction writers have pondered this exciting possibility. For instance, in their award-winning novel *If the Stars Are God*, Gregory Benford and Gordon Eklund pictured an alien race arriving in our solar system in order to learn about the intelligence and spiritual essence of our star, the sun. Their quest completely baffled Earth's scientists. When a representative of Earth told the alien beings about the sun's temperature, age, mass, and so on, the visitors from outer space thought the earthling was jesting and teasing them. They had all the physical information; what they wanted to understand was the sun's inner being and humanity's form of worship of the sun. Finally, the alien beings permitted the Earth representative to hear the sun's song. In fact, it was through his own human voice that the song manifested. When he realized what was happening, that the sun was a vastly intelligent being, he reacted with terror.

Astronomers and astrophysicists will dismiss such stories as mere fiction that have no equivalent in the real world. But they are making this judgment on the basis of their overwhelmingly materialistic philosophy. Let us not forget that only a few decades ago, a prominent school in psychology seriously entertained the possibility that one could talk about intelligence without talking about consciousness, purely on the basis of a study of human behavior. This extreme position has meantime been abandoned.

In fact, a new school of psychology — that of transpersonal psychology — is nowadays considering all kinds of phenomena that were previously considered as so much hocus pocus, namely out-of-body experiences, near-death experiences, mystical states, lucid dreaming, and so on. The findings show that consciousness and body (or brain), though interactive, are not inevitably associated. This has been emphasized by the world-famous neurosurgeon Wilder Penfield in his book *The Mystery of the Mind*.[3]

Aivanhov explained the relationship between consciousness and the brain by resorting to modern communication technology. In his customary picturesque language, he observed:

> The human brain is like a radio or television set: it can tune in to all kinds of different transmitters operating on different wavelengths. All you have to do with a transistor radio is to choose the programme you want and turn a little know until you get it: music, a news bulletin or whatever you want. Well, you can do this with your own inner transistor, too . . . and if you push the wrong button you may get nothing but static and clamour or a blast of music straight from Hell! When this happens, switch to another station. It is as easy as can be! All you need do is to use your mind or your imagination to tune in to a programme from Heaven.[4]

Now, if the radio or television set is mechanically or electronically faulty, the programs are either interfered with or do not show on the screen at all. However, this deficiency says nothing about the existence of the programs themselves. For, we can watch them on another, functional set quite adequately. Similarly, while a brain tumor or other physical flaw in the human brain impedes the functioning of the mind, we cannot conclude from this that the mind is entirely a product of the brain. There is every indication that the mind, or consciousness, exists independently and that the brain acts more like a filter for the presence of consciousness, delimiting its functioning in certain ways.

If awareness can exist without a physical body, or if consciousness is not completely exhausted and determined by brain processes, then we are free to speculate about what kind of physical form a particular consciousness may be associated with. Why not an incandescent body like that of a star?

Free from the burden of our modern cosmological knowledge, which makes us predisposed to purely materialistic and reductionistic explanations, ancient sages and seers far and wide have regarded the sun as a very special entity. We generally dismiss their attitude as primitive sun worship, but this pejorative label misses the depth of their insights about the sun.

THE SPIRITUAL SUN IN HINDUISM

There is no telling when humanity "discovered" the sun. We can only assume that at some unknown point in time our earliest ancestors began to become aware of the presence of the solar orb as a great creative and numinous force in Nature. But once the sun had risen on the horizon of human consciousness, it became in due course a cultural symbol of the first order. Only our modern civilization, governed as it is by a coarse materialistic philosophy, has lost sight of the sun as a key symbol of profound spiritual significance.

The sun held a central place in the life and thought of one of the oldest civilizations — that of India, whose beginnings have most recently been dated back to the fifth millennium B.C.[5] As we learn from the *Rig-Veda*, in ancient Vedic times the sun was invoked as Surya, Savitri, and Pushan. The golden-bodied sun served the Vedic people as a guiding symbol of the Divine. For them, the solar Spirit was "God among Gods."

To this day, pious Hindus recite daily the ancient *gayatri-mantra* dedicated to Savitri, the quickening aspect of the solar being, which is found in the *Rig-Veda* (III.62.10): *tat savitur varenyam bhargo devasyo dhimahi dhiyo yo nah pracodayat*, "May we contemplate that most excellent splendor of Savitri, the God, so that He may inspire our contemplations." In this famous and melodious stanza, the Vedic seers advisedly used the word *dhi*, which is often flatly rendered as "thought" but which suggests so much more.

I have translated it with "contemplation," because what the *rishis* most desired was not mere speculative thought but a visual encounter with the Divine, for which the way was prepared by contemplation.

The seers (*rishi*) were visionaries before they were thinkers. As the *Brihad-Aranyaka-Upanishad* (V.14.4), which was composed toward the beginning of the first millennium B.C., affirms: "Verily, truth is sight" (*cakshur vai satyam*). In a dispute, the *Upanishad* continues, we should trust the one who says "I have seen" rather than the one who states "I have heard."

Aivanhov, too, was such a seer. It was on the basis of his own spiritual realization, and of his reading of what he called the "Book of Nature," that he, like the *rishis* before him, discovered in the sun a great secret. In one of his talks he observed:

> As soon as the sun gets up he pours forth his light, his warmth and his life, and it is that light, warmth and life that encourage men and women to get up, too, and go to work ... The daily rhythm of human life is patterned on the rhythm of the sun's movement. And it is the sun, too, who is at the origin of all culture and civilisation.[6]

Aivanhov reproached us moderns for taking the sun's existence for granted, ignoring the fact that without it, there would be no life on earth. Indeed, without the sun, there would be no planets in our solar system. All animate and inanimate things are, Aivanhov noted, nothing but condensed sunlight. By this he meant that they are made of energy — a lesson that, despite Einstein's influential theorem, few of us have as yet imbibed.

The sun is the origin of life. More than that, the sun is the primordial teacher. For, without the sun there would be no human society, religion, morality, arts, philosophy, and technology. In one of his earliest talks, Aivanhov remarked:

Everything good comes from the sun. It is God's highest manifestation and through it, He sends His blessings.[7]

Elsewhere Aivanhov observed:

Deprived of sunshine men could never have existed. They could never have moved or worked. Without the warmth of the sun they could never have experienced feeling. Without his light they could never had had the faculty of sight, and not only on the physical level but also on the intellectual level: they could never have had understanding, for understanding is a higher form of sight.[8]

This view coincides with ancient Hindu teachings. Thus, in the *Bhagavad-Gita* (IV.1), the God-man Krishna explains to his disciple Prince Arjuna that he, Krishna, proclaimed his "immutable Yoga" to Vivasvat who then taught it to Manu, the progenitor of the human race. Vivasvat ("He Who Shines Brightly") is none other than the solar being, more specifically the creator aspect of the sun.

Vivasvat is functionally analogous to Hiranyagarbha ("Golden Germ"), who is hailed as the first teacher of Yoga in the *Mahabharata* epic.[9] The reference to the golden color in his name provides a firm link to the sun, which, as Surya, has anciently been described as having golden limbs. In yogic symbolism, Hiranyagarbha stands for the higher mind (*buddhi*), the seat of yogic intuitions and the receptacle of transcendental truth.

PHARAOH AKHENATON AND AIVANHOV

Two and a half thousand miles west of the Indian peninsula, the solar spirit was venerated in one of the most spectacular civilizations of the ancient world. The Egyptians worshiped the sun, Aton, already in earliest pharaonic times. This is evident from the tall pillars or obelisks — some gold-plated — dedicated to the Sun God in the temples of the fifth dynasty some 4,500 years ago. The most famous sun worshipper of ancient Egypt was unquestionably Akhenaton, which is the adopted name of Pharaoh Amenhotep IV.

Aivanhov is for our modern age what the Egyptian boy pharaoh Akhenaton was, if only for a brief spell, to the empire of Egypt. The British historian Jaquetta Hawkes commented:

> Akhenaten, born with a native genius that one might well recognize as a spark of divinity, lifted the religion of the sun to the greatest height it was ever to attain. Indeed, in my eyes the religious vision which found living expression at [the pharaonic city of] Akhetaten was as true and fine as any ever realized in the mind of man.[10]

Akhenaton was a mere boy of ten years when he ordered a temple to be built dedicated to Aton. In doing so he made many enemies among the Amun worshippers. Just as old as the worship of Amun is that of the solar deity Ra. Later the two became unified as Amun-Ra.

Both Akhenaton and Aivanhov were heralds of the sun. But Akhenaton was a young and frail epileptic who sought to replace the pantheon of Gods and Goddesses with his new solar monotheism, whereas Aivanhov was blessed with a robust constitution and carefully maintained his health into old age through a strict diet and exercise regimen. He was as much of an idealist as the young Akhenaton, but he was also more than that.

Unlike the pharaoh, he was an adept in esoteric matters. His love for the sun burned not only brightly in his heart, it also reached deep into the mysteries of the cosmos. Aivanhov was a mature visionary, not merely a romantic. Hence, in contrast to Akhenaton's religious teaching, we can expect Aivanhov's message to endure beyond his death. The "solar age" of which he so often spoke is yet to come, and it is not bound to his personal life and destiny, as Akhenaton's teaching had been.

Akhenaton's religious influence hardly extended beyond the limits of the capital city, and the great fervor for solar worship he had stimulated died with him. Although the worship of the sun by no means vanished from Egyptian religion after Akhenaton's premature death, it does not appear to have reached the same spiritual heights again.

THE SOLAR SPIRIT IN GNOSTICISM AND CHRISTIANITY

Some of the esoteric teachings and symbolism of the Egyptian religion survived in Gnosticism — a tradition to which Aivanhov broadly aligned himself. Gnosticism was a religious movement that emphasized, as its name suggests, knowledge, or *gnosis*. The Greek word *gnosis* stands for wisdom that saves, heals, or makes a person whole. It signifies the kind of knowledge that was passed on in the mystery traditions.

The metaphysicians of Gnosticism recognized two ultimate principles — Good and Evil — which were often also designated as Light and Darkness. The latter was equated with matter into which the Spirit had descended. The Spirit was considered to be in its essence one with the Divine. The Dead Sea scrolls, found in a cave in 1947, frequently refer to God as the Light. The members of the sacred community of Essenes, to whom these scriptures belonged and who can be broadly grouped with the Gnostics, called themselves the Sons of Light who were destined to war against the Sons of Darkness. The faithful disciples were promised a Crown of Glory, a phrase that is reminiscent of the sun's corona.

The Gnostics deemed the material realm as an unfit place for the Spirit. Hence they recommended that people aspire to the Light through the cultivation of spiritual knowledge. The *Book of Thomas the Contender*, one of the apocryphal Christian works discovered in 1945 at Nag Hammadi, contains this enigmatic saying attributed to Jesus: "It is in light that light exists."

Then Thomas is recorded as putting the following question to Jesus: "Why does the visible light rise and set on behalf of human beings?" Jesus answered, in paraphrase: "It shines so that you might come forth. When all the elect have abandoned their lowly ways, then the light will withdraw into its essence, since it is a good servant." The *essence* of the visible light, the sun, is the Divine itself. In the *Teachings of Silvanus*, another Nag Hammadi scripture, we find this passage: "For the sun shines on every impure place, and yet it is not defiled. So it is with Christ."

Gnosticism exercised a great influence on Christianity, although from the outset it was sharply opposed by the Church Fathers. When we examine the symbols engraved in the Christian catacombs of Rome, we find that many relate directly to the most ancient solar symbols.[11] Thus the well-known monogram for Christ, a P whose stem is crossed with an X, can be found already in the Neolithic Age, where it represents the sun. The X is really a tilted cross, which represents the four-spoked wheel of the year.

Christ, who is addressed as the "Light of the World," was commonly represented with a corona (halo) around the head, similar to the Buddha. Like Horus in Egypt or Mithras in Persia, his birth is celebrated on December 25, marking the winter solstice. We know that the early Christians wore pendants depicting a lamb, which corresponds to Aries, the first sign of the zodiac.

The monstrance used by Catholic priests when celebrating mass is clearly a symbol of the sun. Solar symbols are found in many churches, cathedrals, and tombs of the medieval period, and from earliest times Christian houses of worship have been oriented along an east-west axis. Sunday, which was once a favored pagan day, is celebrated by Christians as the "Lord's Day," the day on which, according to the biblical account, he rested after creating the world. In his famous *Canticle of Brother Sun*, St. Francis of Assisi sang:

> All praise be yours, my Lord,
> through all that you have made.
> And first my lord Brother Sun,
> Who brings the day.[12]

Finally, to conclude this inventory of Christian solar symbolism, we may recall that the right white glove worn by the

Pope when he blesses the people bears a radiant sun woven in gold threads. The sun stands here for the blessing power of the divine Light.

All these instances indicate how intricately solar symbolism is interwoven with Christian belief and practice. Christians should therefore be the least surprised by Aivanhov's solar gospel. As we will see in Chapter 11, Aivanhov considered himself a Christian, even though his religious beliefs and practices were closer to the teachings of the Gnostics than they were to modern Christianity. In many ways, he offered a daring symbolic reinterpretation of current Church dogma and practice. For instance, he pointed out that the bread and wine consumed during mass, which commemorate Christ's death and resurrection, should be understood as solar symbols:

> It is not a question of the physical reality of bread and wine, but of the two properties of the sun: light and heat, which combine together to create life. But the heat is love, the light, wisdom. And so we can see that Jesus meant that if we ate his flesh: wisdom, and drank his blood: love, we would have eternal life.[13]

For Aivanhov, the sun exemplified perfectly the three aspects of the Holy Trinity, for it combines within itself life (Father), light (Holy Spirit), and warmth (Son).[14] He criticized theologians for preaching a trinity that is a mystery, because people seldom relate to mystery rightly; they tend to ignore what they cannot comprehend, which merely reinforces their spiritual lethargy. The theological God is, as he argued, too abstract and thus too discouraging. He therefore proposed that in place of such a remote figure, we should put the concrete daily experience of the sun. He felt that in contemplating the sun, we could truly discover — in our feelings — the mystery of the Divine. On a humorous note, Aivanhov once remarked:

> Why cannot Christians understand that the greatest truths are all there, before them, visible to the naked

eye? Before long everyone will have understood . . .
except Christians![15]

To worship the visible solar orb would be primitive idolatry and superstition. To respect the sun as a symbol of the
greater Light of which it is but the visible manifestation is a
rewarding spiritual attitude. Neither did Aivanhov equate the
sun with Christ. On the contrary, he made it very clear that the
two are to be carefully held apart. In his own words:

> Of course, Christ is a far greater entity than the sun.
> He is the Son of God, Second Person of the Blessed
> Trinity. And nor does he manifest himself only
> through the sun. There are innumerable suns in the
> universe and most of them are much bigger and more
> brilliant than ours.
>   Christ is in all of them; he is everywhere in the
> universe, but for us human beings who live on the
> planet earth he manifests himself in our sun.[16]

"Behind the light of the sun," said Aivanhov, "is the light
of God."[17] For him, God was not only the Light behind all light
but the utterly unknowable Reality.[18] However, in his philosophy, the incomprehensible nature of the Divine does not
create an unbridgeable chasm between God and the human
being, leaving us in dread isolation.

Since, as Aivanhov affirmed again and again, the Divine
is the quintessence of all beings and things, we cannot truly be
separated from it. It is merely incomprehensible to the mind
with its limited frame of reference. While we can never *know*
the Divine, we can *merge* with it. As he stated:

> No one has ever seen God, because God is infinite,
> limitless. It is possible to sense His presence; it is even
> possible to glimpse His manifestations in a flash of
> lightning, a ray of light, but the Author of those
> manifestations cannot be seen. . . . When shall we
> understand the limitless, the infinite? When we lose
> ourselves in it, when we become one with it.[19]

But in order to become one with the Divine, we must first polish the mirror of our body-mind. Only then will we be able to realize our true essence, which is the Spirit that is an inalienable aspect of the Divine. As Aivanhov observed:

> Only by cleansing ourselves of the accumulated layers of impurities within us can we become one with God, can we, in other words, "see God."[20]

Aivanhov spoke of the soul as a magic mirror in which we can behold our own divine nature, providing we keep the mirror free from stains.[21] But we cannot be entirely successful at purifying ourselves without also taking into account the environment in which we live. As we are finding out the hard way, we are inextricably interconnected with all things. We can no longer pursue our own pleasure, or even our own salvation, at the expense of others and the natural environment.

Thus, if we truly understand the symbolic significance of the sun we will change our lifestyle and practice what has recently been called Eco-Yoga, or eco-spirituality.

The modern temper is gradually, almost perforce, converging with the ancient vision of the sun, recently restated so convincingly by Aivanhov. For our world is beginning to realize that we cannot continue to despoil our planetary habitat and that solar energy offers a clean technological alternative to oil, coal, and gas.

Equally important is the fact that avant-garde medicine is slowly discovering solar rays as an unintrusive healing force, which does not require a huge, wasteful, and self-serving chemical industry to sustain it. Thus we see Aivanhov's sweeping prediction that the science of the future will be entirely based on sunlight beginning to come true.

To some extent, these developments reflect significant changes in our thinking. However, as individuals and collectively we must be prepared to work for a much more radical inner transformation, so that we will not fall into the trap of thinking of the sun in merely utilitarian terms. Beyond the materialistic usefulness of the sun's rays for warming our homes and healing our bodies, we must also discover the great spiritual truth it represents. Only then can we muster the wisdom necessary to solve the monumental problems of our increasingly complex technological civilization.

NOTES

1. Aivanhov, *Toward a Solar Civilisation*, pp. 11–12.
2. Aivanhov, *The Splendour of Tiphareth*, p. 226.
3. W. Penfield, *The Mystery of the Mind* (Princeton, NJ: Princeton University Press, 1976).
4. See Aivanhov, *The True Meaning of Christ's Teaching*, p. 201. Aivanhov also likened the brain to a piano, "the instrument thorough which the Spirit manifests (like a virtuoso)" (*Freedom, the Spirit Triumphant*, p. 29).
5. See the summary of the evidence by D. Frawley, *Gods, Sages, and Kings: Vedic Secrets of Ancient Civilization* (Salt Lake City, UT: Passage Press, 1991). See also G. Feuerstein, D. Frawley, and S. Kak, "A New View of Ancient India," *Yoga Journal* (July/August 1992), pp. 64–69, 100–102, and, by the same authors, *In Search of the Cradle of Civilization* (Wheaton, IL: Quest Books, 1995).
6. Aivanhov, *Toward a Solar Civilisation*, p. 11.
7. Aivanhov, *The Second Birth*, p. 72.
8. Aivanhov, *Toward a Solar Civilisation*, p. 19.
9. See, e.g., *Mahabharata* XII.337.60.
10. J. Hawkes, *Man and the Sun* (New York: Random House, 1962), p. 125.
11. See H. R. Engler, *Die Sonne als Symbol: Der Schlüssel zu den Mysterien* (Küsnacht-Zurich: Helianthus-Verlag, 1962), pp. 230ff.
12. Cited after J. Pelikan, *Jesus Through the Centuries: His Place in the History of Culture* (New York: Harper & Row, 1987), p. 138.
13. Aivanhov, *Toward a Solar Civilisation*, p. 142.
14. See *op. cit.*, pp. 133ff.
15. Aivanhov, *Toward a Solar Civilisation*, p. 135.
16. Aivanhov, *The True Meaning of Christ's Teaching*, p. 136.
17. Aivanhov, *Toward a Solar Civilisation*, p. 79.
18. See *op. cit.*, p. 79.
19. Aivanhov, *Looking Into the Invisible*, pp. 135–136.
20. Ibid., p. 137.
21. See *op. cit.*, p. 143.

8
THE SPIRITUAL
WORK

LEARNING THE LESSON OF LIFE

Consciously or unconsciously we are all looking for happiness. Sometimes our quest for happiness assumes strange forms, but it is never ending. From a deep spiritual point of view, as Aivanhov reminds us, this quest for happiness is really a ceaseless search for our authentic being, or Self. St. Augustine expressed this long ago in theological language in his *Confessions* (I.i):

> Thou hast created us for Thyself, and our heart is restless until it rests in Thee.

In our essential nature we are at peace with ourselves and the world. There is joy, even bliss. As all the spiritual traditions of the world tell us, in our essential nature we are perfectly in tune with the greater Being, which is called the Divine or Reality. But how many people realize this truth?

For the most part, our ordinary, unconscious or semiconscious ways of seeking happiness merely lead us to experience fleeting moments of pleasure, often promptly followed by disappointment, frustration, sorrow, anguish, and pain. The reason for this is that, by and large, we confuse happiness with pleasure. Pleasure is inherently short-lived, whereas happiness is abiding because it is the very fabric of Reality. In our desire to make pleasure last as long as possible, we hanker after the impossible and set ourselves up for emotional difficulties.

Human life is a protracted school. As Aivanhov said:

Life on earth is a school and so what you find in school
is lessons, lessons on all sides. Until you have understood that, you will be harassed by destiny.[1]

The lessons we must learn are very simple, yet they are not
easily learned because we approach life wearing blinders. We
all tend to be reluctant learners. In fact, the way in which most
people learn the lessons of life are by bad experiences ham-
mering away at them, thereby forcing them to face reality more
squarely. Of course, in the end all bad experiences turn out to
be good, because they shape us and finally bring us closer to
who we really are.

The single most important lesson of life is the insight that
we are here to learn and grow into whole human beings who
are not merely clever or successful but in touch with their
deepest roots. Those roots are anchored in the ultimate Reality
itself. We are, in other words, born to discover our spiritual
destiny.

Once we accept that life is not just about having a good
time but a far more serious matter of evolving into spiritually
mature beings, we must also accept responsibility for our
personal growth. This is the beginning of spiritual life. To
assume responsibility for our personal maturation means to
adopt a course of life that is molded according to the spiritual
principles, as they have been revealed to us for millennia by
the great sages of humankind. We must work for our tranquillity and illumination. In Aivanhov's words:

What counts most is the way in which you spend your
energies: how do you use them and to what end? If
you are depressed and unhappy it is because you
move in too narrow a circle. Expand your sphere of
interest and you will attract forces and living entities
to instruct and help you.... Let your interest embrace
the solar system, the whole cosmos all the way to its
creator, and you will no longer feels so small and
wretched, so abandoned and neglected. You will become creative, a positive, beneficial influence
amongst men.[2]

Peace of mind and happiness are one-tenth grace and nine-tenths effort. As the the British writer and sage Paul Brunton put it:

> He who can unite self-effort with dependence on grace in a constant balance is able to gain peace. The key to success lies in maintaining balance.[3]

It is clear from Brunton's statement that we must be careful not to mistake effort for tiresome toil, struggle, and stress. All struggle signals a lack of balance and is inimical to happiness. The effort we are required to make is the work of self-understanding and self-transcendence through the conscious cultivation of harmony.

This is a difficult concept for many Westerners, since in our part of the world we are brought up to look upon work as an expenditure of energy on external tasks, with little consideration of the inner attitude with which we perform those tasks. How often do we, as Emerson advised, rejoice in our work? How often does it lend dignity to our lives?

INNER WORK, OUTER WORK

As Westerners with an average life-span of, say, seventy-five years we spend roughly 80,000 hours at work, which amounts to about one-eighth of our life. Even if we add another 10,000 hours for commuting to the work place, compared to the 220,000 or so hours that we sleep during our lifetime, this still seems almost insignificant. But it is not! What is so significant is that during those 80,000 hours, we are *conscious*. That is to say, we have the opportunity to determine *what* we do with our lives; *how* we work.

How *do* we work? To wit: every year businesses lose billions of dollars through absenteeism; hundreds of millions of dollars through employee error, irresponsibility, or plain disinterest, and probably as much through employee theft. Bureaucracy has become synonymous with inefficiency and apathy. Business is about profit rather than service. The truth is many people do not really want to be at work, and so their minds are not on the job. They knowingly or unself-consciously sabotage their work. And by sabotaging their work, they sabotage their own growth.

True, many workers have good reason to complain about meaningless tasks, intolerable work conditions, long commutes, inadequate pay and health benefits, and so forth. So many people are alienated from their work and thus from themselves. And such alienation always spells unhappiness and suffering.

Many people feel they can do nothing about their situation. It is true: We may not always be able to precisely choose our circumstance. If you are a single parent with three children and without professional skills, you will be glad to take any odd job that comes along to help keep the family hale. Yet, even in such a dire situation we can seek to improve our lot, for instance by trying to find more meaningful or remunerative work in a benign environment.

But most important, even if our work is difficult or dull, we can always cultivate a new relationship to it. Thus, we may not necessarily be able to change our external circumstance immediately, but we can still change our inner "environment" — our attitude. This is one of the illuminating messages conveyed by Aivanhov. He observed that what most people consider work is not truly work. They may be tinkering or doing hard labor, yet so long as they are merely active with their arms and legs or even with their heads but not with their whole being, they cannot be said to be engaged in genuine work.

For Aivanhov, true work has to do with the human Spirit. "Work," he stated, "is the meaning of life."[4] It is the meaning of life, because human life is about the realization of the spiritual dimension of existence. As Emerson said:

> The only path of escape known in all the worlds of God is performance. You must do your work before you shall be released.[5]

In the final analysis, only the Divine is at work. And it takes much discipline to even begin to comprehend that divine work. God's work, he once remarked, is "immense, gigantic! Even I lay no claim to have understood it. It makes one's mind spin only to think of it."[6] Although God's work is barely comprehensible, we must nevertheless attempt to duplicate it in our lives. This is the essence of the spiritual path. I will show shortly what this means.

WORK AS CONSCIOUS PARTICIPATION IN THE DIVINE

At whatever level of spiritual understanding and discipline we may be, we cannot help but be active. "Nature has no patience with creatures who do nothing," Aivanhov noted. "Every being must be committed, busy."[7] This comment echoes the following well-known verses of the *Bhagavad-Gita* (III.5), the New Testament of Hinduism:

> Not even for a moment can anyone ever remain without performing action. Everyone is unwittingly made to act by the qualities issuing from Nature.

Given this universal dynamics from which we cannot escape, we might as well make our actions, our work, a fully conscious effort involving our entire being. In other words, we might as well turn our work into *spiritual* work. This is exactly the sentiment taught by the God-man Krishna to Prince Arjuna in the *Gita* almost three thousand years ago. It is the ideal of the Yoga of Action (*karma-yoga*). To quote from the *Bhagavad-Gita* (III.9 and 19) again:

> This world is action-bound, save when this action is [intended] as sacrifice. With that purpose . . . engage in action devoid of attachment.
> Therefore always perform unattached the proper deed, for the man who performs action without attachment attains the Supreme.

The Yoga of Action is *conscious participation* in the work of the Divine. It is conscious cooperation with the Divine. This is what is meant by "duplicating" the divine work, or "imitating" the Divine.

In practice, spiritual work means that we must overcome the artificial gap between inner and outer as well as between sacred and profane. Notably, we must find the right balance between handling our worldly obligations and pursuing our contemplative needs. This is how Aivanhov put it in his characteristically simple style:

> Each person must be free to work, earn his living, marry and have a family but, at the same time, each one should have an inner light, a discipline, a method of work.
>
> It is a question of giving both the spiritual and the material dimension their due; so far very few have ever really reached this ideal . . . The important thing is to combine the two: to live a divine life and to live it in the world.[8]

Aivanhov pertinently observed that "spiritualists" tend to have a negative relationship to material existence, which often makes them ineffectual. By contrast, "materialists" know how to accomplish things, because they like to work with matter, but they ignore the spiritual dimension, and so are in the final analysis also ineffectual. In a talk entitled "Yoga: The Alchemical and Magical Significance of Nutrition," he noted:

> An initiate must be both a "spiritualist" and a "materialist." But he must not only know how to work with matter, he must also *refine* it, and he must be able to make the spiritual realities *tangible* in the world.[9]

"Spiritualists" are forever attempting to get away from matter and work. This has been the classic error of many schools of Gnosticism in the past: to pit the Spirit against matter and then to devalue the material realm accordingly. Spiritualists like to escape into the inner dimension, the psyche, and not least into fantasy. For, there they can safely imagine that they have no responsibilities in the external world. This is really a form of narcissism.

Similarly, "materialists," who deny the existence of the spirit and celebrate matter as the ultimate reality, are escapists as well. They flee from the responsibilities that a spiritual point of view would impose on them. They do not like to take responsibility for the hidden aspects of their actions and thoughts. They point-blank deny their existence.

Genuine spiritual life unfolds in the balance between accepting that we are embodied in the material realm and understanding that our life's journey does not end there but that our material being is continuously immersed in a vast invisible dimension where all things and being are instantly interlinked. After observing some of his disciples working hard on a new building, Aivanhov tried to assist their self-understanding by proffering them the following simile:

> For the outside of the house, you build from the bottom up. And for the inside of the house, what do you do? Do you clean the floor first? No, you begin with the ceiling, and afterwards you paint the walls, wash the windows, and finally, you clean and wax the floor. So for the interior, it is the opposite, you work from the top down. . . . The house teaches us how to work with the two currents of evolution and involution.[10]

By "evolution" Aivanhov meant the process of cosmic, biological, psychological, and spiritual unfoldment — from the most primitive to the most exalted. "Involution" refers to the process by which the most subtle realities are rendered visible in the material realm. Aivanhov summarized this as follows:

> So there are two movements: one movement which begins at the center and directs itself towards the periphery, and a second movement which goes from the periphery to the center. The first movement travels through space to the very limits fixed by God. By

this movement God created the universe . . . Involution is the process of materialization, while evolution is the process of dematerialization. In nature, these two movements never cease taking place together; they meet and their interference gives birth to life in all its forms.[11]

The evolutionary process and the involutionary movement revolve around the principles of spirit and matter respectively. These are the two ultimate forms of life, the *yin* and the *yang* that together weave the web of existence. Therefore, we can never escape either of them. The challenge is to respect both movements in our own life. Aivanhov used himself as an example of such an integrated approach. He once commented:

Every kind of work can become a spiritual work. For me, everything I do is work. The word "work" is always in my mind; I try to make use of everything. I never discard anything: I use it all. Even when I am motionless and apparently idle, I am working with my thoughts, sending life, love and light throughout the universe.[12]

The above quote in a way answers the question: What does spiritual work consist of? For Aivanhov it is to recapture our original condition, our true, pure, luminous nature. That deepest or highest condition is coessential with the Divine itself. The task before us, remarked Aivanhov, is "to impregnate oneself with Heaven so that it can come and manifest here on earth through us."[13]

SPIRITUAL METANOIA

Spiritual work involves a profound reorientation. Hence it can never be a mere compromise. It must become our principal work, which then affects all our other activities. As Aivanhov stated:

Even if your job is exceptionally important and interesting, start doing this inner work which will give meaning to all the other things you do on the side. Keep your job, but do this spiritual work as well, for it is the only thing that can really improve you in depth and give a new flavour to all your activities. If you don't do this, little by little, you will lose your appetite for life, and that is the greatest of all misfortunes. This is why I say, in all sincerity, that this is the only thing that counts for me: this work that has to be done day after day and which will, eventually, set the whole universe in motion.[14]

Spiritual work sets, as Aivanhov put it, "the whole universe in motion," because it restructures our very perception of things. This principle is easy to understand when we consider how our pessimistic views tend to color our experience and turn out to be self-fulfilling prophecies. But when we behold the world around us in the divine light, it loses its gloom. While there may still be countless negative forces surrounding us, they no longer trouble us or determine our course of action. Thus we become capable of changing the world and our life in a positive, divine direction. We can bring a piece of heaven down into hell and establish an oasis for ourselves and those of our fellow beings who resonate with the spiritual dimension.

We become alchemists who transmute the cosmos — however local that transmutation may appear to be. Who said that the universe can be transformed overnight? But, according to Aivanhov, it must be transformed, uplifted, made to resonate more and more with the Divine. Our concern should never be over the seeming insignificance of our efforts, or the time it takes for things to change. Rather, we should simply focus on doing what obviously needs to be done in the moment.

Aivanhov recalled how his teacher, Peter Deunov, used to say to him often: "Work, work, work. Time, time, time. Faith, faith, faith." In the course of his life as a disciple and then as a master in his own right, Aivanhov had many occasions to ponder these words. This is how he came to understand them: We must always be active for our spiritual upliftment and liberation. This inner work *will* take time, in fact an entire lifetime, and it can succeed only when there is faith that the principle behind this inner work is utterly reliable and that no effort is ever lost.[15]

Spiritual work involves, first of all, self-inspection or self-analysis. We must be aware of what is going on inside us. We must understand our motivations and resistances, our feelings, and the mechanics of our thoughts. Without such vigilance, we are like blind persons stumbling in the dark. As Aivanhov explained:

> Self-analysis should become a habit with you. Anyone who imagines that their psychic life is going to organize itself without any analysis or lucidity on their part, is due to be disappointed. It is no use expecting great spiritual achievements if one lacks the most basic qualities even to begin the work.
>
> And the beginning is just that: to be constantly wide awake and vigilant, to recognize the nature of a current of thought or feeling just as soon as it starts moving within you.[16]

The next step of spiritual practice is to take charge of what is happening inside us. We must learn to control our inner or psychic life and replace our negative habits with positive attitudes. Aivanhov called this the art of "spiritual gold-plating" or "spiritual galvanoplasty." Gold-plating is achieved by a chemical process in which an electric current is run through a basin filled with a gold solution. The current flows from the positive to the negative pole and deposits gold particles on the negative pole (or cathode). Aivanhov ingeniously transposed this electrochemical process to the spiritual plane:

> The phenomenon of Galvanoplasty teaches us how to work with the forces of life. By putting the anode in our minds, that is, by having only the most incorruptible thoughts (pure gold) and by nourishing the highest ideal, an image of perfection in our hearts (the solution of love), and by linking ourselves to the spirit (battery), or God within, then we receive His strength and life-giving force. We are filled each day with the

current, the subtle substance that develops the qualities we were given by God when He created us, but
which have been lying dormant. As they develop
they change the form of our body. . .[17]

This aspect of the spiritual discipline is of the nature of
self-sacrifice. To sacrifice means literally to render sacred. The
self must be rendered sacred. That is to say, we must submit
our human personality to the current of the larger Reality: We
must die in order to live. Aivanhov spoke of this transformation also as the second birth. He said:

> When our intellect becomes like the sun and our heart
> like the water which flows from the spring, then we
> will be born a second time. . . . To begin the new life,
> it is sufficient to be full of virtue and to live according
> to the laws of love, wisdom, and purity.[18]

Our second birth calls for self-sacrifice, which is rooted in
a deep willingness to be changed and transformed by the
divine Being. This amounts to a constant openness to the
higher evolutionary possibilities. When asked by a seeker
"How do I work on my consciousness?", the contemporary
spiritual teacher Sri Chinmoy replied:

> Just keep the door of your consciousness open, but
> see whether it is a thief or a friend who is coming in.
> Allow in only those whom you want. Keep out the
> lower thoughts. Open the door to higher, sublime
> thoughts. This is the first step in working on your
> consciousness.[19]

Once we have understood our own psychic pattern and
how we cut ourselves off from the blissful nature of Reality,
we must next reorient our lives by aligning ourselves and all
our actions with the true spiritual north pole, which is the
Divine. We must assume responsibility for all the many ways
in which we seek to deny Reality. As Aivanhov commented:

Most people are aware of what goes on inside them only when they are struck down by tragedy and disaster . . . But when the situation is less dramatic, they are not conscious of their inner lives, so they allow all kinds of negative elements to accumulate and, little by little, these things destroy them; by the time they realize what is happening it is too late to save the situation. . . . [Therefore] when you have glanced into yourself and seen what is going on, you must intervene and reject one element or introduce another; in other words, you must take control of the situation and prevent your enemies from invading and plundering you.[20]

The enemies that ever threaten our inner peace and harmony are of course those thoughts and feelings that run counter to the process of spiritual evolution: fear, anger, hatred, envy, jealousy, thoughts of unworthiness or self-aggrandizement, and so forth. These enemies are combatted by thoughts and feelings of harmony, love, forgiveness, compassion, blessing, and so on. "If a man's face doesn't shine like the sun," remarked Aivanhov, "it is because there isn't enough good in his thinking to give his face a glow."[21]

The first two steps of spiritual life are, as Aivanhov pointed out, captured in the pithy command "Watch and pray," which is attributed to the great God-man of Nazareth. We must be alert, and we must tune in to that which transcends the drama that is constantly unrolling on our inner screen. By attuning ourselves to the Divine, through prayer and other contemplative means, we gradually transform our psychic environment, until we are so suffused with the divine Light that darkness can no longer assail us. As Brother Lawrence, the great seventeenth-century Carmelite mystic, was able to confess:

The time of business does not with me differ from the time of prayer, and in the noise and clatter of my kitchen, while several persons are at the same time calling for different things, I possess God in as great tranquillity as if I were upon my knees at the blessed sacrament.[22]

It is clear from Brother Lawrence's statement that external work is no obstacle to our internal, spiritual tasks. We do not need to abandon our job to cultivate the inner life. The fourteenth-century German mystic Johannes Tauler made the same affirmation:

> Whence comes it then, that we have so many complaints, each saying that his occupation is a hindrance to him, while notwithstanding his work is of God, who hindereth no man? Whence comes this inward reproof and sense of guilt which torment and disquiet you? Dear children, know that it is not your work which gives you this disquiet. No: it is your want of order in fulfilling your work. If you performed your work in the right method, with a sole aim to God, and not to yourselves, your own likes and dislikes, and neither feared nor loved aught but God, nor sought your own gain or pleasure, but only God's glory, in your work, it would be impossible that it should grieve your conscience.[23]

PURIFICATION AND HARMONY

The gradual inner transformation that the spiritual practitioner undergoes can be viewed as a process of purification. Aivanhov used the metaphor of purification very extensively. In fact, he spoke of a "psychic pollution" from which we are all suffering. We have started to notice the environmental pollution and its dire consequences, but we have not yet realized that the pollution of air, soil, and water, and the mounting garbage heaps around us, are only an external manifestation of our inner pollution.

We have not yet recognized that our thoughts and feelings are powerful forces or, as Aivanhov was fond of saying, "living entities." As he put it very graphically:

> Each thought is like a human being, it tries to live as long as it can and, when it has no more strength left, it dies. And all thoughts of the same nature get together and amplify each other.[24]

We tend to regard our thoughts and feelings in the abstract. What this means is that we consider them as irrelevant because we do not see them, and as true materialists we only believe what we can see and touch. However, this is a foolish position to take. After all, it was a thought — or a series of thoughts — that led to the formula that made the hydrogen bomb possible, which had a greater impact on modern life than any other invention. It is thoughts and feelings that give rise to struggle, conflict, and war. Aivanhov once remarked:

> If there are so many sick people in the world today, it is not only because of the pollution of air, water and food. No, if the psychic atmosphere were not so polluted, human beings would be capable of neutralizing the external poisons. The problem is primarily within. When a human being lives in a state of harmony, his inner forces react and reject impurities...[25]

Inner purity is a matter of harmony or balance. Harmony was indeed the focus of numerous of Aivanhov's talks over the years. As he affirmed:

> In harmony all the blessings are found: happiness, light, energy, health, joy, unfoldment, ecstasy, inspiration... If you want to be happy, to grow and unfold, you must think of harmony and put yourself in harmony with the whole universe. You won't be able to do it right away, but if you persevere, one day you will feel that from head to foot everything within you is in communication with cosmic life and vibrating in unison with it. Then you will understand what life, creation and love really are.[26]

Harmony is the essence of our being. But we must discover or realize this. And to realize our harmonic essence, we must work with ourselves, our thoughts, feelings, desires, and intentions. We must discover a central thought or idea that, like a powerful current, polarizes all other psychic acts. Aivanhov proffered this explanation:

Truly spiritual people work for an idea, for a divine idea. . . . If you do not have a divine idea to work for, even if you are paid, you will have neither joy nor happiness because you are not linked to Heaven [i.e., to the Divine].[27]

Aivanhov next said:

I, myself, work for an idea! If I am different from most people, it is not because I am more intelligent, or stronger, or more knowledgeable, certainly not; there are so many who surpass me in all these realms, but it is because I work for an idea, that's all. But try to make people understand the power and effectiveness of an idea, how it works and how alive it is![28]

That divine idea is the idea, the force of harmony itself. Harmony should be our first thought or intention and our last. It should be our guiding impulse and experience throughout the day. Even during sleep, our body-mind should be established in harmony. This is the quintessence of the spiritual work as taught by Aivanhov.

In the Yoga tradition of India we find an identical notion. Thus the *Bhagavad-Gita*, the oldest extant Yoga scripture, defines Yoga as balance, or equanimity. The Sanskrit word is *samatva*, which literally means "evenness," suggesting harmony. This eveness is the mainstay of Krishna's Yoga. As I commented in another book of mine:

It is a positive state of mind in which we are able to look with balanced serenity on all the many things that would ordinarily upset us and stir up unwholesome emotions and becloud our judgement.[29]

Harmony is the opposite of stress, hecticness, restlessness, competitiveness, unease, and the myriad other conditions that characterize the modern psyche and culture. Harmony is both the *process* of spiritual life and the ultimate Reality itself, which is the "goal" of all disciplines. As Aivanhov said:

There is a world of harmony, an eternal world, from which all forms, all colors, all music, and all beauty come. I have penetrated into this world. Years ago, I was wrenched out of my body and I heard the harmony of the spheres. I have never experienced such feelings, such beauty, such intensity. Nothing can be compared to it; it was so beautiful, so divine, that I felt afraid. I was afraid of that splendor because I felt that my whole being dilated to the point that I risked dissolving and disappearing into space. So I interrupted this ecstasy and returned to earth. Now I regret it. But at least for some seconds I lived, I saw, I heard how the whole universe sings. . . . Pythagoras, Plato, and many other philosophers have spoken of this harmony, but I wonder how many of them have been able to hear it. And now, merely remembering this experience fills my soul, and it is as if it were sufficient by itself to maintain, support and nourish my whole spiritual life.[30]

We need not, however, have had this experience to take up spiritual practice. We can consider the argument put forward by Aivanhov and other spiritual adepts and then, on the basis of an intelligent, open consideration, make our resolution. Harmony can be our reference point in life even without the prior mystical experience of it. The idea of harmony, or peace, makes intrinsic sense. The German mystic Meister Eckhart, a great luminary of the thirteenth century, offered his disciples the following words of radical wisdom:

Man can offer God nothing better than peace. Unlike peace, God does not need or want waking, fasting, praying, or any penance. God calls for nothing more than that one gives him a peaceful heart: Then he brings about such secret and divine works in the soul that no creature is able to serve or observe that [process].[31]

In a similar vein, Aivanhov was insistent that if we work with the idea and ideal of harmony, we do not need to work separately with any other "divine idea" or virtue. Harmony entails them all. If we try to actualize other virtues without first having found the harmony within, we will inevitably fail. We cannot be loving and compassionate, for instance, without being attuned to the higher Reality. We will only come across as presumptuous fakes or hypocrites, and will end up despising ourselves.

When we are in harmony, our actions are whole and become healing for ourselves and others. In harmony, we transcend the ego, and our body-mind becomes a conduit for the higher reality. Aivanhov once said:

> I only want to live in harmony, and all at once I realize that I have all the virtues, because harmony forces me to be intelligent, wise and understanding. But try to be wise or lovable when you are inwardly in a state of confusion and you won't be able to, just because you are in a terrible state of disharmony . . . Harmonize everything within yourselves, and you will become capable of acting with such wisdom, such depth, such intelligence, that you will wonder, "How did I do it?"[32]

The question is: Will *we* do it?

NOTES

1. Aivanhov, *What Is a Spiritual Master?*, p. 94.
2. Aivanhov, *The True Meaning of Christ's Teaching*, pp. 90–91.
3. *The Notebooks of Paul Brunton*, vol. 13: *Relativity, Philosophy, and Mind* (Burdett, NY: Larson Publications, 1988), part 2, p. 185.
4. Aivanhov, *Freedom, the Spirit Triumphant*, p. 57.
5. R. W. Emerson, *The Conduct of Life* (New York: E. P. Dutton, 1908), p. 267.
6. Aivanhov, *The Powers of Thought*, p. 25.
7. Ibid., p. 25.
8. Ibid., p. 119.
9. Aivanhov, *Hrani Yoga: Le sens alchimique et magique de la nutrition*, p. 108. Available in French only.
10. Aivanhov, *Harmony*, p. 100.

11. Ibid., p. 103.

12. Aivanhov, *The Powers of Thought*, p. 26.

13. Aivanhov, *La nouvelle religion: solaire et universelle* (Part 1), p. 163. Available in French only.

14. Aivanhov, *The Powers of Thought*, p. 35.

15. See *op. cit.*, p. 36.

16. Aivanhov, *The Powers of Thought*, p. 46.

17. Aivanhov, *Hope for the World*, p. 17.

18. Aivanhov, *Spiritual Alchemy*, p. 45.

19. Sri Chinmoy, *Yoga and the Spiritual Life* (Jamaica, NY: Agni Press, 1974), p. 94.

20. Aivanhov, *The Powers of Thought*, pp. 45–47.

21. Aivanhov, *Cosmic Moral Laws*, p. 22.

22. Brother Lawrence [Nicholas Herman of Lorraine], *The Practice of the Presence of God* (New York: F. H. Revell, 1895), p. 20.

23. Johannes Tauler, *Life and Sermons of Dr. John Tauler*, transl. by Susanna Winkworth (New York, 1858), pp. 409-410.

24. Aivanhov, *The Powers of Thought*, p. 71.

25. Ibid., p. 58.

26. Aivanhov, *Harmony*, p. 16.

27. Ibid., p. 18.

28. Ibid., p. 18.

29. G. Feuerstein, *The Bhagavad Gita: Its Philosophy and Cultural Setting* (Wheaton, IL: Quest Books, 1983), p. 158.

30. Aivanhov, *Harmony*, p. 28.

31. From the sermon *In omnibus requiem quaesivi*, ed. by J. Quint, *Meister Eckehart: Deutsche Predigten und Traktate* (Munich: Carl Hanser Verlag, 1963), p. 367.

32. Aivanhov, *Harmony*, p. 34.

9
THE DISCIPLINE
OF LIGHT

THE TRANSFORMATION OF ORDINARY LIFE

As we have seen in the previous chapter, spiritual life is a conscious endeavor requiring great vigilance, dedication, patience, and a willingness to inspect our life and make it conform to spiritual principles.

First and foremost, as Aivanhov explained, spiritual life is a matter of dealing, in the full light of consciousness, with the most mundane aspects of our existence — our means of livelihood, diet, exercise, and sexuality. All too often people imagine spiritual life to be something spectacular and extraordinary for which they themselves are ill-qualified. But this may only be a lame excuse for not taking the first step on the spiritual path. When we examine the great spiritual traditions of the world, we find that they all begin not with rare mystical experiences but with the conscious transformation of the most ordinary activities of one's daily life.

If spiritual life is difficult it is not because we are asked to accomplish at once the inner realizations of advanced mystics or sages, but because we must cultivate a new understanding of, and orientation toward, our routine tasks and obligations. As Aivanhov would say: We must cultivate simplicity.

> Ah, simplicity! What is simplicity? It is to live; only to live but live divinely. There are too many complicated, sophisticated, untruthful things in the world. People boast and bluff and deceive each other with high-flown speeches.[1]

As the Zen masters put it, we must develop "beginner's mind," which is the attitude of looking at life and ourselves with uncomplicated naturalness rather than sophisticated and self-important learning. The internationally respected German psychotherapist and Zen teacher Karlfried Graf von Dürckheim observed:

> Whether in the kitchen or working at an assembly-belt, at the typewriter or in the garden, talking, writing, sitting, walking or standing, dealing with some daily occurrence, or conversing with someone dear to us — whatever it may be, we can approach it "from within" and use it as an opportunity for the practice of becoming a true man [or woman]. Naturally, this is possible only when we are able to grasp the real meaning of life and become responsible towards it. . . . In everything one does it is possible to foster and maintain a state of being which reflects our true destiny. When this possibility is actualized the ordinary day is no longer ordinary. It can even become an adventure of the spirit. In such a case the eternal repetitions in the exterior world are transformed into an endlessly flowing and circulating inner fountain.[2]

The problems that many, perhaps even most, people experience in life concern the basic stuff of work, food, and relationships, especially sexual relationships, which make up our daily round. Spiritual practitioners are expected to, step by step, bring consciousness, prudence, and balance to all these areas.

We have already dealt with work in the preceding chapter. In addition to what has been said there, we must remember the Buddha's eightfold path, which includes "right conduct" and "right livelihood." The former moral demand consists mainly in one's abstention from antisocial practices such as stealing, illicit sexuality, and killing. The latter moral demand seeks to ensure that spiritual practitioners harmonize the way in which they earn their living with their spiritual ideal. Thus they are expected to abstain from treachery, deceit, usury, and fortune telling. In light of these ethical principles, how many politicians, money lenders, cattle breeders, and so-called psychics would have to radically reform their professional and personal lives!

THE SECRET OF NUTRITION

"Nutrition," noted Aivanhov, "is the beginning, everything starts with the food you allow into your system."[3] According to an ancient Sanskrit maxim, the quality of our mind is determined by the quality of our food: *yatha annam tatha manah*. This is exactly what the German philosopher and theologian Ludwig Andreas Feuerbach proposed in the nineteenth century. He wrote:

> Food becomes blood, blood becomes heart and brain, thoughts and mind-stuff. Human fare is the foundation of human culture and thought. Would you improve a nation? Give it, instead of declamations against sin, better food. Man is what he eats.[4]

This sounds like a grossly materialistic doctrine, and in some sense it is. But it also happens to echo one of the most profound insights in the spiritual traditions. According to the traditional understanding, all life forms are food for each other. That is to say, we depend for our individual existence on the sacrifice of others. We take the life of plants and animals to feed our bodies and sustain our own life.

In the ancient *Taittiriya-Upanishad* (II.2), composed almost 3,000 years ago, an anonymous sage instructs his disciple in the secret of existence. He tells his pupil that it is food that sustains life. Life itself can be understood in terms of nutrition. Our primary yearning for freedom and happiness is a kind of hunger. Happiness is nutrition. In fact, when we are happy we are less likely to consume vast quantities of food because the radiance of bliss nourishes our body-mind. Happiness is the immortal nectar (*amrita*) sought by the yogic alchemists. When we do not obtain an adequate amount of this food of happiness, we must turn to lesser forms of nutrition, notably the ordinary food stuffs that our civilizations supplies in such profusion.

The food we eat is, however, not merely the visible matter but also invisible radiation. That radiation interacts with our personal energy field. But even the material properties of the food we eat impacts on our system through the chemical interaction that occurs by means of digestion. This is very evident, for instance, when we try to do mental work on a full stomach. While our stomach juices are hard at work, our mind tends to be quite sluggish and our thoughts are barely uplifting. On the other side, light fasting tends to produce a wonderful clarity of mind.

Spiritual practitioners who have been vegetarians for a long time are sensitive to the psychic effects of food, and, if they happen to deviate from their vegetarian diet, they quickly experience the dulling and disquieting effect of meat. This effect goes beyond a mere upset digestive system.

There is no question that what we eat influences us in profound ways. Eating is a form of energy exchange that is particularly crucial. As Aivanhov stated:

> The food we eat goes into our bloodstream and from there attracts entities that correspond to it in nature. The Gospel says, "Wheresoever the carcass is there the eagles will be gathered together," and this truth applies on all planes, the physical, astral and mental. If you wish to be healthy, do not attract eagles (or vultures) with carcasses on any plane! Heaven will not manifest through anyone who is open to physical, astral or mental impurity.
>
> Meat corresponds to a certain element in our thoughts, feelings and actions.[5]

If we remember that everything is energy, we can see that meat represents a particular level of vibration. By ingesting meat, we inevitably begin to resonate with its vibratory rate. Aivanhov put it this way:

> You should know that everything you absorb in the
> way of food becomes a sort of inner antenna that
> captures different waves ... [and] meat links you with
> the lower regions of the astral world and the beings
> who devour each other like wild beats. Meat is an
> invisible link to brute fear, cruelty, sensuality: the
> animal world. Anyone who is able to see colours
> would be distressed at the colours in your aura.[6]

But much more is involved in meat consumption. There is
also a moral and an ecological dimension to our nutritional
habits of which we must become fully aware. John Robbins,
author of the bestselling book *Diet for a New America*, was
groomed to run the Baskin-Robbins business empire but gave
it all up to devote his life to the welfare of his fellow humans,
animals, and the environment. In his celebrated book, he
exposed the inhumanity and utter wastefulness of the meat-
producing industry as well as the unhealthiness of a non-
vegetarian diet. He wrote:

> There have at last been enormous breakthroughs in
> the science of human nutrition, and for the first time
> now we are receiving irrefutable scientific evidence
> of how different eating patterns affect health. . .
> Few of us are aware that the act of eating can be a
> powerful statement of commitment to our own well-
> being, and at the very same time to the creation of a
> healthier habitat. In *Diet for a New America* you will
> learn how your spoon and fork can be tools with
> which to enjoy life to the fullest, while making it
> possible that life, itself, might continue. In fact, you
> will discover that your health, happiness, and the
> future of life on earth are rarely so much in your own
> hands as when you sit down to eat.[7]

If it is our goal to vibrate in harmony with the universe, we
must be selective about what we admit into our body-mind
system, whether it be food or thoughts. What is important to
realize is that our choices affect not only us individually but
all other life forms on this planet and possibly beyond the

boundaries of the globe as well. We either promote benign vibrations within and around us, or we assist, consciously or unconsciously, the forces of disharmony and disorder in the cosmos. There is no in-between position. The secret of a spiritual approach to nutrition was spelled out by Aivanhov as follows:

> To receive the most subtle particles in the food, you must be fully conscious, wide awake, full of love. If the entire system is ready to receive food in that perfect way, then the food is moved to pour out its hidden riches. Like someone you receive with love, he opens himself and gives you everything he has; if you are cold, he remains closed. . . . Food also remains open or closed depending upon the attitude of the one who partakes of it: when food opens itself, it gives you all that it has in the way of pure, divine energies.[8]

THE FOOD OF LIGHT

Food, Aivanhov noted, is light. But we convert that light in accordance with our psychomental condition. Hence the challenge before us is to approach food and eating with a new understanding. When we regard food as sacred, and eating as a spiritual discipline, the matter we ingest not only does not weigh us down but positively uplifts us. In his fine book *Anna Yoga: The Yoga of Food*, Jack Santa Maria described the traditional Hindu attitude to food very well when he said:

> Brahman is the giver of life too and the sustainer of life in the form of Food. For this reason Krishna describes one who eats without first offering to the Divine as a thief . . . and for Hindus it is the ritual of offering that has the central place in the act of consumption. . . . Since life is built upon the body of food it should always be respected and never spoken ill of. The Yoga aspirant is advised to foster this respect for food, to feel glad and serene at the sight of it and to appreciate it in every way.[9]

Aivanhov reminded his disciples:

> If I have been insisting for years on one thing, one
> little thing: how to eat, it is because I have a reason. .
> . . How many times have I not repeated it! But no one
> has understood what I am asking. You continue to eat
> without thinking or meditating, without linking
> yourselves with God, or even remembering to thank
> him. Here, I would like this act of nourishment to take
> place in a way that is truly Initiatic, because that is
> what will make it possible for you to absorb other,
> subtler nourishment, the nourishment of the stars,
> mountains, rivers, plants, trees; the nourishment that
> comes from the fragrance of perfumes, the sounds of
> music, the light from the sun. It is all nourishment, it
> is always a form of food, with the same correspond-
> ing laws.[10]

The Yoga of Nutrition taught by Aivanhov is a means of
getting in touch with the subtle realm of all of Nature, not
merely with the food on the dinner table. It consists in our
effort to create a conscious link with the Divine, which is our
ultimate form of sustenance. More than that, however, by
subjecting our nutrition to spiritual laws, we not only maintain
our body-mind in good health but also contribute to the
transmutation of Earth itself. As Aivanhov made clear:

> This earth is made of such dense, crude matter that it
> will take millions and millions of creatures to trans-
> form it. But the question is: "How? How can they
> transform it?" My answer is, "By eating it!" Yes, I
> mean it. This is something else that science has not
> yet discovered: why we eat. It is the earth we are
> eating. . . . Oh, it has been dressed up a bit and made
> to look appetizing in the form of fruit and vegetables,
> but it is still earth. And that earth has to go through
> us: it has to be swallowed, digested and excreted,
> swallowed, digested and excreted over and over
> again until every particle is charged with the emana-
> tions and vibrations of our human thoughts and

sentiments. Once the earth is impregnated in this way it will become luminous and transparent.[11]

What a remarkable vision! In the above passage, Aivanhov furnished us with a most practical, down-to-earth program for the spiritualization of matter, which is at the core of spiritual life. Of course, we must remember that, in his understanding, eating is far more comprehensive than the act of introducing food into our mouths.

A similar attitude must, for example, also inform the sexual life of spiritual practitioners. Sex, too, is a kind of energy exchange, a way of feeding and being fed, a means of transmuting matter. Because of the importance of sexual discipline, we will examine it separately in the next chapter.

At the basis of all of Aivanhov's spiritual recommendations lies the recognition that Nature is energy, or vibration. Aivanhov also spoke of it as a manifestation, or variation, of the primordial light. As he explained in one of his first talks:

> Light descends from the subtle regions toward the increasingly denser regions until it reaches solid matter. As it travels, it advances with more and more difficulty.[12]

Pointing to the Book of Genesis in the Old Testament, Aivanhov noted that light was the "very first creature that God brought from the original chaos."[13] He further explained that that first-born light was not the visible light of the sun or the stars but the invisible primordial light. That light is all-pervading. He remarked:

> At the origin and source of all things is light. And light is Christ, the Solar Spirit.[14]

Elsewhere he said:

> Light is matter in its subtlest, most tenuous form, and what we call matter is simply highly condensed, concentrated light. In every zone and region of the

universe, therefore, we have the same fundamental matter — or the same light — in varying degrees of condensation or subtlety.[15]

This teaching was not invented by Aivanhov. Rather, we find it in many different traditions, notably Gnosticism, in which light is deemed the very essence of creation. On a certain level, this ancient truth is now understood by modern science. The American physicist Roger S. Jones wrote:

> I often think that light is the key to the mystery of spacetime. That which gives us the sight and knowledge of our world is so thoroughly enmeshed in space and time that we can have no vision without them or outside them. In relativity, light plays such a pivotal role in the integration of space and time that it is difficult to think of light as some mere physical phenomenon occurring *in* space and time. It seems almost as if light were the source of space and time.[16]

What scientists, on the whole, have not yet begun to appreciate is that light is, in the final analysis, a spiritual reality. Physics distinguishes between different frequencies of light — from the infrared to the ultraviolet and beyond. But all these frequencies are only manifestations of the same invariable, eternal Energy that creates and sustains the cosmos and that spiritual practitioners can experience directly in higher states of mystical elevation.

The visible light, especially the light of the sun, can serve as a concrete symbol of that transcendental Light. This brings us to a consideration of Aivanhov's Solar Yoga.

SOLAR YOGA

Aivanhov called his approach to spiritual life "Solar Yoga." What does this mean? First of all, the term *yoga* stems from the Sanskrit language, which was the learned medium of the brahmins of India. It means literally "union" or "conjunction." In the spiritual context, it stands for "discipline." The verbal root *yuj*, from which the word *yoga* is derived, can mean both "to join" and "to yoke."

Yoga is a richly textured tradition, which comprises a great many different orientations. It also happens to be one of the oldest continuous spiritual traditions in the world, reaching far back into antiquity. It is probable that an early form of Yoga was known already to the people of the Indus/Sarasvati civilization, who lived four thousand and more years ago.

The great historian of religion Mircea Eliade has rightly called Yoga a "living fossil," for to this day the ancient yogic teachings find their dedicated practitioners. Indeed, the yogic practices and ideas continue to be refined and adapted to suit the needs of contemporary seekers.

This creative process of elaboration and innovation of the Yoga tradition is by no means confined to India, its land of origin. Ever since the missionary activity of that great charismatic Hindu leader Swami Vivekananda, who was active in America and in India at the turn of the century, millions of Westerners have become attracted to Yoga. Because Aivanhov freely referred to the various branches of Yoga in his talks, it seems appropriate to briefly consider the traditional yogic schools.

In Western countries, men and women turn mostly to Hatha-Yoga, the Yoga of physical disciplines, which is taught by many teachers. A good many people practice Mantra-Yoga, the Yoga of reciting sacred sounds, which in the West has been made popular by Maharishi Mahesh Yogi, the originator of Transcendental Meditation. A respectable number of people are adherents of Kriya-Yoga, which is a Yoga of meditation and energy techniques, as taught in the first decades of this century by Paramahansa Yogananda.

Bhakti-Yoga, the Yoga of devotional self-surrender, is practiced by the numerous followers of the Hare Krishna movement. Then there are thousands of practitioners of Siddha-Yoga, as taught by Swami Muktananda, which seeks to awaken the "serpent power" (*kundalini-shakti*), the dormant psychospiritual energy of the human body. There are also those who dabble in Tantra-Yoga, notably its left-hand variety, which was made notorious in Western countries by the late Bhagawan (Osho) Rajneesh.

This catalogue by no means exhausts the various schools that have taken root in the Western hemisphere. The West has even spawned its own hybrid schools mixing Yoga with Taoism, Zen Buddhism, and Paganism. These developments notwithstanding, the Euroamerican world has produced few genuinely great adepts with original teachings that are informed by their personal realization.

One of these rare exceptions is Mikhael Aivanhov. When, in 1959, Aivanhov visited India, he was greeted by a renowned Hindu sage as a "solar *rishi*." Although he was not familiar with Aivanhov's teaching, he could not have characterized Aivanhov better. For, he made the life-giving sun the focus of his life and teaching.

As we have seen in Chapter 7, Aivanhov seriously regarded the sun not merely as a giant star, a massive conglomeration of atoms whose internal combustion produces the phenomenon of light, but as an intelligent entity. He believed that everything in the universe is alive, ensouled, or enspirited; that everything harbors a great intelligence, which (or who) manifests in beings and things and is apparent to the degree that their structures permit.

The visible solar orb is merely the physical body of the being we call "sun." It tabernacles a vast intelligent being, whose only purpose is to generously irradiate the cosmos with life-giving energies, by an act of incomparable compassion and love.

Aivanhov saw in light the first emanation of the Divine, retaining the Divine's qualities more than any other manifestation. As he insisted:

> Light is a living spirit which comes from the sun and which establishes a direct relationship with our own spirit.[17]

Aivanhov further claimed that, as a supremely intelligent being, the sun is completely responsive to our spiritual intentions and aspirations. He viewed the sun as an "open door to Heaven."[18] Aivanhov also stated that the sun has been his principal teacher and that "the sun's replies are given in a flash, like an electronic machine."[19]

Aivanhov gave the name *surya-yoga*, "Solar Yoga," to the conscious cultivation of that solar umbilical cord to the Divine. As he observed:

> By the practise of Surya yoga you establish a link between yourself and the power that governs and gives life to the whole Universe: the sun. That is why you must necessarily get results! ... No book can give you what the sun gives you if you learn to have the proper relationship with him. ... If you want to create a bond between you [and the sun], you have to look at him in all consciousness. If you do that there will be a communication of vibrations between the sun and you in which forms and colours, a whole new world, will be born.[20]

An important part of *surya-yoga* is to contact the sun at dawn, which requires proper mental preparation. In order to be able to approach the rising sun in a meditative disposition, the *surya-yogin* should live a balanced life, involving dieting, perhaps even fasting, adequate sleep, and, above all, an un-cluttered mind. Making peace in his own heart, the *surya-yogin* is able to gather his energies and project himself into the sun.

This projection is made possible by the fact that, on subtler planes of existence, we are already fully in touch with the solar being. Aivanhov put this fact more succinctly when he said that the human being already dwells in the sun. In his own words:

> That part of ourselves, that entity which lives in the sun, is our Higher Self.[21]

This mystical statement has its striking counterpart in the *Brihad-Aranyaka-Upanishad* (II.3.3ff.), which speaks of the "person" (*purusha*) in the sun. The exact wording of this passage is as follows:

> Now, formless is the breath and the mid-space (*antariksha*). It is immortal; it is infinite; it is the beyond. The essence of that which is formless, immortal, infinite, and beyond is the Being (*purusha*) who is in the [solar] orb (*mandala*). He indeed is the essence of that. Thus is the divine [revelation]. (vs. 3)

> The form of that Being (*purusha*) is indeed [bright] like a deep saffron-colored cloth, like white wool, like the firefly, like a fire's flame, like the lotus flower, [or] like a sudden flash of lightning. Verily, the glory of him who knows That is like a sudden lightning-flash. (vs. 6)

In the same scripture (V.15.), we also find the following ecstatic prayer to the solar being:

> The face of Truth is covered
> with a golden vessel.
> O Nourisher! Remove that
> so that he whose law is the Truth may see.

> O Nourisher, solitary Seer, Controller, Sun,
> Offspring of the Creator! Arrange your rays! Gather
> your brilliance! I [desire to] behold that most beautiful form of yours. He who is yonder, yonder Being —
> I myself am He!

Esoterically, the human being is modeled after the sun. We participate in the sun's splendor, though we are habitually unaware of this fact. Our "Higher Self," the *atman* or *purusha*, is one with the Divine. This is the key message of the Upanishads and the Vedanta metaphysics built upon these scriptures. It is also the central message of Aivanhov, whose liberal Gnosticism has numerous points of contact with Hindu teachings. Aivanhov's unique contribution is that he has made that esoteric knowledge accessible to modern students.

PRACTICING AT SUNRISE

Aivanhov affirmed countless times that by focusing on the sun, and by attuning ourselves to the solar "wavelengths," we are made whole. He spoke of "eating" and "drinking" light, the primordial food of the universe. As he put it:

> We go to the sunrise in order to nourish ourselves with light ... Man needs to feed on light in order to nourish his brain ... Light awakens those faculties that enable man to penetrate the spiritual world.[22]

Aivanhov, who was a very practical man, recommended this exercise:

> In your thought, with your imagination, try to draw some of these divine particles [of the sun] into yourself. In this way, little by little, you will completely regenerate all the materials of your being.
>   Thanks to the sun you will think and act as a child of God.[23]

Aivanhov's *surya-yoga* furnishes us with a vision of our solar system that is truly magnificent. It replaces our egocentric view, which sees everything revolving around the human individual. Simultaneously it relieves us of the burden of having to play God, instead facilitating our native ability to transcend the self (*ahamkara*) and to find the bliss of the Divine in our life. The ego is the ultimate black hole. It sucks in light but emits none.

The sun is the exact opposite of the ego. It ceaselessly bestows life upon the world. Its life is a true sacrifice (*yajna*). This secret message was clearly understood by the ancient seers and sages. Perhaps our civilization has gone so astray because we have forgotten their subtle understandings and intuitions.

Aivanhov reminded us of the fact that we inhabit a far more wondrous universe than science would have us believe — a universe that is patiently waiting for our conscious, mature collaboration. It is tragic that we are looking for intelligent life in far-distant galaxies when there is a supreme intelligence so close to our home planet and so inextricably interwoven with our own lives. We need not even construct multibillion-dollar spaceships but merely open ourselves up to the ever-present spiritual dimension.

The great adventure awaiting us in the third millennium is not the exploration of outer space, even though technology will undoubtedly open up the solar system and even find pathways to more distant stars. Rather, it is the far more rewarding and awe-inspiring exploration of inner space — the human psyche. It is even doubtful that we can conquer the vast lonely expanse between planets and between our sun and neighboring stars without some form of psychic discipline. Our astronauts will have to be psychonauts as well.

More importantly, we will only emerge from the present global crisis healed in body and spirit if we learn the secret of light, if we become collaborators of the sun. As Aivanhov expressed his noble vision:

> There is no more worthy, more glorious or more potent work than this work with light.[24]

NOTES

1. Aivanhov, *Life Force*, p. 39.
2. K. Graf von Dürckheim, *The Way of Transformation: Daily Life as Spiritual Exercise* (London: Allen & Unwin, 1971), pp. 16–17.
3. Aivanhov, *Hope for the World*, p. 78.
4. Cited in H. Hoffding, *History of Modern Philosophy*, transl. by B. E. Meyer (London, 1900; repr. New York, 1955), vol. 2, p. 281.
5. Aivanhov, *The Yoga of Nutrition*, p. 5.
6. Ibid. pp. 53–54.
7. J. Robbins, *A Diet for a New America* (Walpole, NH: Stillpoint Publishing, 1987), pp. xvxvii.
8. Aivanhov, *The Yoga of Nutrition*, p. 38.
9. J. Santa Maria, *Anna Yoga: The Yoga of Food* (London: Rider, 1978), p. 83.
10. Aivanhov, *Love and Sexuality* (Part 2), pp. 118–119.

11. Aivanhov, *The True Meaning of Christ's Teaching*, pp. 113–114.
12. Aivanhov, *The Second Birth*, p. 153.
13. Aivanhov, *Looking Into the Invisible*, p. 105.
14. Ibid., p. 107.
15. Aivanhov, *Light Is a Living Spirit*, p. 21.
16. R. S. Jones, *Physics as Metaphor* (Minneapolis: University of Minnesota Press, 1982), p. 113.
17. Aivanhov, *Light Is a Living Spirit*, p. 27.
18. Ibid., p. 28.
19. Ibid., p. 35.
20. Ibid., p. 30.
21. Ibid., p. 33.
22. Ibid., p. 75.
23. Ibid., p. 72.
24. Ibid., p. 64.

10
TAMING THE
SEXUAL DRAGON

LIGHT BEYOND SEXUAL PLEASURE

In our quest for happiness, we often get sidetracked on the path of mere sensual pleasure. Aivanhov once traveled on an ocean liner and was "staggered to see all the different kinds of entertainment that were available all day and all night."[1] He compared the pleasure cruise on a luxury liner with the kind of self-indulgent life that most people have chosen or would like to live.

Aivanhov told his students that in choosing pleasurable sensations over true happiness they were merely preparing a life of poverty for themselves. He pointed to the drunkard whose only future is in the gutter. He put it graphically thus:

> If only there was a pair of scales in which you could put on one side what you had gained in tasting all these sensual pleasures and on the other side what you had lost by giving way, you would see that you had lost practically everything and gained practically nothing.[2]

One pleasure in particular exerts an eternal fascination on almost everybody — sex. It affords the ordinary person the most intense pleasurable sensation, and unknowingly is used as a substitute for the bliss that springs from the mystical realization of the higher Self. Sex is the Golden Calf that people have worshipped for millennia. The thrill of orgasm is the means whereby people stave off feelings of loneliness and meaninglessness. What they fail to realize is that orgasm is a frighteningly efficient way of squandering life energy.

No one can accuse Aivanhov of having been a dour-faced ascetic. His lifelong celibacy neither stifled him emotionally nor whipped his mind into feverish private fantasies. Rather than denying the sexual force, he consciously worked on its sublimation, learning to control and harness it.

Aivanhov's sex-positive philosophy is best illustrated in his advice to a young girl who saw male genitals everywhere and was very distressed about her unusual visions. She had consulted several psychoanalysts who had been quite unable to effect a cure. At somebody's recommendation she finally came to see Aivanhov. Greatly embarrassed and feeling weighed down by guilt, she confided in him. He burst into good-natured laughter and then said to her:

> Don't be upset; that is all quite natural and normal; it is the kind of thing that happens to some extent to everybody. I shall show you how to clear up the whole business very quickly, but you must not go on wrestling with it like that. Nature is very powerful; for millions of years, she has organized things in such a way that men and women shall be attracted to each other, and there is not the slightest hope of your changing all that at this stage! Everything that Nature has done is well done, but men and women don't understand. Images of this kind come into the minds of all human beings; the only difference is that some know how to react and others don't. Now, this is what you should do: the next time this image comes into your mind, instead of getting all upset, look at it calmly, but from a different point of view. Remember that this organ is something beautiful, powerful and divine, for it is the organ that transmits life. Reflecting and meditating on this, you will be so moved to admiration at the intelligence and wisdom of the Creator, that you will forget all the rest. You will simply be using the images that come into your mind as a springboard to leap up to your Creator.[3]

Of course, the girl was helped by such sagacious counsel. Aivanhov's advice clearly shows his acceptance of sexuality as a natural aspect of human existence. He disfavored any forced asceticism, and found fault with those traditional attitudes that seek to deny the sexual self-presentation of the cosmos. He remarked:

> Most of the religious ascetics and hermits of the past have bequeathed us a truly disastrous philosophy: they fled from women and hid themselves away in forests or mountain retreats because, in their view, women were creations of the devil. But when the poor wretches ran away from women of flesh and blood, they were pursued and tormented by other women from the astral plane . . . and from them there was no escape! Yes, you have all heard of the temptations of St. Anthony![4]

When visiting Greece in the summer of 1969, Aivanhov also went up Mount Athos.[5] While he admired the works of art created by the monks there, he felt that their monasteries exuded an aura of sadness and boredom. In their rejection of the feminine principle as harmful and diabolical, they had deprived themselves of an entire aspect of their own nature. Aivanhov felt that their puritanical philosophy was quite misguided.

In another talk he noted that by "fighting against sexual energy as most religions advise us to do, and repressing these energies mercilessly, you end up as a case for psychiatrists and psychoanalysts!"[6] Repressed impulses sooner or later emerge in the form of neurotic obsessions.

The spiritual path is therefore not about denying or repressing anything but about voluntary self-transcendence, which increases delight and light. Renunciation, observed Aivanhov, is not about deprivation. Spiritual initiates do not deprive themselves; they merely assume a new relationship to all the many functions that keep the ordinary individual entrapped.[7] Aivanhov spoke of "replacement" and "transposition," which refers to a process by which one's actions are not merely cut off but made purer and more luminous: the spiritual art of sublimation.

Our fascination with sex and orgasm largely springs from the fact that we are unaware of the invisible realities behind them. We focus on the sensations they provide. But these physical manifestations conceal a much vaster dimension of interaction, which is grounded in genuine love as a great participatory force in the universe. We confuse sex with love and orgasm with bliss, because we are unaware of the true origins of our sexuality.

Physical pleasure is the lowest vibratory manifestation of universal love, which fills the cosmos and which is the essence of the higher Self. Metaphysically speaking, pleasure is a condensation of light. Hence Aivanhov said: "Sexual energy comes from solar energy and is, in fact, the same thing."[8]

When we stop hunting after physical pleasure, our pleasure is, paradoxically, magnified. It becomes greater and simultaneously subtler. As Aivanhov expressed it:

> Of course, you are going to ask me what is left if you do not look for pleasure. The truth is that you will have pleasure. In fact, your pleasure will be ten times greater than any you would have otherwise, but it will be of a purer kind, and the all-important thing is that you will not have burned up all your energies. The result will be quite different. The result will be light, light and still more light![9]

THE SACRED ENERGY OF SEX

Sexual energy is not dirty or evil. On the contrary, it is fundamental to human and cosmic existence. It is not merely the trickle of nervous excitation that we occasionally feel in our genitals. Rather, it is a powerful force of cosmic proportions — eros — that is the pulse of life. "The sexual force," observed Aivanhov, "is essential for life and is the one thing which can make you love life."[10]

Hence we should never attempt to throttle sexual energy, because we would only suffocate ourselves. We would never succeed at damming it up and certainly not at negating it. To deny eros means to choose death. More than that, it means to choose nonexistence, because eros is operative even on the subatomic level as the force of attraction that creates the relative stability of the known universe. Aivanhov put it this way:

> Love is everywhere in the universe. It is an element, an energy, which is distributed throughout the whole cosmos, and it can be picked up by people through their skin, their eyes, ears and brain. A plant revealed to me that love is everywhere! As I have told you, I get my information from plants, stones, insects and birds. One day, in Nice [on the French Riviera], I saw a plant that was suspended in the air, it hung in the air, it subsisted on air and didn't need to bury its roots in the earth. I looked at it for a long time and this is what it told me. "As soon as I found the element which is indispensable for my life — love — in the air, why should I go on burying myself in the earth as my companions do? I have discovered a secret; I can draw all that I need for life from the air." So I meditated on this plant and I understood that people, too, are built to extract this love from the atmosphere and from the sun.[11]

If sexual energy is not identical with genital pleasure but is the cosmic power of love that goes far beyond the individual, we would do well to adopt an attitude of wonder, gratefulness, and awe toward it. Aivanhov suggested just that:

> Try, now, to see love as a divine energy, an energy which is poured out on us from above and which, as it works its way down, triggers different effects according to the different conductors through which it manifests itself. Love is like water flowing from the mountain heights: at the highest levels it is transparent and crystal-clear, but as it passes through different types of soil, it gradually becomes tainted with the yellows and reds of the earth. Love, too, is a pure, crystalline force which manifests itself divinely.[12]

Sexual energy, as eros, is the dynamic counterpart of the Spirit. It is the power inherent in matter. According to the Kabbalah, the ultimate Reality is limitless Light. It is polarized into Spirit and Matter. The teachers of the Kabbalah refer to Matter as Shekinah, the Divine Female who is eternally wedded to the Divine Male. This metaphysical polarization makes cosmic existence and human life possible. For, together God and Shekinah create the universe. This notion is also fundamental to Indian Tantrism, as we will see shortly. It is also a notion with which Aivanhov was thoroughly familiar and which he wholeheartedly endorsed:

> Marriage is a cosmic phenomenon. First and foremost it is celebrated on high, between the Heavenly Father and His spouse, Mother Nature. Human beings, who have been created in the image of God, unconsciously reproduce what happens on high.[13]

The Divine Couple appears on the finite level in the shape of the enspirited human body-mind. This union between Spirit and body is, according to Aivanhov, true marriage. All the other social arrangements we call "marriage" are, in his view, adulterous because they are based on an external relationship.[14] On the highest level of existence, Spirit and Matter are incessantly united, merged, and their intimate embrace is the source of all light. It is this eternal blissful intercourse that we must discover in the depth of our own psyche. This is what is called Self-realization or God-realization.

The road to that ultimate discovery is eros, love, the force of life itself. As Aivanhov stated pithily: "Love must participate if we are to reach nirvana"[15] and "Love can lead to light, but only if they stop thinking of it as nothing more than a pleasurable effervescence."[16] We must cultivate love to realize its divine nature. To discover the eternal spring of the River of Life, we must trace its flow back past the slow, stagnant pools to the ever more pure waters in the higher regions. We cannot hope to find the source by denying its manifestations; we cannot recover bliss by denying pleasure. Rather, we must transform our experiences, sensations, and thoughts to increasingly conform to the most sublime state of existence, the unsurpassable expression of love, happiness, peace, pure Being.

SUBLIMATING SEXUAL ENERGY

In our quest for abiding happiness we must not only not deny sexual energy but enlist it in our spiritual endeavor, harness its tremendous potential, and acquire control over it. Above all, we must not squander it.

While the life force is infinite and inexhaustible, our human body-mind is not. Our cells and organs can receive only so much life force before they burn out, just as a thin filament inside a light bulb flares up and is destroyed when it is exposed to an electric current that exceeds the one for which it was designed. Conversely, without adequate nourishment from the River of Life, our body-mind withers prematurely, becomes ill, and then becomes useless for the difficult task of spiritual practice. That is why Aivanhov once remarked that eunuchs have no energy for creativity.[17] He also stated that when our erotic energy wanes, we want to die.[18]

Adepts of all ages have stressed the importance of "energy management," of carefully cultivating the life force and especially its sexual manifestation. According to the Taoist masters, for instance, each person is born with a limited quantity of erotic energy. When it is wasted, we fall ill and finally die. The nineteenth-century Taoist master Chao Pi Ch'en taught that a spiritual practitioner should consider his body as a country and the units of sexual energy as its population. Through cultivation of the Spirit and the breath, the country's prosperity is increased, which guarantees peace. However, loss of semen, which leads to the diminution of erotic energy, causes rebellion and chaos.

The Taoist adepts believed that through celibacy and proper "energy management" the store of erotic energy could be replenished and increased, which has many desirable effects on the body-mind. This discipline was thought not only to revitalize and heal the body but to actually rejuvenate it, so that the Taoist goal of longevity could be attained.

To be sure, the Taoists were and are no puritans. On the contrary, their attitude toward sex has at times an almost cannibalistic aspect to it. For, while the male practitioners are anxious to preserve their seminal fluid, they do their best to take advantage of the woman's secretions, which run more copiously when she orgasms. Female practitioners, in their turn, try to outsmart their male lovers so as to benefit from their ejaculation. This exploitative attitude, found among the less enlightened Taoists, is just another version of the battle of the sexes, and it has no place in any mature spiritual practice where men and women must regard each other with respect and as equally magnificent manifestations of the Divine.

Whether or not we aspire to become Methuselahs, as do certain followers of Taoism, it would be wise to accept their ancient teaching: Every time we have an orgasm, we waste a percentage of our stock of life energy, depriving our cells of regenerative force and also depleting our psychic being. It is perhaps no accident that the French speak of orgasm as the "little death," *la petit mort*.

Americans, on average, "die" 5,000 and more times during their lifetime. The situation is undoubtedly similar in Europe and most other parts of the "developed" world where sex is approached as a way of releasing stress. From a spiritual point of view, this wastage of erotic strength is deplorable, even fatal.

Hence teachers like Aivanhov strongly argue in favor of sexual conservation. Not everybody is built to stop having sex or orgasms overnight; nor is this necessary to succeed on the spiritual path. However, everyone can appreciate the preciousness of the life force and begin to economize his or her sexual expenditure.

We can adopt this new course by installing a higher ideal in our mind and life. A high ideal is like a good friend to whom we can turn when we are in need and who unfailingly provides us with reliable counsel. As Aivanhov made clear, we cannot conquer the sex drive by sheer willpower. Quite rightly, he said: "... you must not try to fight against it as it will crush you."[19] Instead of fighting windmills, we should befriend the wind that powers the mills so that some good may come of it.

That is to say, we should cultivate our high ideal, because it allows us to commune with the Divine.

When we establish a channel between ourselves and the Divine, whether through prayer, meditation, or pondering our ideal, we have the most powerful ally in the universe possible. It is through that connection that our life is transformed and that our sexual energy is, bit by bit or maybe suddenly and completely, sublimated without our having to undergo the usual agonizing struggle. What this means in practical terms was spelled out by Aivanhov thus:

> When you feel a sexual impulse, concentrate on your ideal, and then this energy will go up to feed your brain; a few minutes later you will be free, you will have won! . . . Make all your energies converge not towards pleasure but to a sublime ideal; then they will be able to serve you and contribute to the realization of that ideal.[20]

To concentrate on one's ideal is to visualize or picture it as concretely as possible, to open oneself to its benign influence, to welcome it bodily, to warmly embrace it. In other words, to evoke one's ideal is not merely an intellectual act. It is a profound emotional gesture, in which we affirm, in our deepest feeling, the desirability of our highest ideal — which is to stand in the presence of the Divine.

We can assist that vivid visualization through deep breathing.[21] Often the life force gets stuck in lower centers because our breathing habits are so poor. By means of deep, rhythmic breathing, we can consciously help it to circulate through the whole body and thus to stimulate the higher centers in the brain.

Sexual energy can either go down and out or in and up. It can either supply our genitals with brief pleasurable sensations, or it can ascend toward the brain, nourishing certain subtle psychoenergetic centers. The downward flow has purely biological import: to ensure the survival of the human species. The upward flow, however, has far greater evolutionary significance, because it is responsible for the conversion of

Homo sapiens into Homo noeticus, of our conventionally intelligent species into a species that is intelligent and creative in consonance with the spiritual laws of the universe. The difference is phenomenal.

Aivanhov compared sexual energy to gasoline, which burns those who handle it carelessly, whereas those who are prudent can harness it to fly into space.[22] Sexual energy in itself is neither good nor evil. It simply *is*. Its effects depend on our use of it. We can employ it to reinforce our addiction to pleasure. Or we can use it to discover lasting joy and freedom. Sexual energy is the hidden key that opens or closes the narrow passage to the spiritual dimension.

Our chosen ideal of self-forgetfulness, harmony, peace, love, and bliss is a constant reminder of the direction in which we should turn that key. Thus, our mental attitude is all-important. As the American-Polish philosopher Henryk Skolimowski, who holds the first professorship in ecological philosophy in the world, wrote:

> Of all the gifts of evolution, mind is the most precious. Yet we have allowed it to become something else than it deserves. Look at yourself. Look how much pollution is poured into your mind daily. Look how much trivia you have allowed to invade your mind. This is not the right ecology of mind. This garbage in your mind has trivialised your existence, is the cause of anxieties, is the cause of confusion that does not allow you to think right and act appropriately. If you care for the gifts of your life, if you care for the gift of your mind — then don't allow your mind to become a garbage container.[23]

These are direct words. Their message is amplified by Skolimowski's further stipulation that ecologically conscious individuals will reflect at least for five minutes every day on who they are, what they consider their highest potential to be, and what kind of world they desire to live in. It is important that in all our spiritual considerations, we always bear in mind that we do not live in isolation from the rest of creation but are dependent and co-responsible for all other beings.

Hence our attitude toward our own sexuality involves so much more. In fact, it involves everyone and everything. It is not merely a personal, private matter. The sexual or erotic force is, as we have seen, universal. We simply partake of it. Depending on our disposition, we merely exploit it or we regard it with reverence. Only if we follow the second option do we open ourselves to higher evolutionary possibilities.

TANTRA-YOGA AND THE SERPENT POWER

Of all the ancient esoteric traditions, one in particular has made sexual energy, eros, an integral part of its spiritual program. That tradition is Tantrism. Its philosophy and practice is expounded in the Hindu and Buddhist Tantras. These are hermetical works composed in the Sanskrit language which are presented as the "new" revelation best suited for the conditions of the present Dark Age (*kali-yuga*). The Tantric adepts understood their teachings as a reformulation of ancient sacred wisdom for the feeble spiritual capacities of "modern" humankind.

The Dark Age is thought to have commenced in 3001 B.C. at the death of the God-man Krishna, who expounded the Yoga teachings to Prince Arjuna, as revealed in the *Bhagavad-Gita*. It will continue for hundreds of thousands of years before humanity will witness the dawn of a new Golden Age of peace and spiritual fellowship on Earth. Thus, within this vast perspective on world history, the present Age of Aquarius is not the promised Golden Age but merely a cycle of relative upswing in a much longer cycle of decline.

The Tantric adepts felt that humanity in the Dark Age required aids and props for spiritual life that were completely unnecessary in previous Ages. The most widely recommended Tantric aid is the recitation of sacred sounds (*mantra*), such as *om* or *ram*. This practice is said to require neither great strength of character nor superlative intelligence or stamina. Anyone can do it, providing he or she has been properly initiated by a qualified teacher (*guru*) who can empower the disciple's spiritual endeavor.

Regular and prolonged recitation of a *mantra* steadies the fickle mind and thus lays the foundation for inner peace and receptivity of divine grace. The underlying idea is that sound can serve as a transformative vehicle in the same way in which sacred gestures (*mudra*) and the invocation and contemplation of light can bring about spiritually favorable conditions. In one of his talks, Aivanhov explained that "the sounds we hear produce geometrical figures within us."[24] He went on to say:

> The effect of sound, the vibratory energy of the waves it creates, causes myriads of minute particles in us to arrange themselves into geometrical figures. This is why, when you listen to the cacophony that passes for music today, the pre-existent structure and harmony within you, the order that was established by the Creator, is disturbed and eventually shattered.[25]

Hence Aivanhov frequently emphasized the importance of harmonious sounds, and music and singing play an important role in his teaching, as they do in the teaching of his master Peter Deunov.

The Tantric adepts knew much more about sound and its hidden effects than does modern science. But their explorations led them to even more remarkable discoveries. The most outstanding discovery of the Tantric masters is the now widely publicized but still ill-understood phenomenon of the "serpent power," or *kundalini-shakti*. This power is fundamental to all spiritual work in Tantrism. If the Tantrics are correct, it is the great secret dynamo underlying all spirituality, in fact all other human expressions as well.

The Sanskrit word *kundalini* means literally "she who is coiled." It refers to the esoteric fact that, in the subtle energy field at a point corresponding to the base of the spine, the human being is linked to the cosmic erotic force. Thus the *kundalini-shakti* is the enormous psychospiritual energy potential lying dormant in the human body-mind. The Tantric work is to awaken the sleeping serpent, to rouse the dormant power, and guide it from the lower psychoenergetic centers to the highest center at the crown of the head.

According to Tantrism, there are seven principal psychoenergetic centers aligned along the bodily axis. The lowest center is at the perineum; the second at the genitals; the third at the solar plexus; the fourth at the heart; the fifth at the throat; the sixth in the middle of the head (the "third eye"); and the seventh at the top of the head. The flow of energy in the ordinary body-mind is polarized into what the Tantrics call "Shiva" and "Shakti" — God and Goddess. The Sanskrit word *shiva* means literally "benevolent," whereas *shakti* means "power."

Aivanhov was well acquainted with the theory and experience of the *kundalini*. He felt that his own mystical experience at the age of seventeen had been a *kundalini* awakening:

> I had this experience when I was very young; I was seventeen and I had been doing breathing exercises for days on end, and one day, all of a sudden, Kundalini awoke. It was a terrible sensation, as if my head was on fire; I was very afraid. I then made gigantic efforts to make it go to sleep again — yes, such efforts; and I succeeded. Kundalini can even wake in those who are not very spiritually advanced; it can also be awakened accidentally, and as it is a terrible force, those who are not ready for it can become mad or be led right to Hell. What happened to me when I was young could have been the greatest disaster for me if I had not been capable of making this force go to sleep once again. Fortunately, Heaven was watching over me.[26]

Just how terrifying the *kundalini* power can be when unleashed in the unsuspecting person has been vividly described by the contemporary Kashmiri sage Gopi Krishna in his fascinating autobiography.[27] Other accidental awakenings of this force are described in *The Kundalini Experience* by the American psychiatrist Lee Sannella, who was one of the first members of his profession to acknowledge that this experience must be distinguished from psychotic states.[28]

Aivanhov equated the *kundalini-shakti* with Hermes Trismegistus's "Strength of all Strengths," and remarked in this connection that the *kundalini* force "is a condensation of light of the sun."[29] Only initiates can deliberately arouse this dormant power with impunity. Aivanhov observed that in the case of the adept who succeeds in this difficult task, the *kundalini* "returns to its etheric state and manifests as light shining through his eyes and brain."[30]

As for beginners on the spiritual path, Aivanhov made it clear in a number of his talks that he advises them not to dabble with this force until they have attained inner purity and self-discipline, which alone will protect them. Otherwise the *kundalini* is likely to cause havoc in their life.

One of the common troubles that a prematurely triggered *kundalini* can cause is overstimulation of the second psychoenergetic center, leading to a highly intensified sexual urge. A young woman reported to me that when this happened to her, she behaved like a nymphomaniac, almost destroying the relationship with her boyfriend whom she genuinely loved. Only when she realized that she was harming him with her insatiable sexuality did she take steps to regain her bodily and mental equilibrium. The *kundalini* fire continued to burn in her for a period of time and then naturally subsided.[31]

While the *kundalini* is the cosmic erotic power manifesting in the human body-mind, it is not in itself exclusively sexual. Rather, it stimulates the genitals, demanding sexual release, whenever it activates the second psychoenergetic center (*cakra*). As the *kundalini* ascends, its manifestations become increasingly refined — until, in the topmost center — they are of the nature of pure, unalloyed bliss.

The Tantric adepts aspired to tap into that bliss, which springs from the mystical unitive state. They realized that desire, especially sexual desire, is not bad or detrimental in itself. On the contrary, they did everything to kindle desire in their bodies. Thus, the adepts following what is called the "left-hand path," even engaged in sexual intercourse to that end.

The Tantric adepts did not engage in sex because they wanted to be comforted or pleasurized but because this is the single most intense way of stimulating the body's natural energy, which is experienced on the psychological level as desire. They deliberately cultivated that desire, carefully avoiding orgasmic discharge of the built-up psychophysical tension.

Even though Aivanhov was a lifelong celibate, he subscribed to a similar point of view. This is evident from the following unorthodox recommendation he made to a man who had admitted to having little self-control in sexual matters.[32] Aivanhov told him to go to the beach and look at all the pretty girls. This would naturally awaken sexual desire in him, but since he could not satisfy it on the spot, he would be forced to practice a measure of self-control. He should then try to prolong this moment of triumph over his sexual appetite. Aivanhov told the man that once he got to the point where he was able to repeat this exercise several times with success, he should test himself in a different way.

Of course, Aivanhov also instructed him in the esoteric use of the awakened sexual energy: Instead of dispersing it through genital orgasm, one should consciously draw it upward along the spinal axis toward the brain, toward "Heaven," as he put it. This is the occult significance of the phrase "making ends meet," because spiritual practitioners are challenged to raise the lower to the higher. As Aivanhov put it:

> Man's highest achievement is to merge his lower self with his higher Self, the tail with the head. Of course, I do not deny that the tail has some good points: it is capable of movement, for instance. . .
>
> The tail must join up with the head. We have to learn to "make both ends meet." Centuries ago the Initiates coined this phrase, but men have forgotten what it means. Nowadays they use it when they have financial problems: money is tight at the end of the

> month and they say, "I can't make ends meet." In
> reality the "ends" in question are the head and the tail
> of the serpent. The true meaning of making ends meet
> is the development of the chakras [psychoenergetic
> centers], one after the other, beginning with Mul-
> adhara at the base of the spine, all the way to
> Sahasrara at the top of the head, in order to create
> unity.[33]

The well-known mythological image of a serpent swallow-
ing its tail is a concise graphic representation of this esoteric
process of inner purification, sublimation, and completion by
which the sexual force, the "winged dragon," is tamed. It also
applies to the Tantric sexual ritual.

SEXUAL COMMUNION

The Tantric sexual intercourse, called *maithuna* ("pairing"),
is a demanding and prolonged ritual. For the duration of that
ritual, male and female initiates regard one another as God
and Goddess. They seek to bring the conditions of Heaven
down to Earth. Aivanhov compared the Tantric adepts to pearl
divers who bravely dive down into the oceanic deeps and
return with precious pearl oysters, without becoming en-
tangled in seaweed or succumbing to other marine dangers.
As he said, "they dare to delve into their own subconscious
and explore the domain of instinct, passion, sensuality and the
deep waters of pleasure."[34] Aivanhov emphasized that the
Tantric path is for the select few — those who have tasted the
universal love and bliss and who, therefore, cannot be tempted
by lesser pleasures.

He advised his students against experimenting with left-
hand Tantric practices, which he did not find suitable for
Westerners. He explained:

> There are yogis who have felt themselves entitled to
> go to great lengths in order to transform their sexual
> energy but, in my opinion, it is unnecessary to use
> such extreme practices. There are other methods . . .
> our Teaching goes a great deal further than the old

traditions of so-called purity and chastity which tried to turn men into eunuchs and, at the same time, it goes further than all those doctrines which claim to be Tantric and which lead to the grossest sexual excesses. In the last century, in England, there was an occultist called Aleister Crowley who, through his experiments with the methods used by Tibetan Tantrists, became a black magician and ended by driving several of his partners out of their minds. He had powers, to be sure, but what depths he sank to![35]

Crowley, like so many other practitioners of his ilk, failed to be inspired by love and so fell victim to his lust for power. Aivanhov condemned the kind of sex magic that Crowley and his disciples employed. Without love, the spiritual path remains barren, and the seeker is likely to encounter obstacles rather than gifts of grace.

Sex without loving regard for one's partner is unfulfilling, disappointing, and depleting. Since the Sexual Revolution of the 1960s it has become dogma in many circles of Western society that sex has to be a high performance that ensures orgasmic release for both partners. Rather than easing the tension between the sexes, this latest standard has led to performance anxiety on both sides. It has also played into the tendency toward emotional dissociation between partners. It is clear from the high divorce rate and the growing number of marriage and sex counselors that the Sexual Revolution has failed in one important respect: It has so far not produced happier, more contented people.

This failure is not surprising, because happiness is never the result of external manipulations, such as sexual versatility. Instead, it is a matter of discovering the great nutrient of life, which is love. Nothing can thrive without the love ingredient, especially not sex. "Love is divine life," Aivanhov once stated, "that has come down into the lower regions to take over, to spread love around, to bring all to life."[36]

For Aivanhov, as for the Tantrics, sex is a sacred act, which involves a profound process. As he explained:

> When a man and woman unite, the man's energies go
> to the base of his spinal column and from thence to
> the woman, ascending along her spine to the brain.
> From there she communicates them back to the man:
> the woman receives the energy below and gives it
> back above. An extraordinary circulation is thus put
> into play.[37]

This energy exchange occurs regardless of whether we are aware of it or not. It is the means by which sexual partners bond. Sexual intercourse involves an energy transfusion between partners. Hence it is always an important step when friends become lovers. More than any other type of exchange between people, sex creates karmic links that can have long-lasting effects. Therefore casual sex, especially one-night stands, are spiritually detrimental to both men and women.

Aivanhov made it clear that casual sex, whether it occurs between intimates or strangers, is of benefit only to lower spirits — "elementals" — who soak up the energy released during such an exchange. He observed:

> All those who have studied the question of sexuality,
> whether they be physiologists, psychiatrists or sexol-
> ogists, have never discovered what happens on the
> subtle, etheric and fluidic plane during the sexual act.
> They know all about stimulations, tensions and emis-
> sions; they have even classified them! What they do
> not know is that when they are dealing with sexuality
> which is purely physical, biological and egocentric, it
> produces on the higher planes all sorts of volcanic
> eruptions which give off thick emanations and coarse
> forms. These emanations have dull and murky col-
> ours; red is the main colour, but it is a dirty red. All
> these emanations are swallowed up by the earth or
> by shadowy creatures who are waiting to feast on
> these vital energies. Creatures at a low level of evolu-
> tion feed themselves at the expense of lovers . . . lovers
> give banquets to the invisible world.[38]

As Aivanhov stressed: "Lovers who are driven only by a desire for pleasure allow burglars free entry."[39] This thought may strike us as fanciful and incredible. But before we pass judgment on it, we should carefully consider the kind of worldview outlined in Chapter 5, which pays due attention to the fact that the visible universe is but the tip of a huge iceberg. At any rate, whether or not we accept the existence of spirit entities that feast on our energies, casual sex is dysfunctional from a spiritual point of view. It squanders our vital energies, and it reinforces in us all those habit patterns that keep us locked out of the delight of the ever-present Reality.

In choosing casual sex, we opt for pleasure; and in doing so, we choose to decline bliss, freedom, and happiness. We also choose to devalue the other person, for we do not see in him or her the presence of the Divine, just as we deny that presence in our own case.

It is only when we respect sexual intercourse as a means of spiritual communion that we can defuse its undesirable side effects and enjoy its mystical properties. For this, we must prepare ourselves properly. Among other things, Aivanhov made the following recommendation:

> Draw close to the one you love, look into her eyes, take her into your arms and propel her Heavenwards; link her to the Divine Mother, or to Christ, the Heavenly Father or the Holy Spirit. If you do this you will never need to reproach yourself for anything; you will feel as though lamps were being lit within you; you will be filled with joy and the most extraordinary sense of happiness.[40]

On a different occasion he stated:

> If, before you take your beloved in your arms, you call on the light exactly as you call on the Lord and invite him to join you at supper, you will be giving her elements that are divine and which she has never before received, and her soul will be eternally grateful because your love is unselfish . . .[41]

As we have seen from previous chapters, this working with the Light is central to Aivanhov's teaching. It is especially significant in regard to our sexual life. One of the reasons for this is that sex releases highly focused energies. Indeed, Aivanhov compared the sexual act to a laser.[42] The male genitals, he said, are like a laser gun, releasing a beam of light into the female organ. The initiate must learn to switch from the horizontal laser of the genitals to the vertical laser of the spinal axis. In the vertical laser, a beam of light — the *kundalini* — is fired from the lowest psychoenergetic center at the base of the spine toward and beyond the center at the crown of the head. Whereas the horizontal laser at best promises a fleeting moment of pleasure, the vertical laser showers upon the initiate the indescribable bliss of Self-realization.

Speaking of the intelligent arrangement of the human sexual organs, Aivanhov shocked some of his listeners when he linked the Holy Spirit with the genitals, Christ with the solar plexus, and the Lord with the brain.[43] In orgasm, we pour out the Holy Spirit through our genitals, and then are surprised when we have no energy left for the pursuit of higher ideals. The secret Yoga of sexual intercourse seeks to honor and preserve the bodily energy reserves — the Holy Spirit — which performs the miracle of inner transmutation by which we come to know our true nature, the higher Self.

The sexual Yoga consists in raising the Holy Spirit to the level of the Christ and then to the level of the Lord. The Holy Spirit, or *kundalini-shakti*, is thus the power by which the original integrity of the Holy Trinity is restored in our own body-mind.

Unconsciously, we all hunger for this wholeness. But unless we recognize this fact, we will always in our ignorance misread this primordial urge for integration, transcendence, and identification with the Divine. In that case, we tend to settle for moments of pleasure, literally forsaking the Holy Spirit, the evolutionary energy within us.

From the perspective of the man, this hunting after pleasure through sexual exploitation amounts to a denial of the spiritual urge in the woman. In our patriarchal society, where sex is often used to express power and the need to control, it is important to emphasize the spiritual obligation that men have toward women. Aivanhov put it very well when he made the following comments:

> Many women would prefer to be stimulated and inspired by a force other than physical force but as few men are conscious enough or enlightened enough to know this, nor self-controlled enough to be inspired on any plane but the physical, women must be content with what they are offered. Man fertilizes woman as the sun fertilizes the earth. Today, man should no longer be content to fertilize woman on the physical plane, but learn to fertilize her on the spiritual plane so that she produces children in her soul and heart, divine children.[44]

Conversely, women must learn to see men in a different light. Spiritual fertilization or conception, just like biological conception, is a collaborative effort. Women, too, must assume full responsibility for their sexual self-expression. Aivanhov said:

> Woman is a pure marvel; nothing in the world will persuade me to change my opinion about her. The day I lose my good opinon of woman, that will be the end of me! . . .
> It is women who are going to transform the whole world. If it has not already happened, it is because they are not yet aware of their mission. . . . But the world needs women who make up their minds to use the power they have over men, not to seduce them but to make them nobler beings.[45]

The mutual ennobling of men and women is one of the greatest tasks confronting our civilization. It is a matter of respect, reverence, and love. "The question of love," noted Aivanhov, "will be the big question set before the generations to come."[46]

NOTES

1. Aivanhov, *A Philosophy of Universality,* p. 145.
2. Aivanhov, *Sexual Force or the Winged Dragon,* p. 61.
3. Aivanhov, *Love and Sexuality* (Part 2), pp. 21–22.
4. Ibid., p. 23.
5. See Aivanhov, *Sexual Force or the Winged Dragon,* p. 52.
6. Aivanhov, *The Key to the Problems of Existence,* p. 192.
7. See Aivanhov, *Sexual Force or the Winged Dragon,* p. 121.
8. Aivanhov, *Hope for the World,* p. 138.
9. Aivanhov, *Love and Sexuality* (Part 2), p. 49.
10. Aivanhov, *Sexual Force or the Winged Dragon,* p. 50.
11. Ibid., pp. 94–95.
12. Ibid., p. 193.
13. Ibid., p. 219.
14. See Aivanhov, *Love and Sexuality* (Part 2), p. 28.
15. Ibid., p. 50.
16. Aivanhov, *Love and Sexuality* (Part 2), p. 195.
17. See Aivanhov, *Sexual Force or the Winged Dragon,* p. 53.
18. See Aivanhov, *Love and Sexuality* (Part 2), p. 89.
19. Aivanhov, *Sexual Force or the Winged Dragon,* p. 117.
20. Ibid., p. 118.
21. See Aivanhov, *Harmony and Health,* p. 140.
22. See Aivanhov, *A New Earth,* pp. 81–82.
23. H. Skolimowski, *Ecological Renaissance* (Ann Arbor, MI: Eco-Philosophy Centre, 1991), p. 4. (booklet)
24. Aivanhov, *Creation: Artistic and Spiritual,* p. 98.
25. Ibid., p. 98.
26. Aivanhov, *A Philosophy of Universality,* pp. 46–47.
27. See G. Krishna, *Kundalini: The Evolutionary Energy in Man* (London: Robinson & Watkins, 1971).
28. See L. Sannella, *The Kundalini Experience: Psychosis or Transcendence?* (Lower Lake, CA: Integral Publishing, 1991).
29. See Aivanhov, *Light Is a Living Spirit,* p. 136.
30. Ibid., p. 136.
31. This case is more fully reported in my book *Sacred Sexuality: Living the Vision of the Erotic Spirit* (Los Angeles: J. P. Tarcher, 1992), pp. 41–43.
32. See Aivanhov, *The Key to the Problems of Existence,* pp. 211–212.
33. Aivanhov, *The Living Book of Nature,* pp. 88–89.
34. Aivanhov, *Love and Sexuality* (Part 2), p. 153.
35. Ibid., p. 158.
36. Aivanhov, *Love and Sexuality* (Part 1), p. 108.
37. Aivanhov, *Christmas and Easter in the Initiatic Tradition,* p. 62.
38. Aivanhov, *Sexual Force or the Winged Dragon,* p. 24.
39. Ibid., p. 69.

40. Aivanhov, *Love and Sexuality* (Part 2), p. 236.
41. Aivanhov, *Love and Sexuality* (Part 1), p. 114.
42. See Aivanhov, *Light Is a Living Spirit*, p. 128.
43. See Aivanhov, *Sexual Force or the Winged Dragon*, p. 129.
44. Aivanhov, *Hope for the World*, p. 138.
45. Aivanhov, *Love and Sexuality* (Part 2), p. 77.
46. Aivanhov, *Love and Sexuality* (Part 1), p. 115.

11
THE TRUE DEPTH
OF CHRISTIANITY

THE THIRD TESTAMENT

Aivanhov was an eminently practical person. Through his teaching he hoped to show contemporary humanity a way out of the cultural and spiritual cul-de-sac in which it is stuck. He provided down-to-earth practical prescriptions for living in consonance with the cosmic and spiritual laws. A very significant aspect of his teaching concerns, as we have seen in previous chapters, the cultivation of right ideas and ideals. As Aivanhov taught: "The great secret lies in the idea, the ideal for which you are working."[1] The ideas and ideals that Aivanhov recommended to his disciples are part of a comprehensive spiritual approach. That approach is thoroughly integrated within an overarching philosophy, or metaphysics, the essentials of which can be gleaned from Aivanhov's published talks.

What is the philosophical framework that Aivanhov tried so hard to communicate? I have already answered this question in part in Chapter 4. We may now examine it in connection with Aivanhov's own spiritual roots, which will provide the historical continuity that allows us to better understand his message and mission. We find that Aivanhov himself understood his teaching as an integral part of the "Third Testament." Jesus of Nazareth reformed the Mosaic law encoded in the Old Testament, bringing his own message, which now forms the core of the New Testament. The prophets of the Old Testament preached about the single God, who is the Creator of all things and whose will must be obeyed. To this Jesus added the law of love, thus tempering the Mosaic demand of "an eye for an

Omraam Mikhael Aivanhov

eye." Aivanhov called Jesus "the most revolutionary of all God's messengers."[2]

But what is the Third Testament? To begin with, the Third Testament is not Aivanhov's personal invention. He never saw himself as a spiritual innovator but understood his mission to make ancient truths accessible to modern humanity. He built his teaching on the bedrock of Peter Deunov's teaching, elaborating and modifying where he deemed it necessary. He was a master at the task of interpreting the ancient esoteric lore to his contemporaries who have all but forgotten their own heritage of wisdom.

Although mainstream Christianity would vehemently deny it, Aivanhov was deeply Christian. They would denounce him, as they denounced Peter Deunov and, before him, the Bogomils and Cathars, who are closely associated with the spiritual history of Bulgaria. Aivanhov belonged to the gnostic tradition, understood in broad terms. Gnosticism has been a dirty word for Christians over many centuries. Today a more dispassionate and accurate appraisal of this age-old tradition is possible, and I will shortly discuss some of its principal ideas and how they relate to Aivanhov's work.

Aivanhov's Third Testament is a gospel in the making, a teaching in the process of being born. Even though its roots reach back into the spirituality of the distant past, it is not a teaching of the past but of the future. The Third Testament is the gospel of the new era of humanity, whose first tender beginnings we are witnessing today. In Aivanhov's words:

> There are changes coming in the philosophic and religious beliefs of humans. For the moment they think it natural to have a distance between themselves and God, they are even convinced that it should be so. . . .
>
> I have often said that in the future there will be a Third Testament which will complete the two preceding ones; in it, this truth that man must come closer to God, will be clear . . . so close that His Presence is felt by man inside himself . . . and then he will never again have the impression of being abandoned.[3]

When we examine Aivanhov's teaching, we are struck not only by its depth but also by its scope. Of course, some cursory readers may be impressed by the intellectual breadth of Aivanhov's books while failing to appreciate their spiritual depth. Aivanhov successfully integrated many different strands of knowledge, experience, and wisdom. This success was undoubtedly the result of his practical orientation and continuous personal testing and verifying.

Some people have described his teaching as "syncretistic," intending this word to convey a certain pick-and-choose quality. However, this label is quite wrong. In his effort to master himself and to understand the world and live in it with wisdom, as well as in his lifelong struggle to communicate the spiritual dimension to others, Aivanhov simply availed himself of any useful and relevant method, technique, and idea. He likened his teaching to "a table spread with food."[4] There is something for everyone's palate: Many roads lead to the Divine.

Thus Aivanhov made use of the *cakra* model, astrology, the Kabbalah, alchemical symbolism, physiognomy, Shiva-Shakti polarity, color symbolism, and a host of other traditional notions.[5] Yet, he was not a Hindu, nor a Kabbalist, nor a pagan astrologer. If he borrowed his ideas from various schools of thought, he also breathed his own life into them, applying to them the touchstone of lived experience.

At any rate, according to his own understanding, Aivanhov was a Christian who lived the Christian teaching. "The things I tell you," he once observed, "are the real Teaching of Christ."[6] He emphasized that nothing in his teaching contradicts the original gospel of Jesus. However, he volunteered that it may well contradict current dogma and belief. It certainly does. To understand Aivanhov's Christian discipleship and his significance for the future of Christianity, we must briefly glance at the historical unfolding of Christianity itself.

THE HIDDEN TEACHING OF JESUS

Christianity has a history of two millennia during which its influence in the world has steadily grown. Today there are an estimated 1.6 billion Christians in the world, and they are found in almost every country. Many are undoubtedly only nominal Christians, but they too are subtly and not so subtly influenced by Christian values and beliefs.

Over the centuries there have been numerous changes in Christian doctrine and practice. The house of Christianity has many mansions, accommodating sometimes vastly different points of view. Moreover, each new generation born in the Western hemisphere and many other parts of the world must find its own response to this great ramifying tradition. There is decline, and there is revival. But revivals are often merely another form of misunderstanding the original gospel of Jesus, by confusing authentic spirituality with the business of religion. The difference between spirituality and religion is crucial and must be clearly understood.

Religion, as widely practiced, is a social club, which makes a minimal demand on people's inner resources. In this sense, Karl Marx was right when he spoke of religion as "opium." However, at the core of the great religious traditions is a set of values, beliefs, and practices that are "spiritual" rather than religious.

In contrast to everyday religion, spirituality is the art of living at the edge of life: of throwing oneself into the human adventure with open eyes, an open mind, and an open heart, stretching oneself to one's ultimate limit. That final limit is none other than the Spirit, or Self. However, the Spirit really represents no limit at all, because it coincides with the ultimate Reality, the Divine, which is omnipresent and omnitemporal.

Spirituality is always esoteric, for the Spirit is hidden and reveals itself only when our minds are calm and our hearts are pure. Spirituality is the mystical quest. Paul Brunton put it this way:

> Religion was devised to assist the masses. Mysticism was designed to assist the individual. When religion has led a man to the threshold of deeper truths behind its own, its task is done. Its real value is attained in mysticism.[7]

Brunton also commented that real religion "is as universal as the wind."[8] As Aivanhov reiterated, true religion is initiatic science, and that science is based on universal principles. Real religion, or spirituality, concerns that which is the highest human potential, which is by nature transhuman or transpersonal. The Spirit cannot be compressed into the individual body-mind. It is never circumscribed by the ego or the personality. On the contrary, it is constantly pressing against all those limitations that we regard as comprising "normal" humanness. "The spirit," said Aivanhov, "never relaxes its thrust from within."[9]

The Spirit is the true agent of evolution. In Aivanhov's gnostic language, the Spirit forever seeks to descend into matter, transmuting it. As he put it:

> The spirit does not need to evolve. On the contrary, its role is to involute, that is, to descend into matter and animate it. In its own sublime region it is perfect ... but it is powerless on the level of matter until the organs of the physical body are ready to allow it to manifest itself.[10]

Aivanhov continued:

> And the spirit is a virtuoso violinist who needs a good instrument in order to produce good music. People expect too much of the spirit: they give it a broken-down body and expect it to do wonders. But it cannot! It is exactly as though you tried to get a spark from a damp match: it cannot be done![11]

From the esoteric perspective, human evolution is the reaction of the material world (which includes the body-mind and culture) to the constant pressure exerted by the spiritual dimension. By and large that reaction is quite unconscious. Spirituality is the conscious response to the demands of the Spirit. "True progress," Aivanhov noted, "is progress of the spirit."[12]

The history of Christianity can be looked upon as a gradual movement from the esotericism of Jesus to the exoteric teaching of the Church, or Churches — from personal spirituality to organized religion. In the course of these changes, as Aivanhov noted, Jesus' message has lost its purity.[13] Christianity has become despiritualized.

In his *The Secret Gospel*, the American theologian Morton Smith offered new evidence that Jesus taught secretly in addition to his public work.[14] In Mark 4:10, Jesus is reported to have said: "To you has been given the secret of the Kingdom of God, but for those outside everything is in parables; so that they may indeed see but not perceive, and may indeed hear but not understand; lest they should turn again, and be forgiven." In his epistle to the Corinthians, St. Paul also indicated that there was a secret teaching reserved for the elect few. The Gospel of Thomas, found in Nag Hammadi, claims to contain secret words uttered by Jesus.

Smith's book is an excellent piece of detective work about a letter written by the famous Christian Gnostic theologian Clement of Alexandria, who lived in second century A.D. In Clement's letter the existence of a secret Gospel of Mark is acknowledged and passages of this lost text are quoted. From the words cited, Smith concluded that the secret Gospel of Mark is probably older than St. John to which it has certain resemblances and that both go back to a common source, possibly in the Aramaic language.

Smith's findings also made it probable that the great secret of Jesus' hidden teaching revolved around baptism at night, while the initiates were wearing only a linen cloth draped over their nude bodies. In fact, the Gospel of Mark (14:51f.) mentions how on his last night in freedom, when the police arrived to capture him, Jesus was with only one disciple while all the others were asleep. That young man wore a linen cloth over his nude body. When the police grabbed him, the cloth fell off, and he ran away. This incident was never adequately explained or even understandable before. Smith's discovery, however, shows us that Jesus was initiating someone in secret. What was the baptism all about? Smith concluded:

Jesus, therefore, was probably the one who made of baptism a rite in which the initiate became possessed by a spirit. By Paul's time the spirit was thought to be Jesus' spirit. Jesus probably had thought so, too.[15]

Smith also showed how the rite of baptism fitted in with Jesus' magical approach to life and the perception of him by disciples and the world as a great magician. However, Smith does not always overcome his scholarly penchant, failing to see the full depth of the spiritual process involved in the secret teaching.

According to Aivanhov, Jesus not only knew the arcane disciplines but had mastered them. He was a fully illumined being and a thaumaturgist possessing untold powers. Aivanhov said:

> Very few people have any idea that Jesus instructed his disciples in the essential disciplines: Alchemy, the Cabbalah, Astrology and Magic. They think the Apostles were ignorant, uncouth fishermen. As though Jesus would have chosen such crude instruments to be the vehicles of the highest, most sublime truth! Outwardly, it is true, the Apostles were simple fisher-folk without learning, but in reality they were very advanced beings who had already been Initiates and played an important role in the history of mankind as prophets and servants of God. Their souls and spirits, therefore, were already prepared for the tremendous task they were destined to accomplish on earth. The Apocalypse contains many examples of St. John's vast knowledge of the Cabbalah and Astrology, and by their healing of the sick, the Apostles proved that they possess very great spiritual powers.[16]

By 200 A.D., the Christian community was ruled by religious specialists who formed a veritable institution — the Church composed of bishops, priests, and deacons who defined and defended the "true" teaching of Jesus, following St.

Paul. The spiritual core of Jesus' gospel became progressively obscured by doctrinal squabbles and routine rituals.

As this official Christianity won the favor of monarchs and empires, the dissenting groups who purported to carry on the secret tradition were increasingly ostracized and persecuted. But they were never completely squashed, as is clear from the appearance of great spiritual masters like Peter Deunov and Mikhael Aivanhov.

THE LIGHT OF GNOSIS

Aivanhov regarded himself as a disciple of St. John rather than the saints Peter and Paul. He said:

> All the Initiates in the past, the purest, most learned men were all disciples of St. John; they were also all persecuted by the official church because of their superiority. But the church of St. John, obliged as it always has been to exist and work in secret, continues to produce sons and daughters of God, and the time is coming when it will manifest itself in the world and show how far above the other churches it is. When it does, the church of St. Peter will have to reform and make many changes, whether it likes to or not.[17]

Aivanhov's preference for St. John is not surprising. He has always been the favored apostle within gnostic circles, which claimed his gospel for themselves. In his commentary on the *Apocalypse*, Aivanhov noted that "Jesus gave St. John a teaching that he did not give to the other disciples."[18] It is a minor miracle that the Church included John's gospel in the New Testament when it ruled, for instance, against the Gospel of Thomas.

As Elaine Pagels suggested in her well-known book *The Gnostic Gospels*, one possible reason that St. John escaped the fate of other gnostic Christian writers is his famous quote from Jesus: "No one comes to the Father except through me."[19] The Church has always interpreted this to mean: "No one comes to the Father except through the ecclesiastic institution I have created."

There is no evidence that this self-serving interpretation of the Church is correct. Rather more convincing is the explanation proffered by the gnostics. Thus, in the Gospel of Thomas, we find this apocryphal saying of Jesus: "There is light within a man of light, and it lights up the whole world. If he does not shine, he is darkness."[20]

The experience of the divine Light is central to Gnosticism. It is the dawning of a superior awareness, or illumination, which thoroughly transforms the individual. This inner transformation is the fruit of the wisdom, or *gnosis*, revealed in the moment of illumination.

The gnostic tradition is difficult to define, since it comprises divergent beliefs and practices, and its boundaries to other similar traditions are at times fuzzy. What all gnostic schools have in common, however, is that they understand their teachings to be esoteric rather than exoteric. Thus, in its basic orientation, Gnosticism is similar to such esoteric traditions as Hindu Yoga and Sufism. It even shares some ideas and attitudes with these traditions.

Scholars have different opinions about the origins of Gnosticism. Many think it arose within Christianity, while some see its roots in Judaism, and other early religious traditions. The most likely explanation is that it was closely associated with Christianity but did not directly spring from it as a heretical movement. It was part of the same cultural milieu in which the original Christian sect arose. Thus there were Christian as well as non-Christian gnostics.

It is not clear to what extent Hindu or Buddhist doctrines have influenced some Gnostic schools. What is known is that the apostle Thomas, Jesus' brother, preached in South India, in the first century A.D. No doubt, there was a steady flow of goods and knowledge between India and the Middle East in those days.

The Gospel of Thomas, found at Nag Hammadi, contains sayings that, according to some scholars, could have been spoken by the Buddha rather than Jesus. We know of Buddhist missionaries in Alexandria about that time. There is also a little known tradition according to which Jesus, after his "resurrection," migrated to Kashmir where he was known as Issa and where apparently his grave can still be found.[21]

Although Gnosticism was persistently attacked and its members were often persecuted, it nevertheless enjoyed as long a life as the Christian Church itself. Thus, the Mandean sect of modern Iraq is a direct descendant of the early gnostic tradition. Gnosticism is also a facet of certain contemporary movements, such as Theosophy. In the heritage of Peter Deunov and Omraam Mikhael Aivanhov we have another modern survival of Christian gnostic ideas.

While Gnosticism existed in many different forms, or schools, we can detect the following shared features:

1. Esotericism, or an unconventional interpretation of religious truths;

2. syncretism, or the willingness to draw from many different sources and create a new unified vision of these diverse materials;

3. emphasis of revealed knowledge (gnosis) to elect initiates;

4. the redemptive value of gnosis;

5. initiatory structure;

6. hierarchic conception of reality, with God at the apex of the pyramid;

7. dualistic notions that are, however, embedded in a more monistic metaphysics;

8. prominent cosmogonic motifs, which seek to explain the fallen nature of humanity;

9. the world, or creation, is inherently negative or evil;

10. double-level theology: the true God is unknown or unknowable, and abides eternally beyond the Creator God (*demiourgos*) and his creation;

11. evil is a degraded level of the Divine, a residue of the process of creation;

12. the human being is both lower, animal nature and "divine spark" (Greek *spinther*);

13. ideal of perfection through progressive purification;

14. idea of the redeemer or savior, who is other than God, but an emanation of God; a divine envoy, mediator, and awakener;

15. apocalyptic sentiments and ideas.

With the laudatory exception of the belief in the evil nature of the cosmos, all these features can also be encountered in Aivanhov's teaching. Aivanhov understood his work as being essentially esoteric, and his interpretation of the gospels, especially the stories found in them, is profoundly spiritual rather than conventionally religious. As was already mentioned, he was also a great synthesizer, drawing freely from a variety of teachings and arcane arts. He placed wisdom above mere intellectual knowledge, and deemed the former to be our saving grace.

Moreover, Aivanhov created a community of spiritual practitioners who were required to live his teaching, thus participating in an initiatory way of life. His understanding of the Divine was clearly gnostic, inasmuch as he taught that God is not only the Creator of the world but also its very essence and that as such He/It is inseparable from our ourselves. To the empirical consciousness, the world appears to be split into countless polar opposites, but these are ultimately unified in the Divine, which exceeds all its creations. Thus, duality is transcended by nonduality, and dualism is eclipsed by nondualism. The Divine is unknowable but can be realized through identification with it. "Wherever there are no limits, where Infinity and Eternity and Immortality exist, that is where God is."[22] This was one of Aivanhov's favorite definitions of the Divine.

Aivanhov often spoke of the fallen nature of humanity, yet he also always emphasized that we can exercise our free will to overcome our present condition and regain the glory of the primordial state of experiencing the divine Presence in every moment. Evil is, in the final analysis, a product of the creative processes issuing from the Divine. It can, therefore, never be eliminated. However, we may transcend it by remembering our divine essence, the "eternal spark" within us. We are able to remember our true nature, the Self or Spirit, by purifying our mind and heart.

Finally, the apocalyptic element in Aivanhov's teaching is expressed in his belief that we are the threshold of a new age and that the birth of the Age of Aquarius may well be attendant with toil and pain.

THE BOGOMILS AND CATHARS

Through Peter Deunov, who resuscitated the ancient gnostic heritage of his homeland, Aivanhov was in touch with a powerful lineage going back to the Bogomils of the tenth century A.D. and earlier gnostic schools. Since Bogomilism played such an important role in Bulgaria, it seems appropriate to consider it here briefly. It is possible that the Bogomils were the continuation of the ancient Paulicians who were widespread throughout the Byzantine world. In c. 872, the Paulicians, who had dared go to war against the Byzantine emperor, were settled in Macedonia (Thracia), Aivanhov's birthplace. They were so named for their followership of St. Paul. They tried to revive primitive Christianity. They had adopted certain Manichean doctrines and practices and were iconoclasts in the literal sense of the term, fiercely fighting against the widespread cult of icons in the Byzantine world. They also opposed the widespread worship of saints.

The Paulicians originally hailed from Armenia and Syria, where we encounter them already in the seventh century.

Despite centuries of persecution, they existed in small numbers in Bulgaria as late as the seventeenth century. Situated between the great powers of Byzantium and Rome, Bulgaria was under the influence of both religious empires. At the time of the Paulicians' downfall, Bulgaria was still steeped in paganism. In earlier centuries, the Bulgarians had even persecuted Christians. This changed under King Khan Boris (Michael), who had himself baptized in 864 or 865 and then converted his people to Christianity by the sword.

It was in the tenth century that we see the earliest concrete evidence of a strong presence of heretical movements in Bulgaria, which had the clergy of Constantinople and Tsar Peter greatly worried. The finger was pointed especially at those who were identified as Paulicians. Theophylact, Patriarch of Constantinople (933–956), had written a letter to Tsar Peter in which the Bulgarian Paulicians were condemned.

At that time, the Church was quite corrupt. One outspoken presbyter, Cosmas, whose sermon has miraculously survived the vicissitudes of time, condemned the bishops as "shepherds who milked and sheared their flocks but took no care of them." Priests lived in idleness and sin, growing fat on the poor folk whom they duped and inspired with fear. Men left their families to become monks, only to divest themselves of the cloth again and return to wife and children. But there were also those few men of the spirit who pursued the ascetical life in remote mountain caves.

It was Cosmas who also first mentioned the "heretic" Bogomil who lived during the reign of Tsar Peter. We also learn from him that the Bogomils rejected baptism, the eucharist, and the doctrine of Mary, the Mother of God. He also mentioned in his sermon that they cut down crosses and used them for profane purposes. This demonstrated their belief that Jesus died on the cross for nothing, and that redemption was to be found only in Jesus' spiritual teaching. For the Bogomils this meant living the austere life of asceticism.

Unlike the Paulicians, the Bogomils did not claim to follow St. Paul. There are parallels between these two movements, but it is unlikely that the Bogomils split off from the Paulicians.

Yet, both were gnostic in character, and undoubtedly the Paulicians were influential in the emergence of Bogomilism which, in turn, was a strong influence in the formation of the Cathars.[23]

At the beginning of the twelfth century, Byzantium started to persecute the Bogomils. Aivanhov spoke of the Bogomils, their greatness and their plight, in one of his first lectures; he said:

> The Bogomils were extremely pure and virtuous, and they preferred to be martyrized [sic] and burned rather than to renounce living according to the rules of the Gospel. Among them were Initiates and great Magi who were heard and followed by the masses. But throughout time it has been known that the enlightened beings have always disturbed the narrow-minded men who wanted to live in darkness, ignorance and greed. The Bogomils were persecuted. Many were killed; others left Bulgaria and settled in Italy and in France...[24]

Aivanhov added:

> Bulgaria was cruelly punished for the crimes it had committed against the Bogomils. For five centuries Bulgaria was under Turkish domination and thousands of people lived in indescribable slavery and were decapitated and hung.[25]

By the middle of the twelfth century, gnostic schools like the Bogomils had spread throughout Western Europe. The Bogomils even managed to found their own Church in Bosnia, which lasted into the fifteenth century.

The Albigensians (named after the city of Albi in southern France) and the Cathars ("Pure") appeared about the middle of the twelfth century, presenting to Rome the same "heretical" threat that the Paulicians and Bogomils had presented to Constantinople. They won many people over to their faith, and in the late twelfth century organized into a Church and soon after started to stagnate.

However, the Cathars changed their Bogomilian heritage in a number of ways. Most importantly, Lucifer is now no longer a fallen angel but the creation of the "God of darkness," a kind of anti-God. Whereas the good God lives in Heaven, the evil God resides in the visible realm, where he is omnipotent.

The Cathars felt revulsion for the physical body. They abstained from marriage for the same reason that they refused to eat meat: namely because animals propagated by sex and because bodies were believed to be the handiwork of the Devil. Another reason why *some* Cathars did not eat meat was their belief in reincarnation. They were allowed to consume fish, however, because they were born of water, not blood. On this point, Aivanhov holds a similar view. However, he did not endorse the Cathars' body-negative philosophy.

The history of the Paulicians, Bogomils, and Cathars was a history filled with oppression and bloodshed. The Church did not tolerate heresy very well and used its considerable material wealth and political power to squash these dissenting voices. There is a simple reason why these heretical movements were so successful: They provided people with a more convincing way of life in which each individual could assume responsibility for his or her spiritual destiny in community with others and realize the Birth of Christ. Apparently the Church failed to provide them with that possibility.

THE COSMIC CHRIST

Esoteric Christianity, or Christian Gnosticism, revolves around the Birth of Christ. The birth of Jesus was an important event, which radically changed human history. But from a mystical or esoteric point of view the only thing that matters is the Birth of Christ. As Aivanhov declared: "It is not enough that Jesus was born 2,000 years ago."[26] It is not enough to believe in Jesus, as TV evangelists would have us believe. Rather, Christians must come to understand the higher spiritual principle that his life and work exemplifies.

The person called Jesus is only the external aspect of something much vaster and more magnificent — the Christ.

Unless Christians encounter and are transformed by the presence of the Christ, they are, strictly speaking, not yet Christians but only followers of Jesus.

The transformative and regenerative encounter with the Christ principle is what is known as the Birth of Christ. Aivanhov spoke of it as "a most important subject" that "should preoccupy all disciples."[27]

The Birth of Christ in one's own life—or soul, as Aivanhov would say — is also known as the "second birth." It is an "upward" birth, into the spiritual dimension. It is the mystical "resurrection," which is accomplished when the psyche — or soul — is elevated through personal purity, love, worship, and singlemindedness to the realm of the Spirit. The union of psyche and Spirit gives birth to the Christ or, in Buddhist terms, recovers our Buddha nature. The Taoists know of the Golden Flower that blossoms within.

Meister Eckhart, one of the finest Christian mystics, often spoke in his sermons about the Birth of the Son or of the Word. He preached:

> It is the greatest gift that we are the children of God and that He begets His Son within us. The soul that desires to be God's child must not give birth to anything within itself; and the one in which the Son of God is to be begotten must not give birth to anything else. God's highest intent is birthing. He will never be content unless He has begotten His Son within us. The soul too is not content unless the Son of God has been born within it.[28]

This mystical realization deeply affects the way we regard and relate to life and death and the cosmos as a whole. Aivanhov remarked:

> Yes, the birth of the divine principle, the event that takes place inside us is so utterly extraordinary that no one can possibly mistake it for something else. All Heaven lies open before you, and a Being supports and upholds you and fills you with Light, protection

and joy. Even under the most terrible circumstances, from the depths of discouragement, you feel the presence of this Being and know that you are being helped and guided. Yes, this feeling, this knowledge of a Presence is the link which is constant from then on, as if you had turned on a lamp that never again is turned off. . .[29]

It is clear from this that the Birth of Christ is not merely a mental event, occurring on a distant spiritual plane.[30] Rather, its transformative power makes itself known on all levels of our being, including the body.

Aivanhov emphasized that for the Birth of Christ, the immortal Child within, to occur in the physical realm as well, we must have reverence for our Earth.

> Anyone who is not aware of his relationship with the earth will not be able to bring the Christ Child into his actions, his physical body. We are inclined to forget that the earth is alive and intelligent, and we consider it only from the geographical point of view: so many inhabitants, so many seas and oceans, lakes and rivers, mountains, and so on. The earth is the most unknown of creatures, the most scorned and disdained; the result is great misfortune for us because we are in error.[31]

This profound eco-theological vision offers another point of contact with Meister Eckhart and contemporary creation spirituality. The American theologian Matthew Fox, a prominent spokesman for creation spirituality, made these pertinent comments:

> I believe the appropriate symbol of the Cosmic Christ who became incarnate in Jesus is that of Jesus as Mother Earth crucified yet rising daily. Why do I believe this? First, because Mother Earth is being crucified in our time and is deeply wounded. . . . She has blessed us for four and one-half billion years by providing water; separating continents; establishing

just the correct amounts of oxygen, hydrogen, and ozone in our atmosphere for us; birthing flowers, plants, animals, fishes, birds to delight us and bless us with their gifts and their work of making air and soil healthy and welcoming to us. In short, earth loved us — and still does — even though we crucify her daily.

Yet, like Jesus, she rises from her tomb every day.[32]

Fox went on to say:

The bottom line is not that Christianity survive into the next millennium. In fact, I propose that Christianity as we know it will not survive for we know it now in wineskins that are brittle, old, and leaking. Nothing will survive if Mother Earth does not survive.[33]

Here Fox expresses Aivanhov's sentiments exactly. Aivanhov's teaching is thoroughly ecological, and his great reverence for Nature should have become clear by now. Nature, after all, is a manifestation of the Divine. Where might we discover the Cosmic Christ if not in the midst of the "buzzing confusion" of the universe?

REINCARNATION: TO BE BORN AGAIN ... AND AGAIN

The Birth of Christ within the human psyche is the event of spiritual resurrection. As Aivanhov remarked: "Resurrection does not take place in the grave. Once you are buried, that is that."[34] After death, the body is doomed to disintegrate. Resurrection is focused spiritual work here and now. In Aivanhov's words:

In order to be resuscitated, you must come back on earth and learn to abandon your weaknesses and shut yourself up in your cocoon, that is, to give up, to renounce all selfishness and stop feeding on self-centred thoughts and feelings.[35]

What Aivanhov is saying here is quite simply that life is a school — an idea we encountered in an earlier chapter. We must learn certain lessons, and if we flunk the tests furnished by life itself, we must repeat the same class over and over again until the lesson is learned. In other words, death is no escape from the responsibilities of life, for we are being recycled until we are ready for graduation onto higher planes of existence.

The belief in reembodiment, so central to Aivanhov's teaching, was also an integral part of early Christianity. It was only at the First Council of Nicaea in 325 A.D. that this belief was formally ruled anathema. Aivanhov saw in this ecclesiastic resolution one of the principal reasons for the further spiritual decline of the Church and Christendom. He noted that without the belief in reincarnation, "nothing in life makes sense."[36] Thus, the Church deprived people of a deeper understanding of their own lives, effectively closing the door on them to authentic spirituality.

Aivanhov also made this harsh but pertinent criticism:

> When the Church rejected the idea of reincarnation, it made God a despot, a monster. Christianity inherited the image from the Old Testament of a jealous, vindictive, terrible God that ruled the world by punishment. It is not a true picture of God.[37]

Aivanhov argued that it would have made no sense for Jesus to exhort his followers to be as perfect as God unless he had also taught them about reincarnation. For it is through our repeated births in this and other realms that we can gradually purify ourselves over many lifetimes and finally recover our identity with the Divine.[38] Apart from that flawless transcendental condition, there is no perfection.

Aivanhov also pointed out various gospel passages that are difficult to understand without the teaching of reincarnation. Perhaps the most striking evidence is found in the Gospel of Matthew (chapters 11 and 17) where Jesus speaks of John the Baptist as the former Elias. There is also the passage in Matthew 16:13–14 where Jesus asks his disciples: "Who do people say I am?" Apparently some of Jesus' contemporaries thought he was John the Baptist, others that he was Elias, and yet others believed him to be Jeremias.

These responses make no sense unless we assume that at least some of the Hebrews of that time believed in reincarnation. Indeed, many looked upon Moses as a reincarnation of Abel, one of the sons of Adam. They also believed that Adam himself had come a second time as David, and thought that the expected Messiah would be another reincarnation of Adam. Later, this teaching became accepted doctrine with most Kabbalists. It was also part of the belief system of the Bogomils and Cathars.

While reincarnation is still rejected by the official Church, several opinion polls conducted in the United States in the 1980s have shown that a surprising 20 percent of people believe that they may not be incarnated either for the first or the last time. If millions of men and women subscribe to this belief, we cannot help but wonder why so few live a life of high moral quality. They are obviously not concerned about reaping the rewards of their present actions in a future embodiment, or else they are merely toying with the idea of rebirth.

THE BODY OF GLORY

We have learned the lesson of life when we seriously begin to create a body of light for ourselves. Aivanhov called this new form the Body of Glory, or the Body of Resurrection. He said:

> Before forming this body within, man is dark, obscure, weak, vulnerable, sickly; but he carries within him a germ from the Christ that he can deveop. . . . Man must surpass himself to attract the purest particles, the most luminous elements from the cosmic ocean, and solder them onto his body of glory. We can do it right away, today, first in small quantities, then more and more each day.[39]

The Body of Glory exists as a seed in everyone. It is the divine spark of which Meister Eckhart and other mystics spoke so eloquently. Spiritual life is the deliberate cultivation of that seed, or spark. Every time we sincerely meditate, pray, worship, contemplate the lives of the saints, listen to uplifting music, regard a beautiful image, consider higher ideals of living, or feel compassion and love for other beings, we increase the luminosity of the Body of Glory.

Aivanhov assured his disciples that one day this incandescent form becomes so radiant and powerful that it is even capable of levitating the physical body.[40] This esoteric ability is recorded in many traditions, including Christianity. Thus the famous Italian monk Padre Pio is said to have appeared to people who were hundreds of miles away, sometimes seemingly even at the same time.

Aivanhov made these further comments:

> People have been able to see the Body of Glory of certain Initiates when they were in a state of ecstasy and rapture: their faces shone, light emanated from them. In this Body an Initiate is able to voyage through space, cross mountains, even penetrate into the centre of the earth, because no material obstacle can stop him. He can even act from a distance on people in order to help them. . . . It is possible for man to be separated from his physical body and live in his Body of Glory . . . and live eternally.[41]

When the resurrected Jesus appeared to Mary Magdalene at the grave, it was his Body of Glory that she saw and therefore did not recognize her teacher until he had identified himself. Only subsequently did Jesus succeed in materializing his etheric body sufficiently to assume the familiar features of his former physical body.

Aivanhov was completely certain that we all have the possibility of nurturing the Christ seed within us to the point where it blossoms into the incorruptible, immortal body of light. Ravi Ravindra, a professor of physics, observed that as our spiritual life deepens, our physical body undergoes a simultaneous change. Spirit and matter are not radically opposed, and, as Aivanhov insisted, the Spirit constantly seeks to transform matter. Ravindra put it this way:

> Higher consciousness . . . affects the body chemically — although it may be better to say that the effects are *alchemical*, owing both to their subtlety and their transformational character. Conversely, a new body is needed for a higher consciousness to be able to manifest itself. It may be worth remarking that in this essentially spiritual perspective the driving thrust of the process of evolution is from above downwards, the Spirit demanding and forging more and more complex material organization in order to be able to manifest Itself in body. A more sensitive (human) body will be required for a superior manifestation of the Spirit on earth.[42]

For a full manifestation of the Spirit, the body has to be radically refashioned into the Body of Glory. This spiritual accomplishment requires immense dedication. As Aivanhov stated:

> Much time is needed, obviously to build this Body. Look at how much time is needed for an acorn to become a great oak tree! We must feed the Body of Glory abundantly and frequently the nourishment it needs. Which means that you must so arrange your life that you are creating the best conditions for spiritual life. . . . If Jesus rose from the dead, we too can rise from the dead.[43]

Christianity has been characterized as a religion of hope. But hope without rational foundation is merely self-delusion. Esoteric Christianity, as expounded by Aivanhov, provides us with a sound basis for hope. Of course, at the same time, it also undermines the conventional Christian attitude of passive waiting for our own spiritual resurrection on Judgment Day. Esoteric Christianity makes an uncompromising demand on us: to work out our own spiritual destiny by collaborating with the Christ principle in evolution.

NOTES

1. Aivanhov, *True Alchemy*, p. 120.
2. Aivanhov, *The True Meaning of Christ's Teaching*, p. 57.
3. Aivanhov, *Aquarius* (Part 2), p. 58.
4. Aivanhov, *Sexual Force or the Winged Dragon*, p. 11
5. On the *cakra* model, see Aivanhov, *Man's Subtle Bodies and Centres*; on astroloy, see *The Zodiac*; on the Kabbalah, see *The Mysteries of Yesod* and *The Splendour of Tiphareth*; on alchemical symbolism, see *True Alchemy* and *Spiritual Alchemy*; on physionomy, see *The Second Birth*; on the Shiva-Shakti polarity, see *Love and Sexuality* (Part 1 and 2); on color symbolism, see *The Splendour of Tiphareth*.
6. Aivanhov, *Aquarius* (Part 2), p. 44.
7. *The Notebooks of Paul Brunton*, vol. 1: *Reflections* (Burdett, NY: Larson Publications, 1984, p. 216.
8. Ibid., p. 218.
9. Aivanhov, *The Powers of Thought*, p. 127.
10. Aivanhov, *Light Is a Living Spirit*, p. 88.
11. Ibid., p. 89.
12. Aivanhov, *The Powers of Thought*, p. 136.
13. See Aivanhov *The True Meaning of Christ's Teaching*, p. 107.
14. See M. Smith, *The Secret Gospel* (Clearlake, CA: Dawn Horse Press, 1982).
15. Ibid., p. 104.
16. Aivanhov, *Spiritual Alchemy*, pp. 38–39.
17. Aivanhov, *Aquarius* (Part 2), pp. 40–41.
18. Aivanhov, *The Book of Revelation*, p. 21.
19. See E. Pagels, *The Gnostic Gospels* (New York: Random House, 1979), pp. 119–120.
20. Cited in E. Pagels, *op. cit.*, p. 120.
21. See H. Kersten, *Jesus lebte in Indien* (Munich: Droemersche Verlagsanstalt, 1983).
22. Aivanhov, *The Key to the Problems of Existence*, p. 72.
23. So according to M. Loos, *Dualist Heresy in the Middle Ages* (The Hague, Netherlands: Martinus Nijhoff/Prague: Academia, 1974). Some scholars deny the strong link between the Paulicians and the Bogomils.
24. Aivanhov, *The Second Birth*, p. 164.
25. Ibid., p. 164.
26. Aivanhov, *Harmony*, p. 206.
27. Aivanhov, *Christmas and Easter in the Initiatic Tradition*, p. 33.
28. Sermon 12: *Impletum est tempus Elizabeth*, translated into English from the German edition by J. Quint, *Deutsche Predigten und Traktate* (Munich: Hanser Verlag, 1963), p. 208.
29. Aivanhov, *Christmas and Easter in the Initiatic Tradition*, p. 47.

30. See *op. cit.*, p. 34.
31. Ibid., p. 34.
32. M. Fox, *The Coming of the Cosmic Christ* (San Francisco: Harper & Row, 1988), p. 145.
33. Ibid., p. 149.
34. Aivanhov, *Christmas and Easter in the Initiatic Tradition*, p. 102.
35. Ibid., p. 102.
36. Aivanhov, *The True Meaning of Christ's Teaching*, p. 68.
37. Aivanhov, *Aquarius* (Part 2), p. 35.
38. See Aivanhov, *The True Meaning of Christ's Teaching*, pp. 57ff.
39. Aivanhov, *Cosmic Moral Laws*, pp. 107–108.
40. See Aivanhov, *Creation: Artistic and Spiritual*, p. 140.
41. Aivanhov, *Christmas and Easter in the Initiatic Tradition*, p. 133.
42. R. Ravindra, *Science and Spirit* (New York: Paragon House, 1991), p. 50.
43. Aivanhov, *Christmas and Easter in the Initiatic Tradition*, p. 138.

12
AIVANHOV'S TEACHING
AND GLOBAL RENEWAL

THE HOUR OF DECISION

We live in decisive times. The way we choose to live our lives today will shape not only our personal future but the future of our species. There is every indication that too many of us are still making the wrong choices. Hence the specter of planetwide destruction — through the pollution of land, sea, and air — looms large on the horizon. Ours is undeniably a time of great crisis. It is in the nature of crises that they can go either way. In a crisis a patient's condition either noticeably improves or he is wheeled out of the intensive care unit with his face covered. Today our species and our global environment are in the throes of such a life-and-death crisis.

This fact has been acknowledged by numerous concerned scientists, scholars, writers, artists, and other sensitive people, including a handful of farsighted politicians. Their voices, however, have so far fallen largely on deaf ears. The reckless devastation of our environment continues unabated, while every day another 300,000 lives are added to our already overpopulated planet, thus compounding the crisis exponentially.

The population explosion is only one aspect of a much deeper problem — the crisis of the human spirit. As Aivanhov explained:

> For the moment, everything on earth is upside down: anything of real value is scoffed at while things that have no value at all are given first place. . .
> Human beings have reversed all the values: nothing is in its rightful place anymore.[1]

The Hindus summarize the present state of affairs in the designation *kali-yuga*, the Age of Darkness. In this era, humanity is farthest removed from its spiritual origins. As Aivanhov put it, we have broken the bond between Heaven and Earth, and this rupture has deprived us of the power of faith and love, abandoning us to moral uncertainty and instinctual life. He said:

> When men no longer believe in the existence of God, of an Intelligence, a Hierarchy, when they no longer believe in the other world, in the soul's immortality, existence has no more meaning for them.[2]

Aivanhov criticized philosophers and scientists for failing to recognize that by demolishing the foundation of faith they would, unintentionally, cause the collapse of the entire edifice of our civilization. In their ambition to install reason as the ultimate arbiter of human destiny, they have indiscriminately rejected tradition and thus cut themselves off from their own spiritual source. Reason undoubtedly has its place in the scheme of things, but it is a poor substitute for spiritual realization, wisdom, faith, and grace.

The immoderate use of reason implies a deficient exercise of our human faculties. It inevitably involves a lop-sided emphasis on the ego-personality, what Aivanhov called the "lower self," which can never be in the interest of the evolutionary process. Thus, rationalism has driven us into a sinister cul-de-sac. We are now facing countless problems resulting from a rampant technocracy, bureaucracy, imperialistic ideology, and consumerist mentality, which are all the manifestations of an imbalanced, egotistic approach to life. Only a civilization afflicted with severe spiritual myopia could ever regard these shortcomings as progress.

The Swiss philosopher and poet Jean Gebser, one of the few Western thinkers to recognize the spiritual nature of the present-day crisis, offered a trenchant critique of the limitations of reason. Like Aivanhov and others, he also spoke of a new era, which he understood as a new type of consciousness — a consciousness that is neither merely rational nor irrational but *arational* and integral. He wrote:

> This new era transcends the preceding rational epoch, which was strongly antireligious, and it runs counter to the unchristian nihilism of our days. This entails that the new era neither can nor will any longer be antireligious. Only rational thought is anti-religious; the arational consciousness, simply because of its transparency, will gain a strengthened relationship to religion.[3]

An increasing number of thoughtful people are coming to the same conclusion. There is an urgent need to correct the imbalance caused by our civilization's idolatry of reason, its worship of the left cerebral hemisphere, and its denial of the other powers of the human psyche. This need is acknowledged and responded to by the holistic movement, which is steadily winning support.

Individually and collectively, we can hope to survive only as *whole* human beings. Our wholeness must include an open channel to the ultimate Reality, the Divine. As Aivanhov remarked: "Consciously or unconsciously all beings seek one thing: their complementary principle . . . God Himself."[4] It is in our attunement to the Divine alone that we overcome our sense of fragmentation, incompleteness, isolation, and alienation.

Thus, we must recover our lost spiritual anchorage. It is not really lost; but by our own doing we have concealed it rather well. The ultimate Reality, being omnipresent, can never be truly lost. The bond of which Aivanhov spoke cannot snap beyond all repair. It is more like an elastic band that, as it is stretched, becomes thinner and thinner. In the end it is so extended and tenuous that it can barely serve as a communication link between the Divine and us. However, if we stop stretching the band and remember the seemingly remote point to which it is attached, we begin to realize how this link is our vital lifeline.

When we are born, the umbilical cord is severed, and we must learn to live outside the protective environment of the maternal womb. However, when we are spiritually reborn — our second birth — we recognize that we are never entirely separated from the cosmic womb. Indeed, we must learn to foster that umbilical connection to the universal Matrix, the Divine. The lesson is one of mastering the fine line between independence and dependence, or effort and grace.

The reason-bound ego-personality feasts on its own sense of self-importance, and fiercely seeks to be independent. Hence the German philosopher Friedrich Nietzsche could in the last century defiantly declare the death of God. The paramount ideal of the ego-personality is freedom. However, its notion of freedom is strangely warped, tied as it is into the need for self-gratification rather than self-transcendence. But freedom is only possible in the mastery of the lower personality, the ego. And this mastery entails the ability to surrender to the Divine. As Paul Brunton put it dramatically:

> When the ego is brought to its knees in the dust, humiliated in its own eyes, however esteemed or feared, envied or respected in other men's eyes, the way is open for Grace's influx.[5]

The ego must not be killed but brought under the control of the higher Self. In the same way, we must not attempt to discard reason and logic, for we would merely cripple ourselves. Rather, we must seek to illuminate reason with the light of the Self, or Spirit. Then we will be able to restore balance to our inner lives as well as our external environment.

ECO-SPIRITUALITY:
WE ARE THE WORLD WE LIVE IN

The reciprocity of inner and outer life has of late been recognized by a small but growing segment within the ecology movement. The work of philosopher Henryk Skolimowski and ecological thinker Charlene Spretnak is representative of this avant-garde group. They speak of "eco-spirituality" —

the wedding of ecological and spiritual values in order to heal the planet and ourselves.

The great spiritual traditions of the world were created long before the onset of the environmental problems bedeviling our existence today. They were, by and large, focused on individual salvation, based on the ideal of world renunciation. Today, however, a new type of thinking and spirituality is emerging, which is in some respects radically different from the traditional viewpoints. The new orientation was poignantly expressed by Aivanhov thus:

> Anyone who thinks he can settle his own affairs without considering the whole is an idiot, his thinking is all wrong. If there are social problems, as he is part of society, no one asks his permission and he goes down with the rest; if good conditions exist for the whole collectivity, then each individual benefits.[6]

Eco-spirituality is based on the fact that we do not exist in isolation but that life is always a cooperative process. Skolimowski characterized this innovative approach as being part of today's "Ecological Renaissance." This Renaissance, he explained, "celebrates life as part of the flowering of the universe, the human as an intrinsic part of the cosmic design, and the cosmos as home for man."[7] He further stated:

> Spirituality is a sublime subject. Great minds and souls have reflected on it and left behind many illuminating insights. Yet we need to reflect on it again, if only because we wish to prove that we are spiritually alive. Our circumstances and problems are unprecedented and they require a new spiritual response, a new form of spirituality.[8]

The new spirituality, according to Skolimowski, must view the world as a sanctuary and instill in us reverence for life and the cosmos as a whole. For him, ecology is "reverence in action," which bridges the apparent gulf between subject and object, mind and matter, human being and universe. The new ecology thus implies a distinct moral code. Skolimowski expressed that code in the following succinct way:

> We need to treat each other according to what we can potentially become: divine lights uplifting ourselves and helping others to heal, to integrate, to become reverential. Working on ourselves to release and articulate our inner divinity and working in the outside world to heal the earth are complementary aspects of ecological spirituality.[9]

These words, uttered by a philosopher, are befitting of a sage. Skolimowski belongs indeed to the new species of philosopher-sages for whom philosophy is not semantic quibbling and word play but what it was originally: the love of wisdom. It is this kind of serious philosophical work that epitomizes the confluence that is occurring today between modern thought and the ancient sacred traditions. It bespeaks of the new orientation to life, the new consciousness, that Aivanhov not only heralded in his many talks but personally embodied.

Charlene Spretnak, who is a well-known American spokesperson for Green Politics and ecofeminism, has called the new awareness and attitude "ecological postmodernism." In her remarkable work *States of Grace*, Spretnak argued that we must now move "beyond cynicism and postures of despair." Instead we must assume our role as full participants in the unfolding drama of the cosmos. She noted:

> For these existential possibilities the universe has provided the guidance and inspiration we need: the core teachings of the wisdom traditions. Through their practices, their emphasis on process, we can become sensitive to profound dimensions of mind, nature, the body, and community. . . . We are ready as never before to appreciate the great wisdom traditions.[10]

Spretnak's book spells out for us what this means in more practical terms — how we can live in harmony with Nature, how we can *embody* grace, how we can discover the sacred nature of our own body and the Body of Earth. Locked away in the world's spiritual traditions is a treasure of inestimable value. This is the moment to tap into their riches. In Spretnak's words:

> The wisdom traditions can be appreciated for their respective benefits, but also for their potential to bring to a multicultural dialogue about significant issues and ideas a depth of understanding that has been denied by the boundaries of modernity. I believe that ecological postmodernism — the cultural passage beyond the failed aspects of modernity — might itself become a wisdom tradition, contributing to that dialogue the fruits of in-depth exploration of process in various areas.[11]

Aivanhov was in many respects thoroughly traditional. He was a voice for the wisdom traditions, what he called the "initiatic viewpoint." Yet, he was also thoroughly modern — or, rather, postmodern — for he constantly sought to bring the traditional wisdom to bear on today's problems. He felt that the initiatic traditions were clearly relevant to our contemporary dilemma.

At the same time, Aivanhov was not reluctant to modify the teaching he had received from Peter Deunov to better suit it to today's conditions. For instance, unlike Deunov, he addressed the whole matter of sexuality in considerable depth, because he found that it was such a big stumbling block in many people's lives.

Aivanhov was a threshold figure in a twofold sense. First, he served as a signpost beckoning us to look toward the immaterial, spiritual dimension while accepting our embodiment and remaining fully active in the material realm. Second, he stood on that fluid edge between the traditional past and the emerging future, freely giving out the wisdom of bygone ages while always challenging us to work on what he envisioned to be a most glorious future for humanity.

THE DAWN OF A GOLDEN AGE?

When we consider the numerous destructive forces that almost completely unopposed are wreaking havoc in our planetary home, all talk about a Golden Age seems mere millennarian hope. Yet, a new, more benign era is exactly what Aivanhov and other visionaries have been seriously promising us as our allotted future destiny. Aivanhov even went so far as to tell us that the Golden Age is not generations or centuries away, but imminent. In a talk given on December 10, 1966, he said:

> Aquarius will be the new age, the new life. First there will be disastrous events, gigantic upheavals, turmoil and change of all kinds, and afterwards . . . it will be the Golden Age. Aquarius will bring in the Golden Age.[12]

In another talk, given four years earlier, on March 24, 1962, he was still more explicit:

> The Kingdom of God will come, I promise you that, and the Golden Age will come. Astrologers are busy making those calculations, but as I told you years ago, the Golden Age will be here on earth by the end of this century.[13]

Aivanhov also made it clear that the Age of Aquarius will not properly begin until about two hundred years from now, when the vernal point of the zodiac has shifted to the constellation of Aquarius. However, he was sure that we would experience the influence of the new astrological configuration by the turn of the present millennium.[14] Only time will tell whether he has seen correctly.

Aivanhov, like other visionaries of our time, did not foresee an easy birth for the coming Age. Rather, he repeatedly observed that humanity would be undergoing a major purging before the Golden Age is ushered in. He noted:

The Age of Aquarius is fast approaching, and it is going to overturn and shatter all the old forms and values that human beings thought of as permanent.[15]

Aivanhov further stated:

Human beings need to suffer before they begin to wish for harmony and peace and the splendour of the new life. If they are not ground down by all kinds of sufferings, they will never understand or make up their minds to work for the Kingdom of God.[16]

However, Aivanhov never wasted time focusing on the negative side of a situation. He was a lover of beauty and harmony. Thus, while he warned of the trials and tribulations ahead of us, he always preferred to talk about the glory of humanity's future, giving us a positive ideal to work with.

After all, the Golden Age will not click into place automatically. It requires for its birth the collaboration of many far-sighted people, who are not wrapped up in manipulating their own parcel of destiny but have sufficient emotional maturity and inner space to hear and respond to the evolutionary call. In a way, Aivanhov's insistence that the Golden Age will be here by the end of the second millennium is the proverbial carrot dangling in front of us — a powerful image to motivate us.

From this perspective the question of whether the Golden Age is myth or reality has no clear-cut answer. It is both. To the degree that we allow the myth, the guiding image, of the Golden Age to inform our actions, it becomes our reality. Conversely, to the degree that the Golden Age is becoming historical reality, it forfeits its mythic component. If we regard the Golden Age as being "too good to be true," we merely disempower ourselves. Our beliefs and ideas, as Aivanhov vigorously affirmed, shape our reality, our future. We would therefore do well to cultivate those notions and attitudes that are life-enhancing and allow us and future generations to manifest our human potential to the full.

Aivanhov never ceased to remind his disciples of the fact that we inhabit a far more wondrous universe than science would have us believe — a universe that is patiently waiting for our conscious, mature collaboration. We have barely touched our own evolutionary potential.

Aivanhov has rendered our species an invaluable service by sharing with us his long-range view of the future, which alone can provide us with a clue about humanity's true potential. He spoke of the coming solar civilization as founded in a deep spiritual realization. He even equated it with the Kingdom of God. What he meant by this is clearly articulated in the following passage:

> The Kingdom of God is not what the materialists think: it will be a spiritual realization, not a physical one. The Kingdom of God is a state of mind, a state of consciousness; for it to come, man must change his present state of consciousness. I have come with a program, a plan, and if I can give this plan to the world, the Kingdom of God will be easy to realize. This does not mean that it will be installed in all our heads at once, no; for some, it will not come for thousands of years, but when it does, it will be in the form of a reorganization of the world, and once the new organization is firmly installed at the top, all the other "members" will conform to the new order.[17]

It appears from this that the Golden Age will at first be a change of mind and heart and only later manifest on the material plane, bringing peace, harmony, love, joy, justice, and abundance. Aivanhov firmly believed that many invisible beings — the Universal White Brotherhood — are actively creating the conditions for the Golden Age on the spiritual plane. He observed:

> The thoughts and feelings of all the enlightened beings in the world form a powerful light which is spreading and influencing the minds of men and women and, one day, the whole world will be touched and contaminated by this new light. This is

why, as I have always said, when men are unaware of the fact that thought is an active force, their evolution is seriously hampered. But we know how powerful thought, meditation and prayer are, we know how beneficial their effects on mankind can be, and thanks to this knowledge we can participate in this great work of light so that the ideal of the Universal White Brotherhood may be disseminated throughout the world. And the Universal White Brotherhood desires only one thing: that the whole world be united in one family.[18]

THE SAVING GRACE OF UNIVERSAL KINSHIP

The noble ideal of brotherhood between all people has been taught by many sages and saints, but foremost by Jesus of Nazareth, who demanded that our love be extended even to our enemies. This potent ideal is also fundamental in Aivanhov's teaching. He defined brotherhood as "a collectivity animated by love, warmth and mutual support, in which each individual works consciously for the good of all."[19]

Aivanhov regarded the brotherhood founded by him as a reflection of the Cosmic Brotherhood, the body of highly evolved spiritual beings, who guide humanity's destiny from higher planes of existence. "We are," he once remarked, "engaged in a gigantic work for the benefit of all mankind."[20] The visible efforts of the human brotherhood are supported by a vast community of beings in the invisible realms.

To realize the ideal of universal brotherhood — or kinship between all beings — Aivanhov felt that the creation of a world government was indispensable and inevitable. "The whole world must become one family," he observed.[21] Today, at a time when sociologists and psychologists are concerned about the decline of family life, Aivanhov's message is especially important. He believed that the integrity of the family could not be restored without invoking the concept of the larger human family.

Indeed, he maintained that the family has the evolutionary purpose of educating us to become members of the "universal

Family." He noted that hitherto the family has failed in its purpose. Today the family is seldom more than a breeding ground for discontented, egotistical individuals. As is clear from the high divorce rate, the number of juvenile delinquents and teenage truants, the numerous abandoned elderly, and the overwhelming number of emotionally and spiritually immature adults, the modern family is thoroughly dysfunctional. Hence the British psychiatrist David Cooper was able to actually celebrate the "death of the family."[22] What passes for family in our postindustrial society is, in his view, by and large little more than a neurotic "suicide pact," which entraps people and deprives them of spontaneity and genuine love; it is an arrangement between sick souls.

Since the family is regarded as the basic cell of the social organism, social planners are understandably anxious about the breakdown of family life. However, they evidently lack the wisdom to offer practical solutions of lasting value on how we might regenerate the ideal of a stable, harmonious family life.

To be sure, the family can only be salvaged if we place it within the larger framework of spiritual evolution, just as our individual lives are meaningless without reference to their grounding in the spiritual dimension. Aivanhov explained that if we want to save the family, we must broaden our conception of it, so as to "encompass the whole world."[23]

Our typical "nuclear" family — consisting only of parents and children — is a modern invention. When we examine preindustrial, tribal societies, we find that family includes a lot more people. Sociologists have coined the term "extended family" for this type of familial group. But this is really a misnomer. It would be more appropriate to call our own nuclear family a *diminished* family, because it is so highly exclusive.

To realize the ideal of universal brotherhood calls for sweeping changes in our attitudes. As Aivanhov emphasized, these changes must begin with expectant mothers. "Education begins before birth."[24] The medical profession itself is slowly beginning to realize that the baby in the womb is highly sensitive and impressionable to all kinds of external stimuli.

But Aivanhov had something more in mind. He believed that, by their whole orientation to life, parents attract certain kinds of souls. The moment of conception is a faithful reflection of their general attitude and disposition. It is seldom a sacred moment, which would signal to a higher being that the parents offer the right conditions for his or her further spiritual growth. According to Aivanhov, the being about to be born into the human world hovers around the mother until the moment of birth, when the child takes its first breath. Then the subtle body and the young physical body become wedded to each other, creating the new individual.

Mothers, therefore, have an especially important responsibility in creating the right prenatal circumstances for the baby growing in their wombs. This responsibility of what Aivanhov called "spiritual gold-plating," was well understood in the past, and motherhood was celebrated among the women as one of the great mysteries of life. Aivanhov regarded women, more than men, as the spiritual custodians of humankind. He said:

> Nature has given women powers which they use badly or not at all. It is important that they become aware of these powers and realize that the future of the human race is in their hands. If women take the trouble to understand what I am saying they will become an unheard-of force in the world, capable of sweeping all before it.... From now on, all the women of the world must unite for the regeneration of the human race. In spite of their intelligence and skill men cannot do very much in this way. It is women, mothers, who have been entrusted with this mission, for it is they who have been given the power of influencing the child in the womb.[25]

That is not to say that men have no obligations in this matter. On the contrary, they must work hard to correct the errors and biases piled up in the course of many generations of patriarchical rule. Patriarchy is the institutionalized dominance of men over women not only within the family but in society at large, depriving women of their power and influence. It is the patriarchal mind-set that is largely responsible for the way in which our civilization is run — including endless wars, competitive business and sports, and not least the ruthless exploitation of the Earth's resources.

The demonstrable failure and injustice of the patriarchal ideology has in recent decades given rise to the rapidly growing feminist movement. A large faction within this movement seeks to redress the balance by ushering in a new age of matriarchy. However, the ambition to create a female-dominant society is merely a reactive stance. It is historically understandable, but not justifiable. If matriarchy ever existed on this planet, it surely has no future, because it is merely another lopsided approach to life.

Rather, today's challenge is to overcome all such intrinsically limiting points of view. The Golden Age is not about power, dominance, control, and exploitation. It is about human beings who are whole and integrated, and a civilization that is rooted not in mutual distrust and exploitation but in the ideals of love, compassion, and voluntary cooperation. Anything less than that has no credibility at this point in human history. We must move forward, unhampered by the ideologies and social straitjackets of the past.

Hitherto human history has been a tragicomedy of tribal allegiance and then, later, national sovereignty, empire building, and capitalist or communist imperialism — all manifestations of the primitive urges to gain material security and exercise power over others. Aivanhov saw world government as a political innovation that inevitably will be connected with humanity's spiritual maturation.

With the creation of the United Nations in 1945, an entirely new political element entered into human history. The United Nations was a direct response to the senselessness and inhumanity of World War II. Although in its present form this organization is less than perfect — and some have declared it completely dysfunctional and a travesty — it nevertheless represents an ideal that must be kept alive under all circumstances. That is the ideal of universal brotherhood, as articulated in the Charter of the United Nations, which was signed on June 26, 1945, in San Francisco:

> . . . to practice tolerance and live together in peace with one another as good neighbors.

Although the Charter, couched in legal language, does not mention the words "brotherhood" and "love," it would be quite easy to reformulate its wide-ranging objectives in these terms. This is borne out by the fact that the very first article of the Universal Declaration of Human Rights, which was adopted without opposition by the United Nations in December 1948, states unequivocally:

> All human beings are born free and equal in dignity and rights. They are endowed with reason and conscience and should act towards one another in the spirit of brotherhood.

The spirit of brotherhood, or kinship, is indeed the single most important value in international relations as well as in our private lives. Without it, we will forever remain strangers to one another. The world government of which Aivanhov spoke can be understood as the external crystallization of the principle of universal brotherhood. There are many aspects to the present crisis of our civilization, and there are also numerous remedial actions that we must now take. So long as we approach this serious matter in piecemeal fashion, however, as if each problem could be handled separately, we will accomplish very little. This is like putting Band Aids on a burn victim.

The only way to heal ourselves and our ailing planet is by going to the root of the problem — which is our spiritual dislocation, our frivolous and by now habitual attitude of disregard for the Source of all life. We must recover our connection to the Divine, which alone can give us primal trust and the strength and wisdom to live our lives in harmony. It seems fitting to conclude with a quote from Aivanhov:

Men must understand the importance of the link, the little piece of thread that they must fit into place, to restore the circulation between Heaven and earth. Then everyone would become magnificent, full of love, and humanity would change its direction.[26]

NOTES

1. Aivanhov, *Man, Master of His Destiny*, pp. 97–98.
2. Aivanhov, *Cosmic Moral Laws*, p. 227.
3. J. Gebser, *In der Bewährung: Zehn Hinweise auf das neue Bewusstsein* (Berne/Munich: Francke Verlag, 1969), p. 65.
4. Aivanhov, *Hope for the World*, p. 25.
5. *The Notebooks of Paul Brunton*, vol. 1: *Perspectives* (Burdett, NY: Larson Publications, 1984), p. 98.
6. Aivanhov, *A New Dawn* (Part 1), p. 30.
7. H. Skolimowski, *Ecological Renaissance* (Ann Arbor, MI: Eco-Philosophy Centre, [1991]), p. 8.
8. Ibid., p. 21.
9. Ibid., pp. 22–23.
10. C. Spretnak, *States of Grace: The Recovery of Meaning in the Postmodern Age* (San Francisco: HarperSanFrancisco, 1991), 1991.
11. Ibid., pp. 230-231.
12. Aivanhov, *A New Dawn* (Part 1), p. 14.
13. Aivanhov, *Aquarius* (Part 2), p. 158.
14. See Aivanhov, *A New Dawn* (Part 1), p. 13.
15. Aivanhov, *A Philosophy of Universality*, p. 27.
16. Aivanhov, *Love and Sexuality* (Part 2), p. 296.
17. Aivanhov, *Aquarius* (Part 2), p. 174.
18. Aivanhov, *A Philosophy of Universality*, p. 107.
19. Ibid., p. 175.
20. Ibid., p. 178.
21. Ibid., p. 106.
22. D. Cooper, *The Death of the Family* (Harmondsworth, England: Penguin Books, 1973).
23. Aivanhov, *A Philosophy of Universality*, p. 97.
24. "Education begins before birth" is the title of volume 203 as well as the title of a talk printed in that volume.
25. Aivanhov, *Education Begins Before Birth*, p. 46.
26. Aivanhov, *Cosmic Moral Laws*, p. 230.

APPENDIX

Important Dates in the Life of Omraam Mikhael Aivanhov

Largely based on the chronology compiled by Violet Nevile

1900	*January 31:* At approximately 0:25 a.m., Aivanhov is born in the village of Serbtzi, Macedonia, Bulgaria.
1907	His village is burned by Greek marauders.
1909	Death of Aivanhov's father.
1916	Experiences the Music of the Spheres — an experience of lasting influence.
1917	First encounter with his teacher, the Bulgarian Peter Deunov whose spiritual name is Beinsa Deuno (July 12, 1864 to December 27, 1944).
1923 or 1924	University studies for "eight or ten years."
1930 or 1932	Professor of psychology and philosophy at a Bulgarian college.
1935 or 1936	Principal of a college near Sofia.
1937	*July 22:* Arrival in Paris where he taught for the rest of his life at the request of his teacher.
1938	*January 29:* First public talk at the Place de la Sorbonne, Paris, on the subject of astrological and color symbolism and spiritual life.
1939	*June 9:* First public talk in Lyon, France. The theme is "spiritual galvanoplasty."
1945	*Spring:* Beginning of the Swiss branch of the brotherhood.

1945   *Christmas:* Publication of the first book of talks, entitled *Amour, Sagesse, Verité* (*Love, Wisdom, Truth*), with an introduction by Lanza del Vasto.

1948   *January 16:* The association is officially registered as Fraternité Blanche Universelle.
January 21: He is arrested on trumped-up charges of espionage.
July 17: He is sentenced to four years in prison.

1950   *March:* Release from prison after 26 months, following recognition that the charges against him had been false.

1953   First summer congress at the Bonfin, the fraternity's center at the French riviera.

1958   First visit to Swiss students since the trial.

1959   *February 11:* Leaves for India where he stays for one year, meeting various masters.
March: Visit to Japan, Taiwan, and Sri Lanka.
June 17: Meets the legendary adept Babaji and the German-born Tibetan Lama Anagarika Govinda.

1960   Visit to England.

1962   *May:* Visit to Spain.

1964   *May:* Visit to Italy, Greece, and Yugoslavia.

1965   *June:* Visit to King Simeon of Bulgaria in Spain.

1967   *May 5 or 6:* Visit to North America (Hawaii, Florida, Yosemite, and Montreal).

1968   *Spring:* Visit to Heidelberg, Germany.
May: Spends two weeks in Israel (Haifa, Sea of Galilee, Dead Sea, Eilat, Qumran, Jerusalem, and Tel Aviv where he meets Prime Minister Ben Gourion).

1969   *May:* Visit to Greece (Delphi, Patmos, Mount Athos) and Istanbul.

1970   *April/May:* Visit to Japan.

1971   *May 6:* Visit to Morocco, Egypt, Ethiopia, Lebanon (Baalbek), and Greece. He returns via Yugoslavia where he meets his mother.

1971   *Summer:* Charges his students to do all they can "to propagate the Teaching for the happiness of the entire world."

1973   *August 5:* Death of his mother in Bulgaria at the age of 97.

1977   *March 5/6:* Participates in an interreligious convention in Paris, organized by the Sufi teacher Pir Vilayat.
        December 20: Visit to the Caribbean, Northern California, and Hawaii. Returns six months later.

1981   *Spring:* Visit to Canada (two weeks) and the United States (one month). In Virginia Beach he meets Hugh Lynn Cayce, son of the famous American clairvoyant and prophet Edgar Cayce.
        June 18: Visit to Bulgaria at the invitation of the Minister of Culture. Participation in the thirteenth centenary celebrations (foundation of Bulgaria and commemoration of St. Cyril and St. Method).
        October 12: Visit to the United States (Greenwich in Connecticut, New York, Arizona, and Los Angeles).
        Christmas: Visit to Thailand.

1982   *April/May:* Visit to India (New Delhi, Amritsar).
        November: Visit to England and Scotland.

1983   *January:* Travels from England to Egypt.
        April 28: Visit to Norway, Sweden, and Finland.

1984   *January 18:* Visit to the United States (Texas, Los Angeles, New York, Washington, and Greenwich). Meets President Reagan and clairvoyant Jeanne Dixon.
        May 6: Visit to Canada.

1985   *January:* Visit to the United States (Denver, Los Angeles, and Northern California) and Canada.
        July: Brief message broadcast by satellite (LIVE AID).

1986   *December 25:* While at the Bonfin in France, departs from this world at 9:25 pm. His final admonition to students is that they should preserve unity and harmony and continue to spread the Teaching in the whole world.

SELECT
BIBLIOGRAPHY

The following works have been particularly meaningful or useful to me in writing the present book. Please also refer to the literature cited in the end notes to each chapter.

Aivanhov, Omraam Mikhael. *Complete Works*. Frejus, France: Prosveta, 1976–. In progress.

Aivanhov, Omraam Mikhael. *Collection Izvor*. Frejus, France: Prosveta, 1982–. In progress.

Banchi, Ugo. *Selected Essays on Gnosticism, Dualism and Mysteriosophy*. Leiden, The Netherlands: E. J. Brill, 1978.

Berendt, Joachim-Ernst. *Nada Brahma: The World Is Sound — Music and the Landscape of Consciousness*. Rochester, VT: Destiny Books, 1987.

Brunton, Paul. *The Notebooks of Paul Brunton*. Burdett, NY: Larson Publications, 1984-1988. 16 vols.

Chopra, Deepak. *Quantum Healing: Exploring the Frontiers of Mind/Body Medicine*. New York: Bantam, 1990.

Dossey, Larry. *Space, Time, and Medicine*. Boston, MA: Shambhala, 1982.

-----. *Recovering the Soul: A Scientific and Spiritual Search*. New York: Bantam, 1989.

-----. *Meaning and Medicine*. New York: Bantam Books, 1991.

Douno, Beinsa [Peter Deunov]. *The Master Speaks*. Los Angeles: Sunrise Press, 1970.

Ferguson, Marilyn. *The Aquarian Conspiracy*. Los Angeles: J. P. Tarcher, 1987.

Feuerstein, Georg. *Yoga: The Technology of Ecstasy*. Los Angeles: J. P. Tarcher, 1986.

-----. *Sacred Paths*. Burdett, NY: Larson Publications, 1991.

-----. *Wholeness or Transcendence? Ancient Lessons for the Emerging Global Civilization*. Burdett, NY: Larson Publications, 1992.

-----. *Sacred Sexuality: Living the Vision of the Erotic Spirit.* Los Angeles, CA: J. P. Tarcher, 1991.

Fox, Matthew. *The Coming of the Cosmic Christ.* San Francisco: HarperSanFrancisco, 1991.

Gebser, Jean. *The Ever-Present Origin.* Transl. Noel Barstad with Algis Mickunas. Athens, OH: Ohio University Press, 1985.

Harman, Willis. *Global Mind Change.* Indianapolis, IN: Knowledge Systems, 1988.

Hedrick, Charles W. and Robert Hodgson, Jr., eds. *Nag Hammadi, Gnosticism, and Early Christianity.* Peabody, MA: Hendrickson Publishers, 1986.

Hixon, Lex. *Coming Home: The Experience of Enlightenment in Sacred Traditions.* Los Angeles: J. P. Tarcher, 1989.

Houston, Jean. *The Possible Human.* Los Angeles: J. P. Tarcher, 1982.

Hubbard, Barbara Marx. *The Revelation: Our Crisis Is a Birth.* Sonoma, CA: Foundation for Conscious Evolution, 1993.

Jonas, Hans. *The Gnostic Religion: The Message of the Alien God and the Beginnings of Christianity.* Boston, MA: Beacon Press, 2nd enl. ed. 1963.

Liberman, Jacob. *Light: Medicine of Our Future.* Santa Fe, NM: Bear & Co., 1991.

Lorimer, David, ed. *Prophet For Our Times: The Life & Teachings of Peter Deunov.* Shaftesbury, England/Rockport, MA: Element Books, 1991.

-----. *The Circle of Sacred Dance: Peter Deunov's Paneurhythmy.* Shaftesbury, England/Rockport, MA: Element Books, 1991.

M. P. [anonymous]. *Beinsa Douno [Peter Deunov]: Reminiscences — Talks with the Master.* Los Angeles: Sunrise Press, 1968.

Murphy, Michael. *The Future of the Body.* Los Angeles: J. P. Tarcher, 1992.

Pagels, Elaine. *The Gnostic Gospels.* New York: Random House, 1979.

Pearson, Birger A. *Gnosticism, Judaism, and Egyptian Christianity.* Minneapolis, MN: Fortress Press, 1990.

Petrement, Simon. *A Separate God: The Christian Origins of Gnosticism*. San Francisco: Harper & Row, 1990.

Robinson, James M., ed. *The Nag Hammadi Library in English*. San Francisco: Harper & Row, 3rd rev. ed., 1988.

Rudolph, Kurt. *Gnosis: The Nature and History of Gnosticism*. San Francisco: Harper & Row, 1987.

Smith, Morton. *The Secret Gospel: The Discovery and Interpretation of the Secret Gospel According to Mark*. Clearlake, CA: Dawn Horse Press, 1982.

Tart, Charles. *Waking Up: Overcoming the Obstacles to Human Potential*. Boston, MA: Shambhala, 1987.

Wegscheider Hyman, Jane. *The Light Book: How Natural and Artificial Light Affect Our Health, Mood, and Behavior*. New York: Ballantine Books, 1990.

White, John. *The Meeting of Science and Spirit*. New York: Paragon House, 1990.

INDEX

USEFUL ADDRESSES

The following organizations carry the English versions of Omraam Mikhael Aivanhov's books and also are able to provide information about programs in their respective countries.

United States
Prosveta U.S.A.
P.O. Box 49614
Los Angeles, CA 90049
(Publishes *Circle of Light* newsletter)

Canada
Prosveta Inc.
1565 Montée Masson
Duvemay est
Laval, Quebec H7E 4P2

Great Britain
Prosveta
The Doves Nest
Duddleswell, Uckfield
East Sussex TN22 3JJ

Ireland
Prosveta Irl.
84 Irishtown
Clonmel

France
(International Headquarters)
Prosveta S.A.
B.P. 12
83601 Fréjus Cedex
(Correspondents should write in French)

ABOUT THE AUTHOR

Georg Feuerstein, Ph.D., M.Litt., is internationally known for his interpretative studies on the Yoga tradition. He has authored over twenty books, including the award-winning *Encyclopedic Dictionary of Yoga, Sacred Paths, Wholeness or Transcendence?, Holy Madness,* and *Sacred Sexuality.* Together with his wife, Trisha Lamb Feuerstein, he has edited the volume *Voices on the Threshold of Tomorrow.* He is a contributing editor of *Yoga Journal* and *Intuition* magazine and is on the board of the Healing Buddha Foundation, Sebastopol, California. His ongoing interest is in articulating a practical spirituality that satisfies both the rational mind and the heart of the contemporary seeker. Since 1981 he has been living in Northern California, finding that the natural quietness of the mountains promotes both his intellectual work and a more contemplative way of life.